The Bible Speaks Today

Series editors: J. A. Motyer (OT)
John Stott (NT)
Derek Tidball (Bible Themes)

The Message of Judges

Grace abounding

The Bible Speaks Today: Old Testament series

The Message of Genesis 1 – 11
The dawn of creation
David Atkinson

The Message of Genesis 12 – 50
From Abraham to Joseph
Joyce G. Baldwin

The Message of Exodus
The days of our pilgrimage
Alec Motyer

The Message of Leviticus
Free to be holy
Derek Tidball

The Message of Numbers
Journey to the promised land
Raymond Brown

The Message of Deuteronomy
Not by bread alone
Raymond Brown

The Message of Judges
Grace abounding
Michael Wilcock

The Message of Ruth
The wings of refuge
David Atkinson

The Message of Samuel
Personalities, potential, politics and power
Mary Evans

The Message of Chronicles
One church, one faith, one Lord
Michael Wilcock

The Message of Nehemiah
God's servant in a time of change
Raymond Brown

The Message of Job
Suffering and grace
David Atkinson

The Message of Psalms 1 – 72
Songs for the people of God
Michael Wilcock

The Message of Psalms 73 – 150
Songs for the people of God
Michael Wilcock

The Message of Proverbs
Wisdom for life
David Atkinson

The Message of Ecclesiastes
A time to mourn, and a time to dance
Derek Kidner

The Message of the Song of Songs
The lyrics of love
Tom Gledhill

The Message of Isaiah
On eagles' wings
Barry Webb

The Message of Jeremiah
Against wind and tide
Derek Kidner

The Message of Ezekiel
A new heart and a new spirit
Christopher J. H. Wright

The Message of Daniel
The Lord is King
Ronald S. Wallace

The Message of Hosea
Love to the loveless
Derek Kidner

The Message of Joel, Micah and Habakkuk
Listening to the voice of God
David Prior

The Message of Amos
The day of the lion
Alec Motyer

The Message of Jonah
Presence in the storm
Rosemary Nixon

The Message of Zechariah
Your kingdom come
Barry Webb

The Message of Judges

Grace abounding

Michael Wilcock

formerly Vicar of St Nicholas' Church, Durham

Inter-Varsity Press

Inter-Varsity Press
38 De Montfort Street, Leicester LE1 7GP, England
Email: ivp@ivp-editorial.co.uk
Website: www.ivpbooks.com

First published 1992
Reprinted 1994, 1996, 1999, 2000, 2002, 2003, 2004

British Library Cataloguing in Publication Data
A catalogue record for this book is available from the British Library.

ISBN 0-85110-972-1

Set in 10/11 Garamond by Intype, London
Printed and bound in Great Britain by CPD (Wales) Ltd, Ebbw Vale

Inter-Varsity Press is the publishing division of the Universities and Colleges Christian Fellowship (formerly the Inter-Varsity Fellowship), a student movement linking Christian Unions in universities and colleges throughout Great Britain, and a member movement of the International Fellowship of Evangelical Students. For information about local and national activities write to UCCF, 38 De Montfort Street, Leicester, LE1 7GP, email us at email@uccf.org.uk, or visit the UCCF website at www.uccf.og.uk.

| BST | The Bible Speaks Today

GENERAL PREFACE

THE BIBLE SPEAKS TODAY describes three series of expositions, based on the books of the Old and New Testaments, and on Bible themes that run through the whole of Scripture. Each series is characterized by a threefold ideal:

- to expound the biblical text with accuracy
- to relate it to contemporary life, and
- to be readable.

These books are, therefore, not 'commentaries', for the commentary seeks rather to elucidate the text than to apply it, and tends to be a work rather of reference than of literature. Nor, on the other hand, do they contain the kinds of 'sermons' that attempt to be contemporary and readable without taking Scripture seriously enough. The contributors to *The Bible Speaks Today* series are all united in their convictions that God still speaks through what he has spoken, and that nothing is more necessary for the life, health and growth of Christians than that they should hear what the Spirit is saying to them through his ancient – yet ever modern – Word.

ALEC MOTYER
JOHN STOTT
DEREK TIDBALL
Series editors

To Geoff and June

Contents

Author's preface

The book of Judges is full of paradox. It contains some of the most famous of the Bible's stories and some of the least known. In them there is much that is attractive, perhaps more that is repulsive. Their lessons are at once simple and difficult. They show us man's blackest sin, but we see it by the light of God's most luminous grace.

Having preached on them in various places over a number of years, I have come to the conclusion that this last contrast is the one that best sums up the message of the book. One might give it the title which, twelve years before the publication of *The Pilgrim's Progress*, John Bunyan gave to his own spiritual autobiography: *Grace Abounding to the Chief of Sinners*. There can be no message in the pages of Scripture more searching or more rewarding.

I should like here to record my gratitude to all who have helped me with this exposition, not least by listening and commenting. The dedication page is a way of saying thank you in particular this time to my sister and brother-in-law, in whose home the final chapters were written, for their loving hospitality and prayerful encouragement then and on many other occasions.

Michael Wilcock

Chief abbreviations

Auld   *Joshua, Judges and Ruth* by A. G. Auld (*Daily Study Bible*, St Andrew Press, 1984).

AV   *The Authorized* (King James') *Version* of the Bible (1611).

Boling   *Judges* by R. G. Boling (*Anchor Bible*, Doubleday, New York, 1975).

Bruce   'Judges' by F. F. Bruce, in *The New Bible Commentary Revised* (IVP, 3rd edition 1970).

Cundall   'Judges' by A. E. Cundall, in *Judges and Ruth* by A. E. Cundall and L. Morris (Tyndale Press, 1968).

Davis   *Such a Great Salvation* (expositions of the Book of Judges) by D. R. Davis (Baker, Grand Rapids, 1990).

GNB   *The Good News Bible* (The Bible Societies and Collins; NT 1966, ⁴1976; OT 1976).

Kitchen   *Ancient Orient and Old Testament* by K. A. Kitchen (Tyndale Press, 1966).

Klein   *The Triumph of Irony in the Book of Judges* by L. R. Klein (JSOT, Sheffield, 1988).

LB   *The Living Bible* paraphrased by K. Taylor (Hodder and Stoughton, 1971).

Martin   *The Book of Judges* by J. D. Martin (*Cambridge Bible Commentaries*, CUP, 1975).

NAS   *The New American Standard Bible* (1963).

NEB   *The New English Bible* (NT 1961, ²1970; OT 1970).

NIV   *The New International Version* of the Bible (Hodder and Stoughton, 1973, 1978, 1984).

RSV   *The Revised Standard Version* of the Bible (NT 1946, ²1971, OT 1952).

RV   *The Revised Version* of the Bible (NT 1881, OT 1885).

Soggin   *Judges* by J. A. Soggin (SCM, e.t. 1981).

Webb   *The Book of Judges: an Integrated Reading* by B. G.
Webb (JSOT, Sheffield, 1987).

Except where otherwise indicated, this exposition is based throughout on the RSV – in my view still the most reliable of the modern
translations.

Introduction

The judges[1]

They include one or two of the most familiar characters in the entire Bible story. You scarcely need to be a Bible reader at all to have heard of Samson the strong man. Given a Jewish or Christian upbringing, even a child will know of Gideon, and should in due course become acquainted with the names of Deborah and Barak, of Jephthah and left-handed Ehud. Later the careful reader will see that the book of Judges is not just a string of stories, but that a pattern recurs in many of them. Repeatedly God's people turn away from him, and he responds by mobilizing an enemy against them; then they cry to him for mercy, and he responds by sending a rescuer for them.

Before long you find there is more to it than that. There are pieces which do not fit the pattern. The 'minor judges', the Abimelech narrative, the two chapters of prologue and the five chapters of epilogue, seem unrelated to the rebellion/retribution/repentance/rescue cycle. Furthermore, while you are obviously meant to disapprove of the rebellious doings of Israel, you may be equally dismayed by the kind of retribution that God allows – indeed, sends – and even by the methods that he uses to rescue his people; at many unexpected points you may find yourself saying, 'Can that be *right*?' On the other hand, there clearly were among all the turmoils long periods of peace, such as would form the background to the book of Ruth, but vastly less space is given to the peace than to the turmoil, and to a narrative which grows ever more

[1] On the term 'judges': at any given point the context should make clear in what sense this word is being used. But in addition I have tried to avoid confusion by a careful use of capitals: judges are judges, Judges means the book of Judges, and *the* Judge is the Lord.

disturbing. What really is the significance of these stories? Those of Samson and Gideon were easy, you may have thought, colourful tales with a variety of spiritual lessons. But the book as a whole is not simply the sum of its parts; and the more you try to see what the whole is about, the more obscure it can become.

I speak for myself, and as a preacher. I have many sets of sermon notes on different parts of Judges. Rarely have I been able to use the same set twice. Repeatedly I have had to rethink, revise, even discard and start again. The book before you is one result of that process. If any volume in the 'Bible Speaks Today' series is a transcript of the author's sermons, this is not it! I hope that these more recent meditations on this fascinating though difficult part of Scripture are that much closer to its central message than earlier ones will have been. For it does have a central message. The problem is discerning it.

I am quite sure that Scripture is its own interpreter, that we are meant to see each part in the light of the rest, and that it is by leading God's people into Bible truth with Bible balance that the Holy Spirit fosters the mind of Christ and holiness of life in them. Among other things, this means that we shall try to see how the far end of Scripture illuminates this end, and we shall take seriously what are sometimes called New Testament 'controls', for the way that Christ and his apostles understood the Old Testament is obviously of first importance.

But in the case of Judges such controls are few. What we do have is the book itself, and its immediate Old Testament neighbours. And we shall see most clearly what the judges and their book are about if we find some way of reading it which allows every part to shed light on every other part; in other words, some approach which treats it as a literary unity. The question of how the book is put together can have two different types of answer, and for our purposes one is significant and the other is not. We leave aside the study of whatever sources, contributors, editors, and methods of compilation may have been involved in bringing Judges *to* its present form. Instead we concentrate on the book as we have it *in* its present form, and ask how each part relates to the rest and what Judges as a whole is intended to teach us.

And what might the answer be?

There is one obvious thing about the judges which a newcomer to the book might reckon (not without reason) to be quite misleading. That is the word 'judge' itself, with all its modern overtones – panelled courtrooms, gowns and gavels, legal proceedings which are deliberate, weighty, and venerable. None of the judges in the book of Judges fits into *that* scene; Deborah perhaps comes nearest, but most of them are fighters and adventurers, whose unlikely capers seem far removed from the majestic processes of the law.

Yet on reflection, perhaps 'judge' is not after all so misleading a word. Judgment means arbitration; it means discerning and deciding. Perhaps the deepest questions of the book do have to do with this. Who makes the decisions, the judgments? How do you judge the judgments – that is, how do you know when a decision is right? In particular, what results from the ignoring of a right judgment and the following of a wrong one? And as such errors multiply, what sort of final judgment will be made upon them?

These considerations underlie every chapter of Judges, not simply those concerning the 'judges' themselves but those dealing with Abimelech in the middle and with matters of introduction and conclusion at either end.

The Judge

The first and last verses of the book place it neatly in its historical setting. It deals with the period 'after the death of Joshua' (1:1) and before there was any 'king in Israel' (21:25), that is, between the exodus and the monarchy. Some commentators take it that the first phrase, 'After the death of Joshua', is a title; chapter 1 actually describes events *before* Joshua died, then his death is noted in its proper place at 2:8, and, following these preliminaries, the substance of the book called 'After the death of Joshua' begins at that point. Similarly, some believe that in the final verse of the book 'king' is equivalent to 'judge', and that chapters 17 to 21 show the sort of thing which could happen 'between judges', as it were – in the intervals when there was no ruler (king/judge) in Israel. We shall return to these points in due time.[2] For the moment, we shall assume that the entire book has to do with those instructive years of Israel's history which link the Moses/Joshua era with the setting-up of the kingdom.

If, in the days of the exodus and the days of the monarchy, there was one practical fact of life about which no-one needed to be in any doubt, it was this: you knew who was (or at any rate was supposed to be) in charge. Moses was God's friend, spoke with him face to face, acted as his mouthpiece;[3] Joshua was Moses' God-appointed successor, with a like authority and 'full of the spirit of wisdom'.[4] In the days of the exodus, between Israel's departure from Egypt and her settlement in Canaan, everyone knew where

---

[2] See pp. 18 n. 5, 171 n. 23   [3] Ex. 33:11; Nu. 12:6–8; Dt. 34:10.
[4] Dt. 34:9; Jos. 1:5; 4:14.

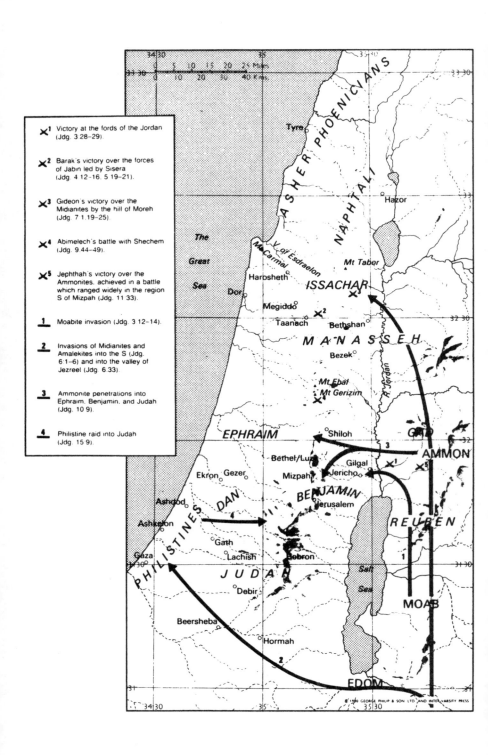

X¹ Victory at the fords of the Jordan
(Jdg. 3.28–29).

X² Barak's victory over the forces
of Jabin led by Sisera
(Jdg. 4.12–16, 5.19–21).

X³ Gideon's victory over the
Midianites by the hill of Moreh
(Jdg. 7.1.19–25).

X⁴ Abimelech's battle with Shechem
(Jdg. 9.44–49).

X⁵ Jephthah's victory over the
Ammonites, achieved in a battle
which ranged widely in the region
S of Mizpah (Jdg. 11.33).

1 Moabite invasion (Jdg. 3.12–14).

2 Invasions of Midianites and
Amalekites into the S (Jdg.
6.1–6), and into the valley of
Jezreel (Jdg. 6.33).

3 Ammonite penetrations into
Ephraim, Benjamin, and Judah
(Jdg. 10.9).

4 Philistine raid into Judah
(Jdg. 15.9).

decisions were to be obtained. The kings in their turn were God's viceroys; he gave them prophets and priests to guide them; and even if the kings and their decisions were often bad ones, it was quite clear in the days of the monarchy, from Saul to Zedekiah, where authority was meant to reside.

But in the intervening years, between the authority represented by Moses and Joshua on the near side and that represented by David and Solomon on the far side, Israel seemed to walk a fragile, swaying rope-bridge slung from one great cliff to another. So then who in that period made the decisions? Small wonder that, as we are told more than once, 'every man did what was right in his own eyes', or that many lost their footing and fell into the abyss. And it scarcely needs to be pointed out how well that quotation describes the world of today, or how sharp a lesson the book of Judges may have for the individualism and anti-authoritarianism of our own society.

Yet the question remains: who, in those lawless times, judged? It does have a positive answer, and not simply the obvious one (the twelve whom the book names). Israel did not need to wait for a crisis, and the consequent raising up of a deliverer, in order to find out that answer. Jephthah, himself one of the twelve, misunderstood much about the God he served, but he understood this, when he appealed to 'the LORD, the Judge' (11:27). That judgment is always available. The fragility of the rope-bridge is in this respect an illusion. God's people are as secure on it as on the cliffs at either end of it. The very first verse of Judges shows them looking to that unchanging authority, the Lord himself, for his judgment as to what should be the next stage in the occupation of the new land. Up to then they have sought his judgments through his servants Moses and Joshua; now 'after the death of Joshua' they go direct, before they have even heard of the judges, to the Judge himself.

We have here, as the primary theme of this relatively obscure book, one of the great fundamental facts of Scripture. The psalmists rejoice in the prospect of God's coming to judge the earth, anticipating those mighty, dynamic decisions by which he will one day cause all things to be what they ought to be: 'He will judge the world with righteousness'.[5] The New Testament focuses this in the second coming of Jesus: God 'has fixed a day on which he will judge the world in righteousness by a man who he has appointed'.[6] Two thousand years earlier it had already been recognized that the decisions of God operate in the present as well as the future: Abraham expected that in his own day 'the Judge of all the earth'

[5] Ps. 96:13; 98:9.   [6] Acts 17:31.

would act in the matter of the follies of Lot and the evils of Sodom.[7]

This is the Judge who stands behind the judges.[8] In such testing days, they and all the people of God are given the responsibility of finding and then following the divine decisions. They can no longer blame Moses, they cannot yet pass the buck to their kings; they themselves have to learn to 'judge with right judgment'[9] and to 'think God's thoughts after him'.[10] Their success or failure in this, and the consequences of it, are what the book before us describes. And the fact that Judges shows how helpless man is in trying to live by such judgments, and how faithful God is in preserving his people in spite of that, makes it an outstanding witness to the truth that where sin increases, grace abounds all the more.[11]

[7] Gn. 18:25.
[8] 'From first to last Yahweh had in truth ruled Israel through his judge' (Boling, p. 241).
[9] Jn. 7:24.
[10] Johannes Kepler, of his work in astronomy in the sixteenth century.
[11] Rom. 5:20.

Judges 1:1 – 3:6

1. The Lord, the Judge

Judges, like every other part of the Bible, has to be read before it can be read. That is, the kind of reading which tries to grasp how it is put together and what its message is needs to be preceded by a reading which simply aims to get to know its contents. By the time you start the second reading, you know that the title 'Judges' refers to twelve successive characters in the book, all in some sense leaders among the people of God. Some (not all) are actually called judges;[1] some are spoken of as deliverers or saviours of Israel;[2] with some, the need for them is indicated by the note àt the beginning of their stories that 'the people . . . did what was evil', so that the Lord first punished Israel and then when she repented raised up this or that rescuer for her.[3] Each of the twelve is identified by one or more of these markers. You will also have noticed that there is a great disparity in the lengths of the accounts (Gideon has a hundred verses, Shamgar one); that a whole chapter in the middle of the book is devoted to a man called Abimelech who was not a judge at all; and that two other chapters at the beginning, and five more at the end, also fall outside the category of judge-narratives. It seems, then, that those narratives begin with Othniel at 3:7, and that we should take as the book's introduction the passage 1:1 – 3:6.[4] In those sixty-five verses no-one, apparently, is

---

[1] The verb 'to judge' is used in this connection in 3:10; 4:4; 10:2, 3; 12:7–9, 11, 13–14; 16:31.

[2] 3:9, 15, 31; 6:14; 10:1; 13:5.   [3] 3:7, 12; 4:1; 6:1; 10:6; 13:1.

[4] For literary reasons, which I do not myself find convincing, Klein takes the Othniel story as part of what she calls the 'exposition', and not as part of the central narrative. She does, however, relate this to the more readily acceptable view that it 'establishes a paradigm which shapes the following "major" judges narratives' (Klein, p. 11; also pp. 12–13, 193–195). See below, pp. 36–37.

yet judging Israel.[5] But as we have seen in our own introduction, the one who later in the book will be hailed as *the* Judge is very much in evidence, and that is the Lord. Three times in these opening chapters he speaks, and each time you realize on reflection that what he has uttered is a judgment.

1. The three judgments

The period of the judges can, as I have said earlier, be regarded as a precarious bridge slung between the authoritative certainties of the exodus on that side and the monarchy on this. But we need to be careful what use we make of that metaphor. On the one hand, we should not infer that Judges represents an abnormal situation for God's people, and that the sooner we can hand over the responsibility for decision-making to some authority-figure, the equivalent of Moses the lawgiver or David the king (whether it be in our time a priest, or a preacher, or a 'shepherd', or an unverifiable 'inner light'), the sooner we shall be back on firm ground. Nor, on the other hand, should we so react against that notion that we regard the uncertainties of Judges as the norm, despise those who look to 'Moses' or 'David' for decisions, and find positive virtue in every man's doing that which is right in his own untutored eyes (17:6; 21:25). The truth is, the message of Judges is needed in *every* age. It clarifies for God's people in any situation what is really important in the fundamental matters of authority and judgment.

For this reason one question which may seem very obvious at the start of the book goes, perhaps to our surprise, unanswered. 'Israel inquired of the LORD', and 'the LORD said . . .' (1:1–2). But how? What exactly did they do, and in what way did the Judge answer them? The book is silent. It is not interested in the method. If we are asking about that, we are asking the wrong question. The Lord had spoken in the law, he spoke sometimes by his angel, he would speak repeatedly through prophets; and in due course he would have New Testament ways for New Testament days. When in the time of the Old Testament God and man spoke together, we are often left in the dark as to the mechanism of the encounter,

---

[5] As noted above on p. 13, there are critics both liberal and conservative who take chapter 1 to be dealing with events before, not after, the death of Joshua; hence the assumption that the phrase 'After the death of Joshua' is a general heading or title. But the text makes perfectly good sense as it stands (2:6–10 being regarded as a flashback), particularly since Joshua was Moses' honoured successor not only as leader but also as prophet (p. 13 n. 4). 'Israel inquired of the Lord' in some direct way (1:1) precisely because Joshua *was* already dead; had he still been alive they would have inquired of him. See also Webb, pp. 82 and 203 n. 2.

but what we do know is that there was seldom if ever that it was God who had spoken. As for the utterances Christian times, certainty of that kind belongs only to of Jesus and the apostles as they are embodied in New Testament Scripture; all later words and signs and messages are debatable and fallible extras.

These matters, however, are not the concern of Judges. By whatever methods God's judgments may be made known, the important thing is that they touch the will and the conscience of man, and expect a response both in heart and in life.

So three times in these chapters the Judge speaks, in a directive (1:2), an accusation (2:1–3), and a decree (2:20–22) – each of them, when you come to think of it, in one sense or another a judgment.

2. The first judgment, and what follows (1:1–36)

After the death of Joshua the people of Israel inquired of the LORD, 'Who shall go up first for us against the Canaanites, to fight against them?' ²The LORD said, 'Judah shall go up; behold, I have given the land into his hand.' ³And Judah said to Simeon his brother, 'Come up with me into the territory allotted to me, that we may fight against the Canaanites; and I likewise will go with you into the territory allotted to you.' So Simeon went with him. ⁴Then Judah went up and the LORD gave the Canaanites and the Perizzites into their hand; and they defeated ten thousand of them at Bezek. ⁵They came upon Adoni-bezek at Bezek, and fought against him, and defeated the Canaanites and the Perizzites. ⁶Adoni-bezek fled; but they pursued him, and caught him, and cut off his thumbs and his great toes. ⁷And Adoni-bezek said, 'Seventy kings with their thumbs and their great toes cut off used to pick up scraps under my table; as I have done, so God has requited me.' And they brought him to Jerusalem, and he died there.

⁸And the men of Judah fought against Jerusalem, and took it, and smote it with the edge of the sword, and set the city on fire. ⁹And afterward the men of Judah went down to fight against the Canaanites who dwelt in the hill country, in the Negeb, and in the lowland. ¹⁰And Judah went against the Canaanites who dwelt in Hebron (now the name of Hebron was formerly Kiriath-arba); and they defeated Sheshai and Ahiman and Talmai.

¹¹From there they went against the inhabitants of Debir. The name of Debir was formerly Kiriath-sepher. ¹²And Caleb said, 'He who attacks Kiriath-sepher and takes it, I will give him Achsah my daughter as wife.' ¹³And Othni-el the son of Kenaz, Caleb's younger brother, took it; and he gave him Achsah his daughter as wife.

¹⁴*When she came to him, she urged him to ask her father for a field; and she alighted from her ass, and Caleb said to her, 'What do you wish?'* ¹⁵*She said to him, 'Give me a present; since you have set me in the land of the Negeb, give me also springs of water.' And Caleb gave her the upper springs and the lower springs.*

¹⁶*And the descendants of the Kenite, Moses' father-in-law, went up with the people of Judah from the city of palms into the wilderness of Judah, which lies in the Negeb near Arad; and they went and settled with the people.* ¹⁷*And Judah went with Simeon his brother, and they defeated the Canaanites who inhabited Zephath, and utterly destroyed it. So the name of the city was called Hormah.* ¹⁸*Judah also took Gaza with its territory, and Ashkelon with its territory, and Ekron with its territory.* ¹⁹*And the* LORD *was with Judah, and he took possession of the hill country, but he could not drive out the inhabitants of the plain, because they had chariots of iron.* ²⁰*And Hebron was given to Caleb, as Moses had said; and he drove out from it the three sons of Anak.* ²¹*But the people of Benjamin did not drive out the Jebusites who dwelt in Jerusalem; so the Jebusites have dwelt with the people of Benjamin in Jerusalem to this day.*

²²*The house of Joseph also went up against Bethel; and the* LORD *was with them.* ²³*And the house of Joseph sent to spy out Bethel. (Now the name of the city was formerly Luz.)* ²⁴*And the spies saw a man coming out of the city, and they said to him, 'Pray, show us the way into the city, and we will deal kindly with you.'* ²⁵*And he showed them the way into the city; and they smote the city with the edge of the sword, but they let the man and all his family go.* ²⁶*And the man went to the land of the Hittites and built a city, and called its name Luz; that is its name to this day.*

²⁷*Manasseh did not drive out the inhabitants of Beth-shean and its villages, or Taanach and its villages, or the inhabitants of Dor and its villages, or the inhabitants of Ibleam and its villages, or the inhabitants of Megiddo and its villages, but the Canaanites persisted in dwelling in that land.* ²⁸*When Israel grew strong, they put the Canaanites to forced labour, but did not utterly drive them out.*

²⁹*And Ephraim did not drive out the Canaanites who dwelt in Gezer; but the Canaanites dwelt in Gezer among them.*

³⁰*Zebulun did not drive out the inhabitants of Kitron, or the inhabitants of Nahalol; but the Canaanites dwelt among them, and became subject to forced labour.*

³¹*Asher did not drive out the inhabitants of Acco, or the inhabitants of Sidon, or of Ahlab, or of Achzib, or of Helbah, or of Aphik, or of Rehob;* ³²*but the Asherites dwelt among the Canaanites, the*

inhabitants of the land; for they did not drive them out.

³³Naphtali did not drive out the inhabitants of Beth-shemesh, or the inhabitants of Beth-anath, but dwelt among the Canaanites, the inhabitants of the land; nevertheless the inhabitants of Beth-shemesh and of Beth-anath became subject to forced labour for them.

³⁴The Amorites pressed the Danites back into the hill country, for they did not allow them to come down to the plain; ³⁵the Amorites persisted in dwelling in Har-heres, in Aijalon, and in Sha-albim, but the hand of the house of Joseph rested heavily upon them, and they became subject to forced labour. ³⁶And the border of the Amorites ran from the ascent of Akrabbim, from Sela and upward.

The question which Israel puts to the Lord is a military one. The occupation of the land she has invaded is not yet complete. The armies await orders. What, in the judgment of the commander-in-chief, is to be the next move? ' "Who shall go up first for us against the Canaanites, to fight against them?" The LORD said, "Judah shall go up; behold, I have given the land into his hand" ' (1:1–2).

a. Orders from headquarters (1:1–3)

Although we are not told by what means these orders were conveyed, we learn two helpful things about them from their background in the book of Joshua. The initial invasion of Canaan seems to have been rapid, effective, and in some sense complete; the summary of it in Joshua 11:16–23 is peppered with the word 'all' – all the land taken, all the kings defeated.[6] Even so, at the end of his life Joshua recognizes that there is still land to be occupied[7] and nations to be driven out.[8] If, as seems likely, it took a long time for Israel properly to 'possess' the land, and the Canaanite peoples re-emerged and rallied (they might be dead, but they

---

[6] Many of the commentators who hold that the campaigns of Jdg. 1 took place before, not after, the death of Joshua, hold also that they are the same campaigns which are described (rather differently) in Jos. 1 – 12. Soggin gives a classical statement of this view: 'It is clear . . . not only that these are two parallel versions of the same event, but also that the versions are clearly incompatible' (p. 26); one is idealized, with an army united and successful, the other is realistic, with forces fragmented and struggling. However, Jdg. 1:8 and 1:21 – another contradiction, as some would see it – show in a nutshell how there could plainly be two events, one after the other: the initial taking of Jerusalem did not guarantee the final driving out of its inhabitants. And so both in other details and in the broad overview: Israel 'took . . .' (that is, in effect, what Joshua says), but 'did not drive out . . .' (that is, in effect, what Judges says).

[7] Jos. 13:1–7. [8] Jos. 23:1–13.

wouldn't lie down), then a need for new onslaughts 'after the death of Joshua', as described in Judges 1, is quite understandable. The point is that the orders given in 1:2 are part of a general strategy made known long before to Joshua, and indeed to Moses.[9] That strategy is a 'judgment' already revealed by God, and – equally important – already accepted by his people, as is shown by the very fact that they are here eager to embark on the next stage of it.

The other background information which Joshua gives us has to do with Judah's allies in this campaign. 'The inheritance of the tribe of Simeon formed part of the territory of Judah',[10] so it was natural and right for the leading tribe to invite its brothers to join the enterprise without looking for some specific authorization from God.

In other words, however God's people in later ages may look for instructions equivalent to 'Judah shall go up' (1:2), two other kinds of directive must surely hold good for us all: the plain principles which God has already put into words, and the use of a 'sanctified common sense' which is in line with them.

b. Report from the field (1:4–36)

The first combined force comprises the armies of Judah and Simeon, and perhaps Benjamin (1:21), includes the house of Caleb (1:12ff.), and is accompanied by Moses' Kenite relatives (1:16). It aims at the territory allotted to these tribes, which means the south of Canaan. To use a term made famous many years later by the Greek author Xenophon, the troops engage first in an *Anabasis*, a 'march up-country' (' "Who shall go up . . . ?" . . . "Judah shall go up;" . . . Then Judah went up'), which takes the attackers from Jericho[11] to Jerusalem (1:8), then in what Xenophon would have called a *Katabasis*, a 'march down-country', into the hilly region round Hebron, the Negeb or southern desert, and the lowland (1:9). This campaign is in general a great success, although not quite all the inhabitants of the area can be dislodged (1:9, 21).

Following suit, 'the house of Joseph also went up' (1:22), with what might seem an equally successful campaign against Bethel. This paragraph and the rest of the chapter concern the northern part of Canaan. But the efforts of the six tribes listed in 1:27–35 are

---

[9] Jos. 1:1–9; Dt. 31:1–6.   [10] Jos. 19:9; see the whole paragraph.

[11] 'The city of palms' (1:16). Some think that this well-recognized name for Jericho (*cf.* Dt. 34:3; 2 Ch. 28:15) here refers to some other town. But it seems unlikely that separate Israelite invasions (*cf.* Jos. 2 – 6) should start from two different places both coincidentally called by the same name.

dismal failures so far as expulsion of the Canaanites is concerned.

c. Campaign review

Appropriately for a military report, Judges 1 is entirely factual. It adds no moral, makes no comment. But from its facts there are certain conclusions we are surely meant to draw.

The two phases of the successful southern campaign are based on Judah's obedience to orders (1:2–3). No wonder the Lord's help is experienced from start to finish (1:4, 19), no wonder the sack of Jerusalem is as thorough as any of Joshua's victories,[12] no wonder this is where we see the fulfilling of promises new and old – Judah's victory, Caleb's inheritance, the Kenites' blessing.[13] Only one failure mars the main account of the Judah campaign, the failure to drive out the plains-dwellers (1:19). The little appendix (1:20–21) parallels this by highlighting from the 'march down-country' the expulsion of the Anakim from Hebron, but from the 'march up-country' the non-expulsion of the Jebusites from Jerusalem.

And this leads into the sorry tale of the northern campaign. Is Joseph's sacking of Bethel really a success? The Lord went with his people against that city, and there was precedent for the stratagem by which they penetrated its defences;[14] but the result was that while the old Luz was destroyed, a new one was built, perpetuating the Canaanite culture which God had appointed for destruction. Are we not meant to contrast this first incident in the north with the first one in the southern campaign? There, the lord of Bezek is justly destroyed by Judah (1:6–7); here, the man of Luz is unjustly spared by Joseph (1:25–26). And the contrast continues. Instead of the victories of Judah, we find a dismaying sequence in which Canaanites are allowed to live at a distance from Israelites (1:22–26), Canaanites are allowed to live among Israelites (1:27–30), Israelites are allowed to live among Canaanites (1:31–33), and finally Israelites are allowed to live at a distance from Canaanites (1:34).[15] Here too a tiny appendix, corresponding to 1:20–21, puts the result in a nutshell: the inhabitants of the land are proving so tenacious that for all Judah's successes even the southern border is still thought of as an Amorite one (1:36).

In a word, our review of the field-report has to be 'Disappointing'. An excellent start tails right off. We must get this sobering pattern firmly in our minds, because it will be the pattern of the whole book. We note that chapter 1 begins with the obedience of

---

[12] With 1:8 cf. Jos. 6:24; 8:8,19; 11:10–11.   [13] 1:2; Jos. 14:6–15; Nu. 10:29.
[14] Rahab at Jericho, Jos. 2.   [15] Webb, p. 99.

Judah and ends with the disgrace of Dan, and shall not be surprised to find that the overall history of the twelve judges is likewise an increasingly unsatisfactory one all the way from Othniel the Judahite to Samson the Danite. The Lord keeps *his* promises, but will his people do *their* part? Will they accept his judgment (that is, what he judges, or decides, is to be done – a judgment which comes to them as a directive) and then act on it, or will they ignore him and do their own thing?

We cannot leave chapter 1 without finding some encouragement in the remaining episode included there, alongside those relating to Jerusalem and Bethel. This is the account of the capture of Debir, which has already appeared in Joshua 15:14–19, but is no doubt reproduced here in 1:11–15 because it points forward to so much else that we shall find in Judges. For the moment, we simply note one thing about it. In taking the Canaanite town Othniel wins also the hand of Caleb's daughter, and fruitful farmland with it; that is, in a chapter which is generally rather disappointing we have a tale of a task well done, a promise kept, a gift given, and a marriage made. We are aware of all that marriage is going to symbolize as the rest of Scripture unfolds the relationship between God and his people. Maybe we have here as one key to Judges the bright hope that where her behaviour is wedded to his judgments, and her endeavours to his power, there Israel becomes the bride of her LORD, and things begin to be as they ought.

3. The second judgment, and what follows (2:1–19)

Now the angel of the LORD went up from Gilgal to Bochim. And he said, 'I brought you up from Egypt, and brought you into the land which I swore to give to your fathers. I said, "I will never break my covenant with you, ²and you shall make no covenant with the inhabitants of this land; you shall break down their altars." But you have not obeyed my command. What is this you have done? ³So now I say, I will not drive them out before you; but they shall become adversaries to you, and their gods shall be a snare to you.' ⁴When the angel of the LORD spoke these words to all the people of Israel, the people lifted up their voices and wept. ⁵And they called the name of that place Bochim; and they sacrificed there to the LORD.

⁶When Joshua dismissed the people, the people of Israel went each to his inheritance to take possession of the land. ⁷And the people served the LORD all the days of Joshua, and all the days of the elders who outlived Joshua, who had seen all the great work which the LORD had done for Israel. ⁸And Joshua the son of Nun, the servant of the LORD, died at the age of one hundred and ten years. ⁹And they buried him within the bounds of his inheritance in Timnath-heres, in the hill country of Ephraim, north of the mountain of Gaash. ¹⁰And all that generation also were gathered to their fathers; and there arose another generation after them, who did not know the LORD or the work which he had done for Israel.

¹¹And the people of Israel did what was evil in the sight of the LORD and served the Baals; ¹²and they forsook the LORD, the God of their fathers, who had brought them out of the land of Egypt; they went after other gods, from among the gods of the peoples who were round about them, and bowed down to them; and they provoked the LORD to anger. ¹³They forsook the LORD, and served the Baals and the Ashtaroth. ¹⁴So the anger of the LORD was kindled against Israel, and he gave them over to plunderers, who plundered them; and he sold them into the power of their enemies round about, so that they could no longer withstand their enemies. ¹⁵Whenever they marched out, the hand of the LORD was against them for evil, as the LORD had warned, and as the LORD had sworn to them; and they were in sore straits.

¹⁶Then the LORD raised up judges, who saved them out of the power of those who plundered them. ¹⁷And yet they did not listen to their judges; for they played the harlot after other gods and bowed down to them; they soon turned aside from the way in which their fathers had walked, who had obeyed the commandments of the LORD, and they did not do so. ¹⁸Whenever the LORD raised up judges for them, the LORD was with the judge, and he saved them from the hand of their enemies all the days of the judge; for the LORD was moved to pity by their groaning because of those who afflicted and oppressed them. ¹⁹But whenever the judge died, they turned back and behaved worse than their fathers, going after other gods, serving them and bowing down to them; they did not drop any of their practices or their stubborn ways.

This time Judges does tell us the method by which the Lord's message is heard – not that that is of much help to those who are eager to discover ways and means for the present day: 'the angel of the LORD went up from Gilgal to Bochim' (2:1), and there spoke presumably to some kind of Israelite assembly. Angels are not exactly biddable, in any case, and there are features of this one's coming which make the event unrepeatable. When the angel of the Lord brings messages to Gideon and to Samson's parents, he simply appears, and after the interview vanishes or ascends (6:11–12, 21; 13:3, 20), by which time he has been recognized as being obviously a supernatural visitant. But here the angel is discovered in the process of travelling up the road from Gilgal, as anyone might do – and, significantly, as the armies of Judah and Joseph had done not long before. The book does not identify the messenger (who may indeed have been human, and not supernatural at all),[16] any more than it explains the method. But its note of the geography is loaded with meaning. Gilgal, 'the Circle', was the stone monument marking the place by Jericho where Joshua had first brought Israel across the River Jordan into Canaan.[17] It was the starting point of his own campaigns, and from Gilgal/Jericho likewise the campaigns of Judges 1 will have begun.[18] The location which after this incident was known as Bochim ('Weepers') may well have been the town known to the Canaanites as Luz and to Israel as Bethel.[19] If this is so, then from the place from which both southern and northern armies had gone up, to the place where, as we shall shortly see, the covenant was betrayed, God's messenger in his turn went up, himself following the course of events and seeing what kind of obedience it showed, before he turned to the people with his judgment on it.

a. The charge and the plea (2:1–5)

If the character of the Lord's first utterance was military, the character of this one is legal. Where that was a directive, this is an accusation, with a charge brought, a plea made, and evidence produced. What is more, instead of chapter 1's mere reporting of events, we have here a probing of motives and an exposing of attitudes.

The charge is not what we might have thought. 'You have not obeyed my command' (2:2). What disobedience has the Lord seen as he has followed the progress of his armies in chapter 1? A failure to expel the people of Canaan? Yes, but that is not the substance of the charge. The nub of the matter is the command to 'make no covenant with the inhabitants of this land'. It is of disobedience at that point that Israel stands accused.

Yet the two kinds of failure (tolerating Canaanites, and covenanting with them) cannot be separated. An imaginary dialogue will show us the reason.

---

[16] 'Angel' in both Old Testament and New – *mal'āk, angelos* – merely means 'messenger'. Contexts usually make plain whether these 'angels' are supernatural (Messengers with a capital 'M', as it were) or human.

[17] Jos. 4:19–24.   [18] See above, p. 22.

[19] Most commentaries point out that the Greek Old Testament links Bethel with Bochim in this place, and mention also the 'Oak of Weeping' near Bethel/Luz in Gn. 35:8.

– Why have my plans for occupation not been carried through?

– We lacked the military capability for the final push.

– But did I not say that if your willingness was wedded to my power, I myself would see to the expelling of the enemy? Something has gone wrong with that 'wedding'.[20] If you have not driven them out, then what have you done with them?

– We have had to come to an arrangement. The terms have been as favourable as we could make them.

And that of course was the forbidden covenant, the kind of agreement implied in every paragraph of 1:27–35, the recognition of a Canaanite culture which was determined[21] to stay put. In fact the spirit of compromise is already there, like a worm in the ripe fruit, at the heart of Israel's 'success' at Bethel: the city is taken, but the Canaanite informer survives to build another Luz because the Israelites deal 'kindly', or *loyally*, with him.[22] That is a covenant, a pledge, an accommodation with danger and evil. But 'what partnership have righteousness and iniquity? Or what fellowship has light with darkness?'[23]

The accusation has extra edge to it precisely because it is only an accusation, and Israel is left in suspense as to what the Judge's sentence will be. For although it looks like it in some translations (*e.g.* RSV: 'So now I say . . .'), verse 3 is not his sentence. 2:1 and 2:3 should be read like this: 'I said, I will never break my covenant . . . *and I also said,* If you compromise with these nations I will not drive them out.'[24] It is as though the Lord is saying, 'I have sworn to give you the whole of this land, yet I have also sworn not to give it wholly to a disobedient people. You put me in an impossible position. *What is this you have done?* And by what fearful means do you think I am to solve my dilemma?'

No wonder 'the people lifted up their voices and wept' (2:4). They had dug for themselves a pit deeper than they knew. They had no choice but to plead guilty. Their tears showed their remorse, their sacrifices showed how very devout they were, and their calling the place 'Weepers' showed how mindful of the rebuke they meant to be in the future. But what are we to make of all this contrition? To judge by the evidence that backs up the charge, not much.

[20] *I.e.* Israel's endeavours wedded to the Lord's judgment; see above, p. 24.

[21] 1:27, 35 NIV; better than RSV's 'persisted'.

[22] 1:24. See Webb, pp. 92–97, where the relations between 1:22–26 and the Rahab story in Jos. 2 and 6 are also explored.

[23] 2 Cor. 6:14.

[24] Webb, pp. 102–105. The second 'said' refers to Jos. 23:12–13.

b. The evidence (2:6–19)

Assuming that everything in Judges happens 'after the death of Joshua', I take the further reference to him here in chapter 2 to be a flashback. This assumption makes good sense of 2:6–19. On the basis of it, the passage is understood as a survey of the spiritual state of Israel which covers the whole of those times. As it looks ahead over the entire period of the judges, so it also looks right back to Joshua. True, the accusation at Bochim, which relates to this survey, is made before even the first of the judges has emerged. But the process of decline was continuous. What would follow was of a piece with what had already happened. The survey of evidence covers three 'generations', and the Israelites at Bochim were sufficiently aware of being 'second-generation' people to know what the angel was talking about, and to know what kind of further evidence would be accumulating as the second gave place to the third.

The first generation (2:6–9) was that of Joshua and his contemporaries. It is referred to in order to provide a contrast with what was to follow. It was marked by two things, which belonged together: its people served the Lord, and they took possession of the land he had given them. Joshua's own burial 'within the bounds of his inheritance' (2:9) sums it up – the consummation of a long life of trusting and obeying. Not that Joshua was himself indispensable, for the same desire to find and follow the Lord's plans for them characterized his fellow-Israelites even in 'the days of the elders who outlived Joshua'; the crucial factor was that there were still in Israel a personal knowledge of the Lord's redeeming work, and people who had directly experienced the rescue from Egypt and the moulding of a new nation.

That was the contrast with the second generation (2:10–18). It 'did not know the LORD or the work which he had done for Israel'. Consequently, in the words which will become all too familiar, 'the people of Israel did what was evil in the sight of the LORD'. The evil is simple, but profound, and it has its equivalents in every age. Exchanging the God of classical, historical redemption for the nature-gods who dominate the thinking of most ordinary people around you (2:12) – what could be more sensible? For the nature-gods, of course, wear a variety of disguises. In the days of the judges they were called Dagon and Baal; nowadays they are anything from New Age pantheism to the market forces of economics. All of them are powers which are excitingly bigger than you, but which you can nevertheless manipulate to your own ends.[25]

[25] See pp. 80–81.

We may ask, how could a generation which had simply not been there at the time of the exodus be blamed for being born too late? The answer is that Scripture sees the experience of redemption as being infinitely renewable. As children ask parents and parents teach children, as those 'who have not known it ... hear and learn',[26] the liberating truth of the exodus-gospel can repeatedly become a reality. There is no excuse for the 'second generation' of Judges 2.

Like the phrase 'the people did evil', the total pattern of events which will soon be only too familiar appears first in this generation. Its rebellion against the Lord (2:11–13) brings retribution, as he hands them over to oppressors (2:14–15). Their consequent misery, even if it is expressed only in 'groaning', as here (2:18), and not in a cry for help, still less a real repentance, then moves him to rescue them by means of a judge or deliverer (2:16–18). The rebellion/ retribution/repentance/rescue cycle, which we have noted already, will be a recurring motif in the book.

But unsatisfactory as it may be to resign ourselves to such a cycle, from which Judges appears to offer no way out, something even more disturbing is foreseen here. We note in passing that the judges do have some kind of guiding role, as well as a rescuing one, since we are told the people 'did not listen to' them; that is a second-generation characteristic, in contrast to the obedient first generation (2:17). But then, what we may call the third generation comes into view. These are they who on the death of the judge behave even 'worse than their fathers', and who fresh from the experience of rescue will still 'not drop any of their practices or their stubborn ways' (2:19). What we see then in the period of the judges, which follows the judgment of Bochim, is what we saw in the military campaigns which preceded it – namely, an inexorable decline. If there is anything cyclic about it, it is not a circle but a spiral, and a downward one.[27]

This is the evidence on which the Lord bases his second judgment. What has happened, what will happen, both are known to him, and the people's knowledge, though more limited, equally

---

[26] Dt. 31:13.

[27] Klein, quoting from W. B. Yeats the phrase 'the widening gyre', suggests the equally helpful image of a spiral moving not downward but outward (which is what Yeats' words mean), with 'the separation between Yahweh and his people becoming ever greater' (p. 20). The quotation is from the poem *The Second Coming*:

> Turning and turning in the widening gyre
> The falcon cannot hear the falconer;
> Things fall part; the centre cannot hold;
> Mere anarchy is loosed upon the world.

condemns them, as they recognize. When, having been given the rule of the judges, it is plain that they still will not obey, they must then hear the third judgment.

4. The third judgment, and what follows (2:20 – 3:6)

So the anger of the LORD was kindled against Israel; and he said, 'Because this people have transgressed my covenant which I commanded their fathers, and have not obeyed my voice, ²¹I will not henceforth drive out before them any of the nations that Joshua left when he died, ²²that by them I may test Israel, whether they will take care to walk in the way of the LORD as their fathers did, or not.' ²³So the LORD left those nations, not driving them out at once, and he did not give them into the power of Joshua.

³:¹Now these are the nations which the LORD left, to test Israel by them, that is, all in Israel who had no experience of any war in Canaan; ²it was only that the generations of the people of Israel might know war, that he might teach war to such at least as had not known it before. ³These are the nations: the five lords of the Philistines, and all the Canaanites, and the Sidonians, and the Hivites who dwelt on Mount Lebanon, from Mount Baal-hermon as far as the entrance of Hamath. ⁴They were for the testing of Israel, to know whether Israel would obey the commandments of the LORD, which he commanded their fathers by Moses. ⁵So the people of Israel dwelt among the Canaanites, the Hittites, the Amorites, the Perizzites, the Hivites, and the Jebusites; ⁶and they took their daughters to themselves for wives, and their own daughters they gave to their sons; and they served their gods.

The second judgment was linked to the first, as the angel of the Lord 'went up' to see how the armies' orders had been carried out; and the third is linked to the second, as charge, plea, and evidence are followed by sentence. But each judgment also has its own distinctive character. The first was a military directive, the second a legal accusation; this one is more like a royal decree.

a. The decree (2:20–22)

What the Lord says here is the sequel to what he said at Bochim. We saw there his dilemma. He was not yet passing sentence, or proclaiming a decree, but reminding Israel of the two apparently contradictory things he had covenanted to do. A disobedient people would find that he would not drive out their enemies; yet he had also promised to give Israel the land to be entirely her own. How to reconcile the two?

Here now is his judgment. It will be the former promise, the non-expulsion of enemies, which his people will find fulfilled in their experience. The latter promise, complete possession of the land, must still hold good in some sense, but they are left in the dark as to when and how it will come true, and it will not do so in their time. As with so many other Bible statements about the land, it will be regularly misunderstood as the years go by. But the dangerous and damaging presence of the Canaanite nations (whom he has already, mark you, appointed for destruction),[28] shall now, he declares, continue. After all, co-existence with them is what Israel seems to want!

But the Lord is not being vindictive; he has a purpose, set out briefly in the decree itself and opened up in what follows.

b. The rationale (2:23 – 3:6)

It was part of the Lord's plan even at the time that there should be in Canaan 'nations that Joshua left when he died' (2:21). Joshua 23, which tells us this at greater length, does not tell us the purpose of it, but we might reasonably suppose that it was to allow for a gradual and therefore thorough settling of Israel in her new land, without her having to be over-extended or spread too thinly too soon. Whether or not there was even then a further purpose in mind, that of a testing for Israel,[29] such a testing is explicitly his purpose now (3:1).

We should not be surprised at the connection here between the words 'test' and 'know'. It is a principle in spiritual things as well as in educational that the teacher tests in order to find out what the pupil knows, and even more important, in order to know the pupil himself. The latter point must be stressed. It is easy to react against some styles of Christian faith because they seem to be geared to the brain rather than the heart. But we cannot on that account delete the word 'know' from the vocabulary of the Bible. The use of mind and intellect is intended to lead towards a knowledge of the truth, and therefore towards a personal knowledge of God;[30] while God's knowledge of the believer is more basic still,[31] and the two 'knowings' are in the end seen to be inseparable.[32]

Both combined form the positive and merciful object of the

---

[28] Gn. 15:16; Lv. 18:24–25; 20:23; Dt. 9:4–5.

[29] The original sense of 2:21–22 may have been '. . . the nations that *Joshua* left . . . *in order to test Israel*'; see Webb, p. 242, n. 110.

[30] *Cf.* Jn. 8:32; 17:3.   [31] Ps. 139.   [32] 1 Cor. 13:12.

Lord's third judgment. They are not perhaps stated in an obvious way. It is clear enough (3:4) that one object of his non-expulsion of the Canaanites is that he will know his people that much better: they will have an extended canvas on which to set forth before his eyes their characters and attitudes. But the converse of his knowing them is not, surprisingly, described as their knowing him. The other half of the test is that they should know *war* (3:2). Why should that kind of knowledge be so crucial? The answer must surely be that it is just that, the conflict with other nations, which enables Israel to know her God. Her oppressors in Egypt, her opponents during the wilderness journey, the occupants of the land she was to take over, each in turn compelled the Lord's own nation to recognize something more of what made him, and therefore her, distinctive. Over against every deadly alternative, inadequate or perverse, hectoring or seductive, the God of Israel became increasingly clearly defined as the Way, the Truth, and the Life. It was by recognizing where conflict was necessary – by 'knowing the war' – that she would come to know him.[33] What the Lord says in this third utterance is judgment in the sense of a judge's sentence, but within the doom we can see its freight of mercy.

It is, all the same, a hard judgment, and one which our own generation needs to understand. Had all gone well, the probationary, educational period – the testing – would have been covered historically by just five Bible books, from Exodus 1 to Joshua 24. Moses would have begun it, Joshua would have completed it, and there and then probation would have been followed by fruition. But what 2:21–22 tells us is that in the event probation is followed by more probation, and who knows when the fruition will come?

From a different point of view, it is true of course that already in Joshua's lifetime 'the LORD had given rest to Israel'.[34] But the New Testament 'control' in Hebrews 4 brings together Joshua 23 and Psalm 95, and explains that we have to read these histories on two levels. In one sense probation was followed by fruition immediately, and *in the perspective of the book of Joshua* Israel did find her promised rest. In the same way, once the monarchy was established King David was given 'rest from all his enemies';[35] that is the perspective of the books of Samuel and Kings. But in another, deeper, sense the Lord could say: 'I swore in my anger that they should *not* enter my rest.' His people continued on probation. Indeed even now 'rest' is a thing to strive towards, and 'it remains

---

[33] In the same way, Christian history shows how each successive heresy has led to a sharper definition of the true faith.

[34] Jos. 23:1 – and periodically it is noted in Judges too: 3:11, *etc.*

[35] 2 Sa. 7:1.

for some to enter it'. That is the perspective of Psalm 95, Hebrews 4, and the book of Judges.[36]

In this sense Judges has a message for all time. As Webb rightly says, 'According to 2:6 – 3:6 all these conflicts grow more intense as the judges era runs its course, and at the end no solution to them is in sight.'[37] Or rather, the solution *is* seen, in prospect, by apostles and prophets throughout Bible times, but will not *arrive* until sin and death are finally swallowed up in victory. Till then, for purposes of testing and discipline the Lord leaves perpetual Canaanite thorns in his people's sides, and to claim freedom from them in this life is to claim more than he has promised, and to miss the blessings that can come by no other means.

It will not have escaped the reader that the three utterances of the Judge in these opening chapters of the book are a universal word to his people in every age. First comes the *directive*, when God commands. What is commanded scarcely matters (once, at the beginning of history, it was simply 'Don't touch the fruit'!); in some way or other law is laid down, the will of man is addressed, and obedience is required. By this the sinfulness of man is exposed, since in his self-will he naturally disobeys. The second judgment therefore is the *accusation*. Again, as with the content of the command, the form of the response scarcely matters. Whether the accused are penitent, or merely remorseful, or even quite unabashed, there follows the third word, the *decree*, showing how God deals with his sinful people, using much that is evil to discipline and train them. The threat of the lowering clouds ahead finds an echo in Chesterton's famous lines:

> I bring you naught for your comfort,
>   Yea, naught for your desire,
> Save that the sky grows darker yet,
>   And the sea rises higher.[38]

We may take courage from the poem's subject: the humility of the great Saxon king Alfred, as the heathen repeatedly overran his England, in learning to accept the discipline, to confront the storm, to clarify his aims and to stand against his enemies, however long he might be called to do so.

---

[36] Ps. 95:11; Heb. 4:3–11. Similarly, where Samuel/Kings speaks of David's attaining 'rest', Chronicles says that he is a man of war, and that not till Solomon's time will rest come (1 Ch. 22:9; 28:3, RV; see my *The Message of Chronicles*, pp. 93f., 99).

[37] Webb, p. 121.

[38] G. K. Chesterton, *The Ballad of the White Horse*.

Judges 3:7–31

2. Ehud: the rule of the left hand

And the people of Israel did what was evil in the sight of the LORD, forgetting the LORD their God, and serving the Baals and the Asheroth. ⁸*Therefore the anger of the LORD was kindled against Israel, and he sold them into the hand of Cushan-rishathaim king of Mesopotamia; and the people of Israel served Cushan-rishathaim eight years.* ⁹*But when the people of Israel cried to the LORD, the LORD raised up a deliverer for the people of Israel, who delivered them, Othni-el the son of Kenaz, Caleb's younger brother.* ¹⁰*The Spirit of the LORD came upon him, and he judged Israel; he went out to war, and the LORD gave Cushan-rishathaim king of Mesopotamia into his hand; and his hand prevailed over Cushan-rishathaim.* ¹¹*So the land had rest forty years. Then Othni-el the son of Kenaz died.*

¹² *And the people of Israel again did what was evil in the sight of the LORD; and the LORD strengthened Eglon the king of Moab against Israel, because they had done what was evil in the sight of the LORD.* ¹³*He gathered to himself the Ammonites and the Amalekites, and went and defeated Israel; and they took possession of the city of palms.* ¹⁴*And the people of Israel served Eglon the king of Moab eighteen years.*

¹⁵ *But when the people of Israel cried to the LORD, the LORD raised up for them a deliverer, Ehud, the son of Gera, the Benjaminite, a left-handed man. The people of Israel sent tribute by him to Eglon the king of Moab.* ¹⁶*And Ehud made for himself a sword with two edges, a cubit in length; and he girded it on his right thigh under his clothes.* ¹⁷*And he presented a tribute to Eglon king of Moab. Now Eglon was a very fat man.* ¹⁸*And when Ehud had finished presenting the tribute, he sent away the people that carried the tribute.* ¹⁹*But he himself turned back at the sculptured stones near Gilgal, and said, 'I have a secret message for you, O king.'*

And he commanded, 'Silence.' And all his attendants went out from his presence. ²⁰And Ehud came to him, as he was sitting alone in his cool roof chamber. And Ehud said, 'I have a message from God for you.' And he arose from his seat. ²¹And Ehud reached with his left hand, took the sword from his right thigh, and thrust it into his belly; ²²and the hilt also went in after the blade, and the fat closed over the blade, for he did not draw the sword out of his belly; and the dirt came out. ²³Then Ehud went out into the vestibule, and closed the doors of the roof chamber upon him, and locked them.

²⁴When he had gone, the servants came; and when they saw that the doors of the roof chamber were locked, they thought, 'He is only relieving himself in the closet of the cool chamber.' ²⁵And they waited till they were utterly at a loss; but when he still did not open the doors of the roof chamber, they took the key and opened them; and there lay their lord dead on the floor.

²⁶Ehud escaped while they delayed, and passed beyond the sculptured stones, and escaped to Se-irah. ²⁷When he arrived, he sounded the trumpet in the hill country of Ephraim; and the people of Israel went down with him from the hill country, having him at their head. ²⁸And he said to them, 'Follow after me; for the LORD has given your enemies the Moabites into your hand.' So they went down after him, and seized the fords of the Jordan against the Moabites, and allowed not a man to pass over. ²⁹And they killed at that time about ten thousand of the Moabites, all strong, able-bodied men; not a man escaped. ³⁰So Moab was subdued that day under the hand of Israel. And the land had rest for eighty years.

³¹After him was Shamgar the son of Anath, who killed six hundred of the Philistines with an oxgoad; and he too delivered Israel.

It must be a rare experience to hear a sermon about Ehud and Eglon. I shall not be the only person brought up in a Bible-reading family to have relished since childhood the tale of the left-handed judge and the fat king of Moab. But how often do preachers preach on them?

Here, at all events, they are the main subject of this section of the book, with Ehud's as the first of the judge-narratives to be set out in any detail. So far from being shelved temporarily as something peculiar, therefore, it asks to be considered as something rather important.

Even so, Ehud is the second, not the first, of the judges. It is worth pondering why his story (3:12–30) should be preceded by the brief account of Othniel, the first (3:7–11), and followed by the even briefer one of Shamgar, the third (3:31).

1. The setting: a shift of perception

The book's lengthy introduction of sixty-five verses has set out the background for the period of the judges. We have been given some idea of what sort of people they will be, why they will be needed, and what they may be expected to achieve. There will in the event be a dozen of them. The twelve accounts will be hugely disparate in length, ranging from a hundred verses to a single one; the first three are all here in our present chapter. What are we meant to learn from Othniel and Shamgar, who provide the setting for Ehud?

a. Othniel (3:7-11)

We noted early on that there is a basic pattern which recurs throughout Judges. Rebellion on the part of Israel is followed by retribution sent by God, and when Israel repents God rescues her. But the reader soon sees that these four Rs, though they may be a useful alliteration for the preacher, over-simplify our writer's recurring framework. He has more recently set out for us, in 2:11-19, a second pattern, slightly different and more complex. In this one we may plot six points:
1. Israel sins (2:11-13)
2. Israel angers the Lord (2:14a)
3. Israel is subjected to an oppressor (2:14b-15)
4. A deliverer is raised up (2:16a)
5. The deliverer rescues Israel (2:16b)
6. The deliverer dies (2:19a).

There is of course more to these verses, 2:11-19, than this six-point sequence. But it is a pattern which will surface repeatedly throughout the next fourteen chapters.

We can readily see how the four points of the simpler framework, the four Rs, relate to these six. But in my view it is the Othniel story in chapter 3, not the six points I have highlighted in chapter 2, which sets out the intended pattern – that is, the one we are really intended to look for. If this is correct, then this first judge-narrative is relatively brief precisely because it is meant as a framework. Though brief, it is rather more detailed than the frameworks noted above. Eleven points make it up (I have italicized the five new ones):
1. Israel sins (3:7)
2. Israel angers the Lord (3:8a)
3. Israel is subjected to an oppressor (3:8b)
4. *Israel cries to the Lord (3:9a)*
5. A deliverer is raised up (3:9b)

6. *The deliverer is described (3:9c)*
7. *The deliverer is empowered (3:10a)*
8. *The deliverer judges Israel (3:10b)*
9. The deliverer rescues Israel (3:10c)
10. *The deliverer gives rest to Israel (3:11a)*
11. The deliverer dies (3:11b).

It is obvious how the eleven points amplify the six, just as the six amplified the four. Not all of them will appear in every judge's story; Ehud's shows many, Shamgar's only two. But Othniel's is the basic pattern of judgeship.

The way the points are made reinforces this view. 'Israel sins', and it is the classic sin of preferring the local gods to her own God. 'Israel is subjected to an oppressor', and he is given the name of Cushan-Rishathaim: from Mesopotamia (Aram-Naharaim, Aram of the Two Rivers) comes Cushan of the Two Wickednesses,[1] the classic double-dyed villain. 'The deliverer is described' as a man of the tribe of Judah, the nephew of the great Caleb (a fine pedigree), whom we have already been asked to admire in 1:11–13. 'The deliverer gives rest to Israel' for the forty-five year period often reckoned in Scripture as standard for a full generation.

This, in other words, is a paradigm, a pattern which will be repeated often through the time of the judges, given the two underlying facts of the period. First, we must recognize that authority is not at this time found in a lawgiver like Moses or a king like David. Secondly, we must recognize that never in this book will the people of God be rid of the people of the land; the pressures of that evil influence will persist throughout. Given these two facts, we see how the Lord deals with the situation. He continues to sit in judgment over it. He will raise up leaders of his own choosing, on the model not of Moses or David but of Othniel. Through them he will rescue his people not only from their oppressors but from themselves.

Yet having set up the model, what does he then do with it?

b. Shamgar (3:31)

Shamgar is only the next judge but one, and already the ideal of Israelite judgeship is brought down to this reduced compass! What are we given? The briefest of all twelve accounts. Who is he? We are told his name and his father's name (or the name of his home town), and that is all. Which tribe does he come from? Guesses

---

[1] So the old Jewish scholars, adding vowels to the consonants of the original Hebrew Bible, interpreted the name.

have been made (twelve judges could represent the twelve tribes of Israel),[2] but the fact is we do not know; he may not even have been an Israelite.[3] How did he rescue Israel? 'With an oxgoad'! No doubt this implement could have been a formidable weapon if heavy and well-sharpened, and certainly we are meant to see the incident as a remarkable feat of arms. But it is very odd, and the story is very unlike Othniel's. The one constant that emerges in this single-verse account of Shamgar is that 'he too delivered Israel'.

So we have moved from a classic situation, with a typical villain, an obvious hero and an expected deliverance, to the tiniest, oddest picture of a judgeship unexpected, untypical and far from obvious. And between Othniel and Shamgar the pattern has shifted before our eyes. As with the word-game in which one letter at a time is changed until the last word is quite different from the first, so that (for example) WHITE turns into BLACK,[4] so point by point the story of Ehud takes the pattern of Othniel and alters it, to show us the unexpectedness of God's saving methods. The Lord says to his people: 'This is what I intend to do for you, and this is how you perhaps expect me to do it. Now you may pin me down as to the ultimate object, because that I have promised; but you will want also to pin me down as to the method, because you love things to be manageable and predictable. So watch me alter the *how* in one place, and adjust it in another place, and find a totally different means in a third place, until the only fact you can rely on is my guarantee that I will do *what* I have promised.' He remains the Judge, he is himself the great Deliverer; but how he judges and delivers is up to him.

This means that real theology, theology that governs the way we

[2] If the judges are drawn from all twelve tribes, there may be some value in the following list. It includes some certainties, some educated guesses ('?'), and some pure speculations ('??'):

Othniel	Judah (3:9 with Nu. 13:6)
Ehud	Benjamin (3:15)
Shamgar	Simeon ??
Deborah	Naphtali ?
Gideon	Manasseh (6:15)
Tola	Issachar (10:1)
Jair	Reuben ?
Jephthah	Gad ?
Ibzan	Asher ??
Elon	Zebulun (12:11)
Abdon	Ephraim (12:15)
Samson	Dan (13:2).

But since Judges leaves us in the dark the matter is presumably unimportant.

[3] See Soggin, pp. 57–59; Webb, p. 133, p. 247 n. 37.
[4] It can be done in seven steps – or fewer?

live, will never be the dry academic subject that some think it. Our God is a God of surprises. Out of the Othniel hat he produces the Shamgar rabbit. The judgeship framework is absolutely reliable, but within it he will do things we never bargained for. In the words of Dorothy L. Sayers, in a different (or not so different) connection, 'We may call that doctrine exhilarating, or we may call it devastating, . . . but if we call it dull, then words have no meaning at all.'[5]

So, as we come to the story of Ehud, we remind ourselves that behind his judgeship it is the Lord who makes the judgments as to what shall happen, how it shall happen, and how the story shall be told to us.

2. The story: a tale of surprises

In the *Canaan Times* the headlines scream: 'MONARCH MURDERED BY LEFT-HANDED KILLER . . . Eglon, twenty-stone king of Moab, died today after a knife attack by an Israelite terrorist. First reports indicate that . . .'

Of the abundant details which flow over from the front page to the next, the most memorable may be that Eglon is 'a very fat man' (3:17), but the most significant is that Ehud is left-handed (3:15). We can get an idea of what that implies for the Bible writers if we piece together some of the verses where the words 'right hand' are used. A concordance will list them for us, and will draw our attention especially to the Lord's own right hand. By it he swears to bless his people,[6] and with it he destroys their enemies.[7] At his right hand are pleasures for evermore,[8] and there his Chosen One sits.[9] It is the hand of power, glory, and blessing.

So if we had been told that the Lord, the Judge, stretching out his right hand to rescue Israel, raised up a deliverer who likewise lifted *his* right hand to brandish the sword of liberation, we should have observed 'How apt!' And when we are told instead that the deliverer cannot use his right hand, we shall say 'How odd' – for this is not what the pattern of Othniel will have led us to expect.

But that is why the left-handedness of Ehud is the most significant feature of the story. The whole thing is 'left-handed', unexpected. In every episode of it, what happens is not what we might have thought. I should have preferred to avoid another string of preacher's alliterations, but the story really is about six Ms, as

[5] Dorothy L. Sayers, on the doctrine of the incarnation, in *Creed or Chaos?* (Methuen, 1967), p. 5.
[6] Is. 62:8–9.   [7] Ex. 15:6.   [8] Ps. 16:11.   [9] Ps. 110:1.

natural as the four Rs we noted at the beginning.[10] More important than the recurring initial, what all the elements of it have in common is their unexpectedness.

a. An unexpected misery (3:12–14)

Half a dozen different nations have been named in the introductory chapters as 'the people of the land', those whom Israel should have driven out but whom the Lord is now leaving there as an ongoing trial for his own people. The Moabites are not among them; nor should we have expected them to be. For one thing, Moab is not part of the Promised Land, and the migrating Israelites have long ago left its territories behind.[11] Then the Moabites are not alien to Israel as the Canaanites are, for they are descended from Abraham's nephew Lot.[12] In any case, even if Moab has been thought of as an enemy, it has been a negligible one: 'Moab was overcome with fear of the people of Israel' when Israel first came its way,[13] and trembling had already seized the leaders of Moab long before that, when they had heard of Israel's triumphant escape from Egypt.[14]

How unexpected, then, it must have been to find that 'the LORD strengthened Eglon the king of Moab', of all people, 'against Israel'; and when Eglon and his allies actually 'went and *defeated* Israel', what discomfiture for those who had assumed that Moab was one foe they need not reckon with!

Nor is the defeat merely the losing of a battle. It results in the humiliating loss of the 'city of palms', Jericho, whose capture had been Israel's first great success in the invasion of Canaan. And it has another result also. If we have looked ahead, we know that Eglon will later be portrayed as a comic figure, who will come to a grotesque end. But that still lies in the future. For the moment – indeed for eighteen long years – Eglon is no figure of fun, but a grim tyrant, and the misery that Israel suffers on his account is all the keener because it has come from a quarter so unexpected. Sin has brought punishment, as the Lord has always said it will. But the form in which the retribution has come is not at all what you might have thought it would be.

b. An unexpected man (3:15a)

I said earlier that God's chosen deliverer, when he comes, turns

---

[10] See p. 11. This favourite trick of the preacher lets him down when he travels abroad, and translators, like garden pests, play havoc with his rows of Ps.
[11] *Cf.* Dt. 2:9, 26–29.   [12] *Cf.* Gn. 19:36–37.   [13] Nu. 22:3.
[14] *Cf.* Ex. 15:15.

out to be a man who cannot use his right hand. That is what the Hebrew phrase means. It is not making the positive statement that Ehud naturally uses his left hand, but the negative one that he is 'bound' or restricted in the use of his right. Perhaps it is deformed or paralysed in some way. As an added irony, he belongs to the tribe of Benjamin, whose name means 'son of the right hand'.[15]

We miss the point of the story if, knowing the outcome in advance, we have our eyes fixed from the start on that able left hand with which Ehud is going to kill his enemy. Except for Ehud himself, all the people *in the story* focus on the other one, the withered right hand. No-one is expecting, let alone admiring, dexterity in the left hand; everyone assumes that that belongs to the right – that is what 'dexterity' means; and if Ehud cannot wield a weapon in his right hand, then he cannot wield one at all.

That is why he is acceptable as an envoy to the court of Moab, and why he is admitted to the presence of the king, not only as he leads the group bringing the tribute but as afterwards he asks for a private audience with Eglon. Because of his deformity, he presents no security risk to the Moabites. No doubt that is also why the Israelites have chosen him as envoy in the first place – an eminently suitable person who cannot be seen as a threat to the tyrant they fear.

We, the readers, can see the irony of the call of such a man, and we know that things are not what they seem. But we must also realize that at the time it must have been a perplexing and mind-stretching experience for Israel. God's ultimate objectives do not change: he will do what he has said. But how he will do it is another matter. Othniel, the first judge, has set the pattern of the classic, readily-recognizable hero-deliverer – and the mould is at once broken by his immediate successor, this unlikely southpaw.

c. An unexpected mission (3:15b)

Yet, as a tennis commentator might say, the southpaw has a devastating serve. His supporters are anticipating great things, and they are here in force to cheer him on . . . ?

No, that is not at all the picture. Here too the pattern of Othniel changes. In his case the sequence of events was that the Spirit of the Lord came upon him; he judged Israel; he went out to war; he

---

[15] Since at the end of Judges Benjamin's fighting forces were notable for including 'seven hundred picked men who were left-handed; every one could sling a stone at a hair and not miss' (20:16), left-handedness may have been a characteristic of the tribe rather than a personal characteristic of Ehud's. (Later David's guerrillas would include a similar band of Benjaminites, this time ambidextrous; *cf*. 1 Ch. 12:1–2).

defeated the enemy. It is clear that he was publicly recognized as leader from the start. But in the case of Ehud there is nothing about his being empowered by the Spirit or judging Israel, and he does not lead a military force against Moab until after the assassination of the Moabite king. He first appears on the scene in quite a different role. There is every likelihood that Israel sees him at the outset in the same way that Moab sees him – namely, as a man whose value to both sides lies precisely in what he cannot do. We don't want any trouble; and if hotheads begin talking about a champion who will deliver Israel by the strength of his good right hand, then Ehud is 'the man least likely to'.

He therefore is the one chosen for a task totally different. So far from a crusade of liberation, this is a mission which sums up the abject humiliation of a defeated people – the conveying of tribute payment. It expresses not revolt but submission. A probe behind the English translations reveals a point which nearly all of them miss: it is not simply 'by him' that Israel sends the tribute to Eglon, but *'by his hand'*. Which hand? His left hand, which he alone knows will be bringing something very different? No, his right, which is good for nothing else; a withered hand, fitly representative of a conquered people.

d. An unexpected message (3:16–22)

Here now is the core of the tale. Not many readers would agree with Auld when in connection with it he uses (three times!) the word 'delightful',[16] but there is no denying that it is an unforgettable story.

In three sequences the writer unfolds for us what it is that Ehud, as the envoy of Israel, is bringing to his overlord. We are probably meant to picture the court of Eglon set up in 'the city of palms',[17] in occupied territory west of the Jordan, once captured from the Canaanites by Israel but now captured from Israel by this latest enemy. Enter Eglon, king of Moab, with Moabite courtiers; to him, Ehud, envoy of Israel, with Israelite attendants bearing gifts. The gifts are the message, and the message is that the people of God have become, and accept that they are, an enslaved nation.

---

[16] Auld, p. 148.

[17] Some commentators see a tension between this and 'the traditional theory according to which the city' (*i.e.* Jericho) 'was destroyed by Joshua, only to be rebuilt in 1 Kings 16:34' (Soggin, p. 54). 'The allusion to Jericho here is surprising, since Joshua had pronounced a curse upon anyone attempting to rebuild it (Jos. 6:26)' (Cundall, p. 75). I sense neither tension nor surprise; if Eglon did build a palace on accursed ground, Judges 3 tell us how the curse came home to roost.

Ehud's party then sets off for home, but gets only as far as the 'Sculptured Stones' before it splits up; all but Ehud go on homewards while he himself returns to the Moabite court. So now in the second sequence we have Eglon and his courtiers, but Ehud alone. 'I have a secret *dabar* for you,' he says to the king. A *dabar*? It could mean a 'word', and most of the versions translate it 'message'; it could equally well mean a 'thing'. We of course know what the secret 'thing' is – the short specially-made sword, with two edges but without a crosspiece, hidden under Ehud's robe on his right side where no right-handed man would carry a weapon. The sword is the message, and the message is (as Eglon's most famous predecessor had been told, to his chagrin) that Israel 'shall eat up the nations his adversaries . . . and pierce them through with his arrows.'[18]

But Eglon is not expecting that kind of message. With the other Israelites already gone he now sends away the other Moabites also, leaving himself and Ehud alone in his private rooms at the top of the house for the third sequence. What is this secret *dabar*? he wants to know. It is a *dabar* from God, says Ehud; and with the unexpected left hand he draws the unexpected sword and thrusts it deep into the king's body.

'So perish all thine enemies, O LORD.' But no, not exactly; for though in a sense those words of Deborah and Barak in 5:31 do apply to all the judges' deliverances, in another sense the very point of the account of this assassination is that the Lord's enemies do not all perish just so. He repeatedly rescues his people in ways they would never have thought of.

e. An unexpected method (3:23–26)

The central section of the story, framed between Israelite misery in the introduction (3:12–14) and Israelite deliverance in the conclusion (3:27–30), ends with the escape of Ehud and the discovery of Eglon's body by his servants. It may have seemed to us dramatic, gruesome, comical; it is also highly ironic. The locked door keeps Eglon's courtiers out of the room where he lies dead, not simply by a physical lock but by their embarrassment about intruding if he is really taking his time in the toilet; yet again things are not what they seem. On the other hand Ehud knows, and we know, that every minute they hesitate is another minute in which he can make good his escape. It is a neat plot-line, but it does also highlight a further unexpected feature. For here, and at every other point

[18] Balaam's prophecy to Balak, king of Moab, in Nu. 24:8.

too, as we quickly realize, Ehud has set out to ensnare the tyrant by weaving a web of deception: the guise of an envoy, the left hand, the hidden sword, the pretended message, the locked door. We may raise an eyebrow at the thought that a chosen servant of God should save his people by means of guile, or we may think that that is far too serious a way of looking at a narrative which is after all a first-class yarn. But either way it is unlike the methods we might have assumed the Lord would use, an unexpected shift from the straightforward 'going out to war' of the model judge Othniel.

f. An unexpected mandate (3:27–30)

Only at this stage, apparently, is Ehud's leadership acknowledged by his own people. Even now we are not told that the Spirit of the Lord comes upon him, or that he judges Israel, and these things had certainly not happened before he went with the tribute to Eglon. If we were expecting the second judge to be given the same kind of mandate that was given to the first one, we are disappointed. What his fellow-Iraelites do respond to is the news that the king of Moab is already dead: Ehud's mandate is his success. The Othniel pattern has changed. The enemy has been delivered into Israel's hand, as 3:28 and 30 significantly put it, but it is a left hand. An Israelite force musters at Ehud's summons, and captures the fords of Jordan; with Eglon's death the Moabites are presumably withdrawing from the occupied west bank, and there is great slaughter as they attempt to retreat across the river to their homeland. Ehud adds to his individual exploit this success as a military leader. But it is still not what we might have thought would happen. The Lord does what he has said he will do, and shows himself to be a saving God; but how unpredictably he does it!

3. The principle: the rule of the left hand

Nothing in this bizarre story is what you thought it would be. Moab, which once seemed insignificant, turned out to be the great oppressor; then, when eighteen years later it seemed so powerful, it turned out to have feet of clay. In their security, the Moabites made a series of assumptions which were all belied in the event. The king of Moab assumed his visitor was unarmed and handicapped, but it was not so. His courtiers assumed they ought to leave his door locked, but it was not so. His troops assumed no Israelites would dare attack them, but it was not so. The ambiguities are neatly summed up in 3:29, where the Moabite soldiers are described as *shamen*, 'stout'. The Hebrew word, like the English one, can be taken in two ways: as long as you fear them, they seem 'strong', and indeed they are 'all . . . able-bodied'; but once they are leaderless, they are (metaphorically) merely 'fat' – the fearsome muscle is seen to be nothing but flesh.

Israel, on the other hand, has a leader who seems singularly ill-fitted for the job, so much so that his people are not at first aware of his call. But on his side of the story too things are not what they seem, as we have already seen in considerable detail.

Unexpectedness, then, colours the whole of the Ehud saga. It is important, however, to notice exactly where that colouring is to be seen. It does not appear uniformly throughout; if it did, we should be all at sea as to the ways of God among his people. There must be some constants in a world of flux.

a. What is constant

For a start, there is never anything very original about the sin of Israel. It is worth remembering that although Satan must not be underestimated, his objectives are nevertheless quite boringly predictable. The most varied and exotic of temptations are never anything more than lures into the same old seven deadly sins. Forgetting the Lord their God, and serving the Baals and Ashtaroth, are simply the Israelites' version of these. We noted in connection with Othniel that the sin which led to that classic judgeship was 'the classic sin of preferring the local gods to Israel's own God': the sin, that is, of centring her life on the values of the world around her, and of assuming that in practice they are more important and valid than the Lord is. This is the 'evil' which Israel repeatedly does 'in the sight of the LORD' throughout the time of the judges. We find nothing unexpected here.

Nor is there anything unpredictable about the purposes of God. Just as repeatedly, he makes plain his hatred of sin, his call to repentance, and his willingness to put right those who return to him. In the law he has spelt out what this means in practical daily living. Furthermore he has given clear directions about Israel's attitude to her new land and the present occupants of it. There is neither confusion nor variation in any of these matters.

b. What is unpredictable

What does vary is the way in which Israel is put under pressure, and what is unexpected is the choice of methods by which God rescues her. The successive oppressors of Israel, Cushan-Rishathaim, Eglon, Jabin, Zebah and Zalmunna, and the rest, are distinguished from one another not just by their names but by the very different pictures which Judges paints of them. Even if you had learned to cope with a Moabite occupation, it would not necessarily prepare you to cope with the scorched-earth policy of the Midianites or the assimilation tactics of the Philistines. And if you never knew what form the next trial would take, you certainly never knew how the next deliverance would come. A woman, Deborah; a nonentity, Gideon; a bandit, Jephthah; a hooligan, Samson – each in turn as unexpected a leader as left-handed Ehud, achieving half a dozen different kinds of success by as many different methods.

Although the trials can be seen as Israel's misery and the rescues as God's grace, it is spelt out for us that trials as well as deliverances come from the hand of God. In other words, where there is unexpectedness in the story it is put there by God. It is only the God who set the original pattern (Cushan-Rishathaim and Othniel) who is at liberty to vary it. We see this happening in the ways by which he brings his people low. But we see it happening even more, so that the variety of his methods becomes quite bewildering, in the ways by which he saves, restores, and blesses them.

'For consider your call, brethren,' says the New Testament, underlining the great principle of the left hand; 'not many of you were wise according to worldly standards, not many were powerful, not many were of noble birth; but God chose what is foolish in the world to shame the wise, God chose what is weak in the world to shame the strong, God chose what is low and despised in the world, even things that are not, to bring to nothing things that are'; and the object of such unlikely choices is now what it was then – it is *so that no human being might boast in the presence of God.*[19] He is in charge of his people's world; history is his story; he is the Judge, and he makes the decisions. We can indeed claim from him what he has clearly promised to do, but none of us has the right to dictate to him how he is to do it. We are not to be surprised if he chooses the most unlikely methods, even if we find that such 'left-handed' things as deprivation or illness, frustration or failure, become the instruments of his rule. After all, who would have expected that he would choose to work through such a 'left-handed' crowd of people as the Christian church? Who would have predicted that when the Judge came himself in the flesh, he would

[19] 1 Cor. 1:26–29.

come as such a 'left-handed' person, with 'no form or comeliness that we should look at him, and no beauty that we should desire him . . . despised and rejected by men'?[20]

[20] Is. 53:2–3.

Judges 4:1 – 5:31

3.   Deborah and Barak: the 'us-and-them' distinction

And the people of Israel again did what was evil in the sight of the LORD, after Ehud died. [2]And the LORD sold them into the hand of Jabin king of Canaan, who reigned in Hazor; the commander of his army was Sisera, who dwelt in Harosheth-ha-goiim. [3]Then the people of Israel cried to the LORD for help; for he had nine hundred chariots of iron, and oppressed the people of Israel cruelly for twenty years.

[4]Now Deborah, a prophetess, the wife of Lappidoth, was judging Israel at that time. [5]She used to sit under the palm of Deborah between Ramah and Bethel in the hill country of Ephraim; and the people of Israel came up to her for judgment. [6]She sent and summoned Barak the son of Abino-am from Kedesh in Naphtali, and said to him, 'The LORD, the God of Israel, commands you, "Go gather your men at Mount Tabor, taking ten thousand from the tribe of Naphtali and the tribe of Zebulun. [7]And I will draw out Sisera, the general of Jabin's army, to meet you by the river Kishon with his chariots and his troops; and I will give him into your hand."' [8]Barak said to her, 'If you will go with me, I will go; but if you will not go with me, I will not go.' [9]And she said, 'I will surely go with you; nevertheless, the road on which you are going will not lead to your glory, for the LORD will sell Sisera into the hand of a woman.' Then Deborah arose, and went with Barak to Kedesh. [10]And Barak summoned Zebulun and Naphtali to Kedesh; and ten thousand men went up at his heels; and Deborah went up with him.

[11]Now Heber the Kenite had separated from the Kenites, the descendants of Hobab the father-in-law of Moses, and had pitched his tent as far away as the oak in Za-anannim, which is near Kedesh.

[12]When Sisera was told that Barak the son of Abino-am had gone

up to Mount Tabor, ¹³*Sisera called out all his chariots, nine hundred chariots of iron, and all the men who were with him, from Harosheth-ha-goiim to the river Kishon.* ¹⁴*And Deborah said to Barak, 'Up! For this is the day in which the* LORD *has given Sisera into your hand. Does not the* LORD *go out before you?' So Barak went down from Mount Tabor with ten thousand men following him.* ¹⁵*And the* LORD *routed Sisera and all his chariots and all his army before Barak at the edge of the sword; and Sisera alighted from his chariot and fled away on foot.* ¹⁶*And Barak pursued the chariots and the army to Harosheth-ha-goiim, and all the army of Sisera fell by the edge of the sword; not a man was left.*

¹⁷*But Sisera fled away on foot to the tent of Jael, the wife of Heber the Kenite; for there was peace between Jabin the king of Hazor and the house of Heber the Kenite.* ¹⁸*And Jael came out to meet Sisera, and said to him, 'Turn aside, my lord, turn aside to me; have no fear.' So he turned aside to her into the tent, and she covered him with a rug.* ¹⁹*And he said to her, 'Pray give me a little water to drink; for I am thirsty.' So she opened a skin of milk and gave him a drink and covered him.* ²⁰*And he said to her, 'Stand at the door of the tent, and if any man comes and asks you, "Is any one here?" say, No.'* ²¹*But Jael the wife of Heber took a tent peg, and took a hammer in her hand, and went softly to him and drove the peg into his temple, till it went down into the ground, as he was lying fast asleep from weariness. So he died.* ²²*And behold, as Barak pursued Sisera, Jael went out to meet him, and said to him, 'Come, and I will show you the man whom you are seeking.' So he went in to her tent; and there lay Sisera dead, with the tent peg in his temple.*

²³*So on that day God subdued Jabin the king of Canaan before the people of Israel.* ²⁴*And the hand of the people of Israel bore harder and harder on Jabin the king of Canaan, until they destroyed Jabin king of Canaan.*

⁵·¹ *Then sang Deborah and Barak the son of Abino-am on that day:*
²*'That the leaders took the lead in Israel,*
that the people offered themselves willingly,
bless the LORD*!*

³*'Hear, O kings; give ear, O princes;*
to the LORD *I will sing,*
I will make melody to the LORD*, the God of Israel.*

⁴*'*LORD*, when thou didst go forth from Seir,*
when thou didst march from the region of Edom,

the earth trembled,
  and the heavens dropped,
    yea, the clouds dropped water.
[5]*The mountains quaked before the* LORD,
  yon Sinai before the LORD, *the God of Israel.*

[6]*'In the days of Shamgar, son of Anath,*
  in the days of Jael, caravans ceased
  and travellers kept to the byways.
[7]*The peasantry ceased in Israel, they ceased*
  until you arose, Deborah,
  arose as a mother in Israel.
[8]*When new gods were chosen, then war was in the gates.*
Was shield or spear to be seen among forty thousand in Israel?
[9]*My heart goes out to the commanders of Israel*
  who offered themselves willingly among the people.
Bless the LORD.

[10]*'Tell of it, you who ride on tawny asses,*
  you who sit on rich carpets
  and you who walk by the way.
[11]*To the sound of musicians at the watering places,*
  there they repeat the triumphs of the LORD,
  the triumphs of his peasantry in Israel.

'Then down to the gates marched the people of the LORD.

[12]*'Awake, awake, Deborah!*
  Awake, awake, utter a song!
Arise, Barak, lead away your captives,
  O son of Abino-am.
[13]*Then down marched the remnant of the noble;*
  the people of the LORD *marched down for him against the mighty.*
[14]*From Ephraim they set out thither into the valley,*
  following you, Benjamin, with your kinsmen;
from Machir marched down the commanders,
  and from Zebulun those who bear the marshal's staff;
[15]*the princes of Issachar came with Deborah,*
  and Issachar faithful to Barak;
  into the valley they rushed forth at his heels.
Among the clans of Reuben
  there were great searchings of heart.
[16]*Why did you tarry among the sheepfolds,*
  to hear the piping for the flocks?

Among the clans of Reuben
  there were great searchings of heart.
¹⁷*Gilead stayed beyond the Jordan;*
  and Dan, why did he abide with the ships?
Asher sat still at the coast of the sea,
  settling down by his landings.
¹⁸*Zebulun is a people that jeoparded their lives to the death;*
  Naphtali too, on the heights of the field.

¹⁹*'The kings came, they fought;*
  then fought the kings of Canaan,
at Taanach, by the waters of Megiddo;
  they got no spoils of silver.
²⁰*From heaven fought the stars,*
  from their courses they fought against Sisera.
²¹*The torrent Kishon swept them away,*
  the onrushing torrent, the torrent Kishon.
  March on, my soul, with might!

²²*'Then loud beat the horses' hoofs*
  with the galloping, galloping of his steeds.

²³*'Curse Meroz, says the angel of the* LORD,
  curse bitterly its inhabitants,
because they came not to the help of the LORD,
  to the help of the LORD *against the mighty.*

²⁴*'Most blessed of women be Jael,*
  the wife of Heber the Kenite,
  of tent-dwelling women most blessed.
²⁵*He asked water and she gave him milk,*
  she brought him curds in a lordly bowl.
²⁶*She put her hand to the tent peg*
  and her right hand to the workmen's mallet;
she struck Sisera a blow,
  she crushed his head,
  she shattered and pierced his temple.
²⁷*He sank, he fell,*
  he lay still at her feet;
at her feet he sank, he fell;
  where he sank, there he fell dead.

²⁸*'Out of the window she peered,*
  the mother of Sisera gazed through the lattice:

"Why is his chariot so long in coming?
  Why tarry the hoofbeats of his chariots?"
²⁹*Her wisest ladies make answer,*
  nay, she gives answer to herself,
³⁰*"Are they not finding and dividing the spoil?—*
  A maiden or two for every man;
spoil of dyed stuffs for Sisera,
  spoil of dyed stuffs embroidered,
  two pieces of dyed work embroidered for my neck as spoil?"

³¹*'So perish all thine enemies, O* LORD!
  But thy friends be like the sun as he rises in his might.'

And the land had rest for forty years.

'And the people of Israel again did what was evil in the sight of the LORD, after Ehud died' (4:1). Something old, something new. The first (something old) is highlighted by the word 'again'. By the end of the book the disobedience of God's people will seem to the reader a chronic disease endemic to Israel, the same old problem again and again, never solved. The words 'After Ehud died' bring us to the second, introducing something new. Eighty years of rest (3:30), comprising perhaps a forty-year generation for Shamgar's judgeship as well as one for Ehud's, are followed by a new oppressor and a new rescuer. We remind ourselves that it is the Lord who raises up both, at this and every other critical point in the book. It is no accident that, as we have seen, Judges portrays the wickedness of Israel as desperately unoriginal – it varies only in that it gets worse – while the Lord's ways of dealing with it are endlessly resourceful. This is one aspect of the gospel message as Judges conveys it, the message that Israel cannot save herself – only the Judge can save her; but that he intends to do.

The hill country of Ephraim, where Ehud blew the trumpet to rally Israel against the Moabites (3:27), is also the place where now Deborah sits in judgment under her palm tree (4:5), but whereas the earlier story was set mostly south of Ephraim, around Jericho and Gilgal, this one takes us north of it, to Mount Tabor and the River Kishon.

What happened there we must read first in the words of Scripture. 'Jabin king of Canaan . . . oppressed the people of Israel cruelly for twenty years . . . Deborah . . . summoned Barak . . . "I will draw out Sisera, the general of Jabin's army, to meet you by the river Kishon with his chariots and his troops; and I will give him into your hand" ', said the Lord through his prophetess

(4:2–7). The narrative telling of the subsequent victory and the death of Sisera is followed in chapter 5 by a fine old triumph-song which recounts the same events rather differently, as poetry.

The content of the two chapters could be retold as a traditional fairy-tale. 'Once upon a time there was a wicked king, who had a fierce general, who had 900 iron chariots. Life was hard for the poor folk who had come to live in that land. But three people were going to rescue them. The first was a judge who sat under a tree, the second was a soldier who won a battle in a thunderstorm, and the third was a woman with a mallet and a tent-peg . . .' It would not be quite the kind of tale that appears in most story-books, because God comes into it. But all the same it would be a riveting read.

Then again we might see these chapters as a mirror of real history. The ancient poem which forms chapter 5 is a richly-wrought work of art, but it is based on actual events which took place in lands familiar enough to us, though historically the nations involved are remote from our day. The Middle East was a political melting pot then as now. Its peoples were moving out of the Bronze Age into the Iron Age. Those longest established, and richest and most powerful, were the Canaanites, and their power was matched by their ambition. Here also, following the story-line against the background of secular history, we cannot avoid the name of God, even if it is simply in the term 'Act of God' which modern insurance companies would no doubt apply to the storm and flood which according to the poem destroyed the Canaanite army (5:20–21).

All these are simply ways of familiarizing ourselves with what happened – at least with what was happening on the surface. This is Scripture; it is narrative; it is history. But it is also theology – that is, it has to do with the knowledge of God – and while it is impossible to avoid his presence in the story however we read it, to look at it in this fourth way is to see him and his people as the centre of it, and therefore to see its true meaning. This is how we grasp what is happening not just on but under the surface. We shall begin, not with 'And behold it came to pass', nor with 'Once upon a time', nor with '3,000-odd years ago in the Middle East', but with a theological beginning, which takes for granted that these chapters have to do primarily with God and with the people of God. They deal with a time when it was not obvious how, or even whether, he was in charge; and they show how in a time of real uncertainty questions were being asked, tests were being applied, and lessons were being taught, whose relevance belongs not only to those days but to our own as well.

Judges has already spelt out something of the intentions of God at such a time. He is not sitting passively by, waiting merely to come to his people's help when they choose to call for it. Given their inability from the start to drive out the nations of Canaan as they should have done, he is actively pursuing purposes of his own through the conflict which inevitably keeps erupting between his own nation and the rest. We have been told plainly that the antagonisms are allowed to continue in order first that Israel may 'know war' (3:2) and secondly that the Lord may 'know . . . Israel' (3:4). The stories of the first three judges, especially that of Ehud, have focused our attention on God himself and his methods as Judge and Saviour. The story of Deborah and Barak now points us to God's people – to what Israel comes to know, and to how she herself comes to be known.

1. 'That Israel might know'

As with Othniel and Ehud (though not Shamgar) the first person named in the account of Deborah's judgeship is the king of the nation currently oppressing Israel.[1] With the king in this case is associated his commander-in-chief, and we are also given the names of the seat of government of the one and the home town of the other: Jabin reigns in Hazor, Sisera lives in Harosheth-ha-goiim – Harosheth 'of the nations' (4:2). It is over against a nation represented by these two men that Israel must now learn to define her own character and to recognize her own distinctiveness. She finds herself opposed to – opposite to – Jabin and Sisera and all they stand for.

a. Jabin

Although the name of the king of the Canaanites is mentioned five times in chapter 4, at no point does he appear on the scene in person. But this shadowy off-stage figure is a powerful and threatening one.[2] What do we know about him?

Judges says only that at the outset of this story he is Israel's oppressor, and that at the end of it Israel subdues and destroys him. Joshua, however, fills in some background, for a Canaanite

[1] Canaan was not a 'nation' in the sense of a single political entity, and the title 'king of Canaan' is not found elsewhere; strictly speaking Jabin was king of the Canaanite city-state of Hazor (see Webb, p. 247 n. 39; Kitchen, pp. 67ff.). But of the two names it is Canaan, not Hazor, that has the important overtones for our writer; see below, pp. 57ff.

[2] As the reader will see from what follows, it seems to me a very superficial judgment to say that 'within the context of Judg. 4 Jabin is not a very central figure' (Martin, p. 54). That is like saying that in a history of the European military campaigns of World War 2 Hitler was not a very central figure.

king Jabin features also in chapter 11 of that book. There, an alliance of local kings under his leadership sets out to stem the Israelite invasion, and is annihilated by Joshua's armies.[3] The relation between Joshua 11 and Judges 4 – 5 is much debated by the commentators. Some hold that 'the *one* decisive historic battle for the north between Israel and Jabin of Canaan has been reported to us in two quite separate traditions'.[4] Others take Jabin to be a favoured name (like the Louis of France) or a regular title (like the Pharaohs of Egypt) among the kings of Hazor, and the power of the first-mentioned Jabin, though destroyed by Joshua, to have revived by the time of his successor in Judges 4. Whatever the historical connection between the two accounts, we are surely meant to read the later one against the background of the earlier. When 'after Ehud died . . . the LORD sold them into the hand of Jabin king of Canaan, who reigned in Hazor' (4:1–2), to Israelites of that later time (and to readers of this history) the name of Jabin would have carried all the menacing overtones that derive from Joshua 11:1–5. Against Joshua had been mobilized the kings of Madon, Shimron, and Achshaph, with others from hill country and lowland, from north, south, east, and west, and from all the tribes of Canaan – 'all their troops, a great host, in number like the sand that is upon the seashore' – and Hazor 'was the head of all those kingdoms'.[5]

It should be no surprise that the malign power of Jabin king of Hazor is felt once more when it was thought to have been destroyed. God's people know that there is a sense in which the resurrection of the dead, far from being miraculous, is positively commonplace, not simply because every one of them has experienced it for himself, but because they see on all hands Satan's counterpart of it. John in the Revelation describes this as the healing of the beast which had been fatally wounded.[6] So long as we live in this present world, no victory over evil will ever be final, whether it is oppression by great empires or personal pains and sins that we are combating. This is what 4:2 shows us when we take it as it stands: renewed aggression by an old enemy. There will always be a Jabin. The fact that, in the words of Revelation 13, the beast with the mortal wound yet lives, is constantly surprising to the more naïve of God's people, to those infected by the modern passion for quick results, and to those confused about the meaning of 'Deliver us from evil'. But when Jabins over whom we had once and for all claimed the victory take on a new lease of life, it simply confirms

---

[3] Jos. 11:1–15.   [4] Auld, p. 152.   [5] Jos. 11:4, 10.
[6] Rev. 13:3, 12, 14.

what Scripture has always said about the persistence of Satan and our own need for ceaseless vigilance. I quoted Chesterton's *Ballad of the White Horse* earlier; the horse of the title, marked out on the green hillside long ago, has incessantly to be scoured clean if the inexorable creeping weeds are not to obliterate it, and in the same way the Saxon king and his successors will have to be always on their guard against the inroads of returning barbarism.

> Will ye part with the weeds for ever?
> Or show daisies to the door?
> Or will you bid the bold grass
> Go, and return no more?

Never in this life can the Lord's servant claim immunity from Satan's attacks on a heart which is not yet sinless and a body which is still mortal.

b. Sisera

Where Jabin is an off-stage character in the drama, Sisera is his on-stage representative. The king is master-minding the war behind the scenes, but the general is the enemy whom Israel has to confront in the field. Whatever God's people may or may not understand of Jabin's secret purposes they are all too aware of Sisera's 900 iron chariots. It is that clearly-perceived military supremacy which has cowed them for twenty years. We are at one of the major cultural turning-points of history, as the whole way of life of the Bronze Age yields to the superior technology of the Iron Age. From the point of view of God's people, however, the historical fact serves a theological end. They may never meet King Jabin in person, but the war-machine that embodies his power is real enough, and indeed incorporates the latest thing in military hardware.

The connection between the king and the general, as it relates to Israel, may be illustrated by what is sometimes called the doctrine of the 'invisible church'. The church is 'invisible' in the sense that none but God can see clearly and exactly who does and who does not belong to it; on the other hand those who do comprise it are perfectly real, visible, human beings. The same principle holds good for the church's spiritual enemies. Then, as now, God's people cannot see what is going on at the heart of darkness, where their great Adversary is hatching his devilry behind the scenes, but the troops and the weapons he uses are not only real but also visible.

In New Testament terms, the ruler of this world,[7] our adversary the devil,[8] the pursuing dragon,[9] schemes unremittingly against the church of Christ; and we need to be aware both that we shall never plumb the depths of his cunning or succeed by our own in outwitting him, and also that he will use as his weapons the things and the people of our own familiar world. Here perhaps is a lesson in the use of the 'imprecatory psalms', those songs of cursing which seem so out of place on Christian lips. May we pray for the destruction of our enemies? Yes, we may certainly pray so against the great Enemy whom we cannot see; and wherever he is plainly using the 'iron chariots' which we can see, we are right to pray with equal vehemence against that use. This is surely how Paul tells the Corinthians to regard that member of their church whose immorality is infecting the whole body: so long as he will not be separated from the evil which is using him, he and it together must 'be removed from among you', though of course Paul's desire is rather that the evil be destroyed and the man be rescued.[10]

c. The Canaanites

There is one other way in which those who are at this point the enemies of Israel are identified. The king, known but unseen, has been named; the general, seen as well as known, has been named; and the nation which they lead is also named. We must not ignore the fact that this is a Canaanite oppression. In the sequence of the Judges narratives it marks a return to the prologue. Othniel, the first judge, was raised up against an invader from Mesopotamia, away to the north-east;[11] Ehud, the second, against the incursions of the Moabites from the Jordan side of the promised land, and Shamgar, the third, against those of the Philistines, from the Mediterranean side; but now Canaan itself rises to repel the newcomers.

This has a double significance. On the one hand, Canaan is the territory that God has intended for Israel from the start. For reasons detailed elsewhere he has destined the Canaanite tribes to destruction in any case,[12] and that purpose coincides with his intention also to provide a new land for his own people newly rescued from Egypt. So conflict between Israel and the Canaanites was central to his plan, in a way that conflict with Mesopotamians or Moabites or Philistines was not.

On the other hand, it was Canaanite religion against whose

---

[7] Jn. 14:30.   [8] 1 Pet. 5:8.   [9] Rev. 12:13.   [10] 1 Cor. 5:1–7.

[11] Some commentators think the country mentioned in 3:8 must be Edom, not Aram; an invasion from there would still be non-Canaanite.

[12] See p. 31 n. 28.

seductions the Israelites had been specifically warned. They would of course become all too familiar with the gods of Philistia and Moab also. But the Baals and the Ashtaroth are the characteristically Canaanite lures that draw Israel away from the true God.

In other words, 'Canaan' is the name of all names with arouses in the people of God both antagonism and desire. When Israel is being obedient, she sees that while the land of Canaan is destined for her, the people and the ways of Canaan are working against her, and that therefore she must drive out the one in order to enjoy the other. Conversely, when she is being disobedient, she accepts the people of Canaan and adopts their ways, and is willing to forgo possession of their land. Furthermore, we realize how right is the perception that it is the Lord who 'sells Israel into the hand of its enemies'.[13] For it is only by suffering of this kind that Israel is delivered from the grand Canaanite illusion. Canaan the country is of course eminently desirable; it is the Lord's choice for his people.[14] The illusion is that 'Canaan' the ethos, its people and its ways, is equally desirable. Only by being allowed to get her fingers burnt will Israel come to see clearly that that 'Canaan' is in fact the great enemy.

For all is the work of God. It is he who plans a home for his people, who condemns the corrupt nations that have long occupied it, and who brings in Israel to replace them. It is he who allows Canaanite influence to linger and to test his people, he who when they fail the test allows their enemies to oppress them, and he who each time finally raises up a rescuer for them. It is he who has determined to use the entire process as a means of instruction for Israel. Everything is in accordance with his decisions: in a word, he is Judge.

All this may help us to see why the story of Deborah comes where it does. So far as the named judges are concerned, she comes fourth, after Othniel, Ehud, and Shamgar; with regard to stories told at length, hers comes second, after Ehud's. But as far as the classical outline of a judgeship-story goes, hers is the third.

In this sequence of three, the development between each and the next may be seen like this. Othniel's provides the basic framework, as we know. It shows us Israel sinning, angering the Lord, subjected to an oppressor, and crying for help; a deliverer raised up, described, empowered, judging and rescuing and giving rest to Israel, and finally dying. That will be *the* pattern of judgeship.

But at once it seems to be pulled out of shape. The very next story, Ehud's, is quite different. What is God doing? On reflection,

[13] *Cf.* 2:14; 3:8; 4:2, *etc.*   [14] *Cf.* Dt. 8:7–10; 11:8–12.

we realize that by the end of it the same sort of object has been achieved ('Moab was subdued . . . and the land had rest', 3:30), but the methods have been altogether unexpected. God in his power and his love will certainly save his people, but the way he will do it is always unpredictable. He is bound to his promises, but to nothing else.

Thus far the stories of Othniel and Ehud. The third, Deborah's story, has the basic outline of the first, and strange features like those of the second (for example murder by deception and treachery). But its chief function seems to be to bring us back to the nub of the matter, to a real 'Canaanite' crisis where Israel finds the issues clear-cut. Canaan is the land she should be occupying, true; but the Canaanites' religion is her great temptation, and now through suffering she has come to see that they are her great enemy, powerful and persistent, a foe to be confronted.

2. 'That the Lord might know'

If the facts about her situation are thus being made known to Israel, what are the facts about Israel which at the same time are being made known to God? We have been told that the Lord left 'all the Canaanites . . . for the testing of Israel, to know whether Israel would obey the commandments of the LORD' (3:3–4). Now the challenge to take up arms against the oppressor raises an Israelite army of 10,000 men. But just as the nature of the enemy is focused in three names – Jabin, Sisera, and Canaan – so the opposition to the enemy is also represented by three names. The 10,000 march out bravely against the Canaanite army, but its defeat is ultimately the work of Deborah, Barak, and Jael.

The novelty here, against the background not only of the first three chapters of Judges but also of Bible history itself up to this point, is obvious. The early books of the Old Testament do not lack their famous women, but none has yet been presented in such a leading or crucial role as those we find in Judges 4 – 5. And the novelty is underlined in at least three ways. This, the earliest narrative to describe female leadership of such a kind, does so by presenting not just one but two able women. Secondly, the story's beginning with an expected enemy (the Canaanites) highlights by contrast the unexpected leader (the woman Deborah). Thirdly, at the story's ending the enemy is destroyed by a method which has a precedent (the deadly 'thrust', the same Hebrew word in both 3:21 and 4:21) but by a person who has not (the woman Jael).

We have begun to see that this mixture of the consistent and the unexpected is characteristic of Judges. It reminds us once more that

God keeps his promises as to what he will do, but that we cannot tie him down as to how he will do it. So here are two facts with which we have to come to terms. With regard to our expectations of him, he regularly reveals the 'what', and just as regularly conceals the 'how'. And with regard to both the 'what' and the 'how', the decisions are his; for he is the Judge.

a. *Jael*

Of the three 'rescuers' of Israel, it is Deborah who is introduced at the beginning, as soon as the backcloth of Canaanite oppression has been painted in (4:4). But we shall look first at the other woman, Jael, who holds the crucial place at the climax of the story. Early on, in the conversation between Deborah and Barak, the writer of Judges points forward to that climax. The predicament of Israel has been described in a way that has by now become familiar: the Lord sold them 'into the hand' of their enemies, Jabin and Sisera (4:2; see 2:14; 3:8). The deliverance of Israel will on this occasion be described by an exact turning of the tables: 'the LORD will sell *Sisera* into the hand' of *his* enemy (4:9).

Or is it his enemy? For while the story is thus given a satisfying shape, it is thick with questions of this sort, and its content becomes ever more unsettling. There is an unconventional note struck almost from the start, with the appearance of female leadership. Then there is an ironic note. Did we not know the end of the story already, we might well assume that in 4:9 Deborah is speaking of herself: 'The glory will not be yours, Barak; this woman initiated the campaign, this woman will finish it' – which is not, of course, what actually happens. Then there is the really disconcerting note, hinted at in the question we have just asked: at the start, Israel sold into the hand of her enemy, and at the end, Sisera sold into the hand of his enemy – but *is* Jael his enemy? There is 'peace between Jabin . . . and the house of Heber the Kenite' (4:17). The general of Jabin's army rightly expects help and protection from the wife of Heber the Kenite; and Jael's hammer-blow is as treacherous as Ehud's sword-thrust was, back in chapter 3, if not more so.

We are surely meant to see a continuity between the two killings. Each is the decisive stroke by which God brings about his people's deliverance. But each was done in private, with no-one else present, to an unsuspecting person, by deception, with ferocity; and if there is any kind of development between the two incidents, it lies in the four additional facts that Jael's victim was an ally, a guest, weary, and sleeping. Neither deed can be called admirable (except as one admires resourcefulness), and the second is even worse than the first.

You remember God's purpose in all this? It is first 'that . . . Israel might know war'; but it is also that the Lord might 'know . . . Israel', and (more fully) that he might 'know whether Israel would obey the commandments of the LORD' (3:2,4). From one point of view, Jael stands on the sidelines in that investigation. Although hers is the deed which signals the end of the Canaanite oppression of Israel, she is not herself an Israelite. But from another point of view, it is deeply disturbing to realize that her deed, which God uses, is a plain flouting of half a dozen of his own commandments. We are left with a question which Judges will press upon us increasingly: how does God's concern with the thing he wants done relate to his concern with the motives and methods of the person who does it?

b. Deborah

Now we return to the other woman, at the beginning of the chapter. Deborah is clearly a counterpart to Jael, though a very different kind of person. Like practically every other women of note in the Bible, she is married, but her husband Lappidoth is scarcely more than a footnote in the account of how this formidable lady directed, ruled, and mobilized her people in a time of national emergency.

The writer of Judges is a consummate story-teller. You can analyse in several ways his putting together of the narrative of chapter 4, and all of them are elegant. For instance, Sisera is the thread for a plot-line which connects all five named individuals.[15] It begins and ends with Jabin; his authority sends Sisera out; the campaign against him is initiated by Deborah, carried out by Barak, and rounded off by Jael; and finally Sisera's death brings us back to Jabin and the ending of his authority. Or, leaving Jabin in the background, the other four may be seen as a double pairing: the men join battle as opponents at the centre of the story, and the women join forces as allies from either end of it. Or again, the Canaanites' part in the drama may be seen simply as the occasion for a three-act analysis, showing how the adversary is met first by Deborah, secondly by Barak, and lastly by Jael.

But while the literary patterns of Scripture are a very great help towards grasping its message, the question remains: when you have a choice of patterns, which one conveys the truest meaning? To my mind Deborah is not intended to be seen as one of five equal characters, nor as one of four, nor as one of three. And although

[15] Excluding Lappidoth (4:4) and Heber (4:11, 17, 21).

she is explicitly said to judge Israel (4:4) and therefore stands in the succession of Othniel and the rest of the judges, she is clearly not in this story the *one* central figure around whom it all revolves. No; as we follow the sequence through – Jabin, Sisera; Deborah, Barak, Jael; Sisera, Jabin – we cannot help seeing her as one of *two*. Deborah and Jael differ in obvious ways (the upright public figure and the faithless, ruthless individualist) but it is the likenesses that we ought to note. Female control of events is sufficiently unusual in Scripture for its appearance here to draw our attention to both women equally. Both are powerful and determined; both are used in God's purposes; and with that in view God has given both of them the necessary abilities and opportunities.

Paradoxically, all this makes Deborah both a greater and a lesser figure than her fellow-judges. Scarcely any of them is portrayed as the wise, mature, godly person that she is. Yet it is not she who stands at the centre of the story, and it is not she (a fact which must often have puzzled thoughtful readers of the Bible) who is upheld in the New Testament as the name to be remembered from Judges 4 and 5.

c. Barak

'Time would fail me', says the writer of Hebrews, having celebrated the great heroes of faith from Genesis to Joshua, 'to tell of . . .' The next portraits in his gallery, had he had the time, would have been those from the book of Judges; and of the twelve judges, three do at any rate get a mention. But for Hebrews the memorable name from our present chapters is not that of the judge Deborah. It is that of the colourless character who stands between Deborah and Jael at the centre of Judges 4: 'Time would fail me to tell of Gideon, *Barak*, Samson, Jephthah . . .'[16]

The crucial point is the brief exchange between the judge and the general in 4:8–9. Deborah has conveyed to Barak the Lord's command that he should go out against Sisera. Barak's reply is that he will not go unless Deborah goes too. She answers: 'I will surely go with you; nevertheless, the road on which you are going will not lead to your glory, for the LORD will sell Sisera into the hand of a woman.'

What does this mean?

It has been taken that Barak is drawing back from his high calling

---

[16] Heb. 11:32.

as a deliverer of Israel.[17] On this view, he is no more admirable a character than Ehud or Jael: where they are cunning and violent, he is cowardly. In Webb's interpretation, Barak tries to evade his responsibility and to manipulate Deborah, and in consequence, as a punishment, is caused to miss the chance of killing Sisera and the honour that goes with it. In line with this approach, the NIV relegates to a footnote the translation 'On the expedition you are undertaking the honour will not be yours', and prefers to say *'Because of the way you are going about this*, the honour will not be yours.'

But the text itself, especially in the context of two other closely-related Scriptures, one long before and the other long after, may encourage us to take quite a different view. Barak's words do not after all express flat disobedience; indeed, while it is true that he sets conditions, he does promise that if the conditions are met, he certainly 'will go'. Deborah's response, so far from showing that she is 'clearly taken aback',[18] seems to me to express immediate acceptance of Barak's conditions – 'I will surely go with you'; and what she goes on to say, about Barak's missing the honour of killing Sisera, is not necessarily a rebuke – it is just as likely to be a plain statement of fact.

In this connection we cannot help hearing in the conversation an echo from the first great deliverance of the people of God in the time of Moses. In Exodus 33:12–17 we find the same kind of command, the same kind of reaction, and the same kind of response. There, it is the Lord who says 'Bring up this people', that is, lead them out of oppression into freedom; it is Moses whose reaction is 'If thy presence will not go with me, do not carry us up from here'; and the Lord's response is, like Deborah's afterwards, 'This very thing that you have spoken I will do.' Does not this parallel shed a very different light on Judges 4:8–9? Even before we are told that Deborah is a judge we have been told that she is a prophetess. Her words are identified with God's words, and this is her authority for judging Israel: she knows God's mind. 'The LORD, the God of Israel, commands . . . The LORD will sell . . . The LORD has given . . . Does not the LORD go out before you?' (4:6, 9, 14). So what are we witnessing when Barak refuses to set out without this woman? Not cowardice – far from it – but faith: faith, that is, which is the glorious combination of a humble confession of his own inadequacy and a sure confidence in the grace

[17] At a point where I do think Webb (pp. 134–138) is wrong, let me take the opportunity to say how enormously thorough and helpful his work on Judges generally is.

[18] Webb, p. 135.

of God, known in this case through his mouthpiece Deborah.

And this is of course just what the New Testament says about the judgeship of Deborah, when Hebrews 11:32 tells us how the apostolic church looks back on it. The outstanding example of faith from those years is not Deborah, let alone Jael. It is Barak. He will not have the honour of destroying the enemy, any more than he had the privilege of initiating the campaign; but what does that matter? He does his duty; let others have the glory.[19]

3. The song

Chapter 5 is unique in the book of Judges, though not in the Old Testament as a whole. In several other books poetry is inserted into narrative, as it is here. Examples are the songs of Moses in Exodus 15 and Deuteronomy 32, Jonah's psalm in Jonah 2, and Hezekiah's in Isaiah 38. Judges 5 is a very ancient song, recounting in the form of poetry the events that chapter 4 has already narrated in prose. We need to have read the two chapters in the biblical order; the poem would be pretty obscure[20] if we had not discovered in advance what it was about. But in another sense the poetry makes certain things even clearer than the prose does.

The central question of the book is, we recall, 'Who judges? Who makes the decisions?' In the narrative, the answer is at one level obvious: 'Deborah . . . was judging Israel at that time' (4:4). But at another level it is not at all obvious, since no one of the three 'deliverers' could have taken decisive action had it not been for the other two. Clearly a fourth person was at work orchestrating the piece! And in the poem the answer to our question is indeed clear, right from the outset.

The first section of the song (5:2–5) focuses twice over on 'the LORD, the God of Israel'. Leaders, people, kings, and princes have all been involved in the war of liberation – praise him! But the outbreak of the war was in fact the Lord himself marching forth – praise him! In other words, the Lord who in chapter 4's 'war

---

[19] There is perhaps even more to Barak than this. In that he does in another sense destroy the enemy (4:15–16), and does in the end receive the glory which he had willingly renounced, he reflects something of the Lord's own greatest work as a Saviour-Judge: see p. 123 n. 24.

[20] Over and above the obscurity of its content, there is the obscurity of its language. 'A comparison of any two English translations shows many differences in the translating and understanding of this ancient poetry. One is tempted, therefore, to . . . discuss, explain, amplify, and (occasionally) resolve the problems in vocabulary, grammar, and rendering of the text' (Davis, p. 81). With Davis, I shall resist the temptation, having other objects in view, and refer the reader to the commentaries.

report' is named in only three verses, each time by Deborah, is according to chapter 5 the one who has both set and kept the whole thing in motion from the beginning.

Here is one distinguishing mark of the people of God. They are vividly aware that their God takes on the gods of Canaan, who are intimately concerned with the practicalities of life, and beats them at their own game: he is actually in control, and not only in, but over and behind, everything.

The second section (5:6–8) links the rise of the Lord as Deliverer with the rise of Deborah as 'a mother in Israel'. The Lord is always in control, but will have his people to see that normal life 'ceases' until guidance by his word takes the authoritative place. Here is the next mark of the 'distinct' nation: they have among them, and they respect, the voice that proclaims 'Thus says the Lord.'

The third section (5:9–13) brings us to the point where Deborah and Barak together lead the insurrection, and Israel is called to follow. Now the people march out as the Lord is marching out, and his triumphs will be their triumphs; for they are distinguished as those who not only hear but obey the directives of the true prophet, the infallible word, and align their walk with the ways of God.

It might then be asked, 'If these judgments and decisions are after all being made at such a high level, how come the period of the judges is not one of the most consistently successful in the history of Israel, instead of the exact opposite?' And the fourth section of the poem (5:14–18) replies that for all those who 'jeoparded their lives to the death', there were also those who 'sat still'; the people were deeply divided in their obedience. It is not yet, sadly, a distinctive mark of Israel that she has a united heart to fear God's name.[21]

That disunity is something we were not told of before; and so is the fact that Barak's battle involved the stars, and the waters of Megiddo. According to the fifth section (5:19–23) the rout of Sisera's army was due to a literally heaven-sent flash flood in the Kishon valley. This is God's doing: Barak is not even mentioned. There need be no doubt in the minds of God's people that he who began the good work will complete it.[22] That is the confidence of the 'distinct' nation.

The curse of Meroz at the end of that section (presumably a place belonging to one of the uncooperative tribes of section 4) points forward to the remarkable blessing of Jael in the sixth section (5:24–27). In one way the importance of her deed is heightened by

[21] Cf. Ps. 86:11.   [22] Cf. Phil. 1:6.

the blessing, and by the bloodthirsty relish with which it is elaborated here. If we see it as justified joy in the downfall of evil, this too is something which sets God's people apart from the rest, who are far from clear-sighted in this respect.

But we should note also that the poem demotes Jael's deed from the climactic place it held at the end of chapter 4 ('There lay Sisera dead . . . On that day God subdued Jabin', 4:22–23), and adds something quite new as the conclusion of chapter 5, namely, the seventh and final section of the song (5:28–31).

This serves a double purpose. It is a highly dramatic and poignant ending to the song, describing Sisera's womenfolk awaiting the soldier who will never return, 'clutching at proud reasons for his delay'.[23] But its tragic irony is also a central theme of the entire book. The poem's opening words (5:2–5) tell us that for those who have the eyes to see, there is the never-failing confidence of true Israelites in a Judge who goes forth in majesty to direct all their ways. Its closing words (5:28–31) tell us that for those who cannot or will not see, there is only the 'Canaanite' confidence which is, in the end, illusion. The latter must 'perish'; the former will be 'like the sun as he rises in his might'.

[23]Auld, p. 160.

Judges 6:1 – 8:35

4. Gideon: overwhelming odds

It is probably true to say that, along with Samson, Gideon is the most familiar character in the book of Judges. You may dislike the term 'character', because it makes him sound fictional, and want to stress that he is a real person. But notice the two words 'character' and 'person'. Together they hint at one reason for Gideon's being so well-known. For many preachers, a deceptively easy kind of sermon is the character-study of a Bible personage; some Bible people lend themselves more readily than others to being held up as examples to follow or warnings to note; and the judges we have read about so far are tough nuts to crack as sermon-subjects of that kind. So with some relief we arrive at the story of Gideon, who seems to be (as James says of Elijah) 'a man of like nature with ourselves'.[1] He has to cope, personally, with circumstances to which we ourselves might conceivably know parallels. On that basis, we might expect to learn lessons from Gideon by seeing him as Everyman.

But before we renew our acquaintance with him with that sort of object in mind, we ought to recall that hardly anyone in Judges so far has provided suitable material for a character-study. Othniel, Ehud, and Shamgar are not Everyman, Deborah and Jael are not Everywoman. As we read their stories, we do not say 'I ought to be like that' or 'I must take care not to be like that.' Instead, what the book has been commending 'to every man's conscience in the sight of God'[2] is the attitudes and actions of Israel as a nation, God's people, and still more his own expectations and purposes with regard to them. It is from their situation and their relationship to him, rather than from the personal doings of their leaders, that we are to read off parallels to our own.

[1] Jas. 5:17.   [2] 2 Cor. 4:2.

Gideon is still a great character! As a flesh-and-blood person, as a believer and a servant of God, he develops before our eyes, and we are not wrong to say that in this or that respect his personal story has lessons for us. That is right and proper – as long as we remember the background of it all: what God is doing with his people, not just with Gideon, in the enormously demanding situation in which he has set them. They are torn between the destructive power of the world, the heathen nations in and around Israel's promised land, and the authority of the wise and loving Judge who is Israel's God; and this at a time when they are not protected or cushioned against these ultimate realities by intervening authority-figures like Moses in earlier days or David in later ones. The lessons that Gideon has to learn are the lessons that Israel as a whole has to learn. It is in that sense that we take him as an instructive character-study.

His is the longest of all the Judges stories. Although Samson's has four chapters to Gideon's three, Gideon's has a hundred verses to Samson's ninety-six; and whether or not the writer intended this, it is very apt, because the story is in a sense all about quantities. This is plain at once if we start in the middle, with the best-known part of it, Judges 7.

1. The heart of the story (7:1–25)

Then Jerubbaal (that is, Gideon) and all the people who were with him rose early and encamped beside the spring of Harod; and the camp of Midian was north of them, by the hill of Moreh, in the valley.

²The LORD said to Gideon, 'The people with you are too many for me to give the Midianites into their hand, lest Israel vaunt themselves against me, saying, "My own hand has delivered me." ³Now therefore proclaim in the ears of the people, saying, "Whoever is fearful and trembling, let him return home." ' And Gideon tested them; twenty-two thousand returned, and ten thousand remained.

⁴And the LORD said to Gideon, 'The people are still too many; take them down to the water and I will test them for you there; and he of whom I say to you, "This man shall go with you," shall go with you; and any of whom I say to you, "This man shall not go with you," shall not go.' ⁵So he brought the people down to the water; and the LORD said to Gideon, 'Every one that laps the water with his tongue, as a dog laps, you shall set by himself; likewise everyone that kneels down to drink.' ⁶And the number of those that lapped, putting their hands to their mouths, was three hundred men; but all the rest of the people knelt down to drink water. ⁷And the LORD said to Gideon, 'With the three hundred men that lapped I will deliver you and give the Midianites into your hand; and let all the others go every man to his home.' ⁸So he took the jars of the people from their hands, and their trumpets; and he sent all the rest of Israel every man to his tent, but retained the three hundred men; and the camp of Midian was below him in the valley.

⁹That same night the LORD said to him, 'Arise, go down against the camp; for I have given it into your hand. ¹⁰But if you fear to go down, go down to the camp with Purah your servant; ¹¹and you shall hear what they say, and afterward your hands shall be strengthened to go down against the camp.' Then he went down with Purah his servant to the outposts of the armed men that were in the camp. ¹²And the Midianites and the Amalekites and all the people of the East lay along the valley like locusts for multitude; and their camels were without number, as the sand which is upon the sea-shore for multitude. ¹³When Gideon came, behold, a man was telling a dream to his comrade; and he said, 'Behold, I dreamed a dream; and lo, a cake of barley bread tumbled into the camp of Midian, and came to the tent, and struck it so that it fell, and turned it upside down, so that the tent lay flat.' ¹⁴And his comrade answered, 'This is no other than the sword of Gideon the son of Joash, a man of Israel; into his hand God has given Midian and all the host.'

¹⁵When Gideon heard the telling of the dream and its interpretation, he worshipped; and he returned to the camp of Israel, and said, 'Arise; for the LORD has given the host of Midian into your hand.' ¹⁶And he divided the three hundred men into three companies, and put trumpets into the hands of all of them and empty jars, with torches inside the jars. ¹⁷And he said to them, 'Look at me, and do likewise; when I come to the outskirts of the camp, do as I do. ¹⁸When I blow the trumpet, I and all who are with me, then blow the trumpets also on every side of all the camp, and shout, "For the LORD and for Gideon." '

¹⁹So Gideon and the hundred men who were with him came to the outskirts of the camp at the beginning of the middle watch, when they had just set the watch; and they blew the trumpets and smashed the jars that were in their hands. ²⁰And the three companies blew the trumpets and broke the jars, holding in their left hands the torches, and in their right hands the trumpets to blow; and they cried, 'A sword for the LORD and for Gideon!' ²¹They stood every man in his place round about the camp, and all the army ran; they cried out and fled. ²²When they blew the three hundred trumpets, the LORD set every man's sword against his fellow and against all the army; and the army fled as far as Beth-shittah toward Zererah,

as far as the border of Abel-meholah, by Tabbath. ²³*And the men
of Israel were called out from Naphtali and from Asher and from
all Manasseh, and they pursued after Midian.*

²⁴*And Gideon sent messengers throughout all the hill country of
Ephraim, saying, 'Come down against the Midianites and seize the
waters against them, as far as Beth-barah, and also the Jordan.' So
all the men of Ephraim were called out, and they seized the waters
as far as Beth-barah, and also the Jordan.* ²⁵*And they took the two
princes of Midian, Oreb and Zeeb; they killed Oreb at the rock of
Oreb, and Zeeb they killed at the wine press of Zeeb, as they
pursued Midian; and they brought the heads of Oreb and Zeeb to
Gideon beyond the Jordan.*

God, Teacher as well as Judge, is using this latest predicament of
Israel's to help her to grasp a vital truth about his ways with his
people. The first paragraph of the chapter shows him setting this
lesson before her.

a. The lesson taught (7:1–8)

Verse 1 paints the picture, verse 2 strikes the keynote.

We are to visualize, spread across the whole breadth of the valley
'by the hill of Moreh' (7:1), the hordes of Midian. They are the
enemy. What sort of enemy they are we shall not fully realize till
we go back to read chapter 6. For the moment, here at the heart
of the narrative the crucial battle is about to be joined between
them and (to the south, 'beside the spring of Harod') the Israelite
forces gathered by Gideon, their God-appointed judge and saviour.

Next, the keynote of the story is struck: God says to Gideon,
'The people with you are *too many*' (7:2). Too many? In the
circumstances, surely, no more than a respectable army, considering
the enemy they are up against. 32,000 responded to the summons[3]
when, as 6:34–35 tells us, the Spirit of the Lord clothed himself
with Gideon and the call to arms sounded not only through his
own clan and tribe but through three other neighbouring tribal
territories also. But that is too many, says the Lord. Send home

---

[3] As elsewhere in the Old Testament, the word translated 'thousands' may in fact
mean not a precise number but something more like 'contingents' or 'units'. This
is how Boling's translation regularly renders it; the word refers, he says, to 'the
quota supplied by one village or "clan" ... for the military muster. ...
Originally ... quite small ... finally ... a technical term for a military unit of
considerable size' (Boling, p. 55, on 1:4). See also his notes on 20:15, 35 (pp. 284f.,
287); and compare 6:15, where Gideon says his 'thousand' (RSV 'clan') is the weakest
in Manasseh. The point of this present story remains the same, whether it is 10,000
men or ten units that come to the stream: 'the people are still too many' (7:4).

'whoever is fearful and trembling' (7:3). At once the army is reduced to 10,000! Certainly we must now have made all the defence cuts we can afford. But no, says the Lord, 'the people are still too many' (7:4), and a further reduction is required.

On what basis is this next cut to be made? The famous, simple, but much-misunderstood test is imposed. The 10,000, presumably thirsty after the march from home that has brought them together to Harod, will no doubt in any case be wanting a drink. As they come to the spring and the stream that flows from it, the Lord tells Gideon to watch the way they drink. Whereupon 9,700 'knelt down to drink', while three hundred 'lapped, putting their hands to their mouths' (7:6).

Writers and preachers have differed as to why the Lord should choose those who lapped rather than those who knelt, even debating how exactly we ought to picture the two words. But once we find ourselves asking why 'lapping' was the sign of a better soldier, I am sure we are on the wrong track. The object was to reduce Gideon's army to a force not of a particular kind, but of a particular number. A small corps of crack troops is precisely what God does not want. The three hundred are meant to be not an elite, but a group so inadequate that when the battle is won (God declares) it cannot be a case of Israel's saying 'My own hand has delivered me' (7:2); no, 'I will deliver you' (7:7). Until the numbers are reduced to the level at which it is clearly the Lord and not Israel who wins the battle, they are *too many*.[4]

b. The lesson confirmed (7:9–15)

Once is not enough. God repeats and confirms what he wants Gideon to grasp. This in itself tells us a couple of vital truths. One is that God's servants generally are slow on the uptake, and God is lovingly patient and persistent with them. The other is that these are not side-issues, to be noted merely in passing; it is part and parcel of the main story that Gideon is not very quick at learning lessons, and needs to have them reiterated over and over again. And that is of course equally true of all his people throughout the period of the judges.

So the lesson is to be confirmed by Gideon's being sent into the enemy camp to discover that there also the same message has been coming across loud and clear. The Teacher is kind ('If you fear to

[4] Boling takes 'lapping' to mean lying flat and putting one's face in the water, and so throwing caution to the winds. 'The story thus gives even greater credit to Yahweh, who chose not only a smaller force, but also those less suitable to a military enterprise' (p. 145f.).

go down, go . . . with Purah your servant') but strict ('Arise, go' – that is an order): Gideon is not going to be let off the hook.

Put yourself in the shoes of the two Israelite spies as they creep into the Midianite camp under cover of darkness. What do you see? Verse 12: the flickering fires of an army whose camp seems to stretch to infinity. What do you hear? Verse 13: a dream being discussed by two Midianite soldiers, who foresee the defeat of that entire host, in the dream-image of a tent knocked over by a mere bread-roll which comes tumbling against it. And to make doubly sure that you do not miss the point, what has already been said by the Lord ('I will . . . give the Midianites into your hand', 7:7) is now heard from the Midianites themselves, with the lesson about numbers and quantities underlined: 'This is . . . Gideon the son of Joash, *a man* of Israel' – one man! – and 'into his hand God has given Midian and *all the host*' (7:14). It is God who stands behind Gideon as the Saviour–Judge, and he will defeat so great an army by means of so small a force that the deed will clearly be his and no-one else's – 'lest Israel vaunt themselves', as he had said at the outset (7:2).

Within hours the lesson is demonstrated before the eyes of watching Israel.

c. The lesson demonstrated (7:16–25)

Gideon does what he is told, and there follows a famous victory. There is no success without obedience. Not that the scheme of deploying his three hundred men each with a trumpet in one hand, and in the other a torch hidden inside a jar, necessarily came as a direct instruction from God. It may have done.[5] But Gideon has grasped the principle, already noted in the case of Ehud,[6] that God chooses 'what is weak in the world to shame the strong . . . so that no human being might boast in the presence of God'.[7] It is in obedience to that principle that he willingly accepts the derisory force of three hundred men as God's weapon, divides it again so that each man is now part of a group of only one hundred, and gives them a command which involves no military skill whatever, but simply an ability to blow a trumpet, break a jar, and shout. (So much for the supposed soldierly instincts of those who had lapped water.) Only later will they be concerned with fighting; on the night of the battle it is Midianites who fight each other, and

[5] The curious note in 7:8 seems to say (if the RSV's reconstruction is correct) that jars and trumpets were already in evidence for some purpose or other while the army still numbered 10,000.
[6] See pp. 46f.   [7] 1 Cor. 1:27, 29.

'flee when no one pursues'.[8] In the graphic words of 7:21, Gideon's men 'stood every man in his place . . . and all the army ran'. From three strategic points on the perimeter of the camp had come the sudden flare of torches, the braying of trumpets, and Israel's war-cry, and God saw to the rest.

After that, of course, someone did pursue. At this point came the turn of the discarded thousands, and of others from the tribe of Ephraim also, as the proud invaders who for so long had had everything their own way now fled, a disorganized rabble. Armed bands were quickly mobilized, river-crossings seized, enemy generals captured and killed (7:23–25). With regard to Gideon himself, we cannot help but notice how he has grown in stature in the course of the chapter. True, when possessed by the Spirit in 6:34 he had blown a trumpet and found perhaps to his surprise that an armed rising resulted. But there is something more than that to the Gideon of 7:24, who issues military orders (to a tribe not his own, be it noted), and has them obeyed to the letter. Out of weakness he begins to be made strong, becomes mighty in war, and puts foreign armies to flight, as Hebrews 11:34 will phrase it.

We have not yet put all of this in its context. Exciting and instructive though chapter 7, the central part of the story, may be, it has to be filled out by what has gone before and by what will come after if we are to see things in their proper proportions. As we return now to the beginning of the story, we need to bear in mind the crucial words made so vivid in the scene by the spring of Harod, when the God who wants an army of three hundred looks at a host of 32,000 and says 'Too many'.

2. The beginning of the story (6:1–40)

The people of Israel did what was evil in the sight of the LORD; *and the* LORD *gave them into the hand of Midian seven years.* [2]*And the hand of Midian prevailed over Israel; and because of Midian the people of Israel made for themselves the dens which are in the mountains, and the caves and the strongholds.* [3]*For whenever the Israelites put in seed the Midianites and the Amalekites and the people of the East would come up and attack them;* [4]*they would encamp against them and destroy the produce of the land, as far as the neighbourhood of Gaza, and leave no sustenance in Israel, and no sheep or ox or ass.* [5]*For they would come up with their cattle and their tents, coming like locusts for number; both they and their camels could not be counted; so that they wasted the land as tney*

[8] Pr. 28:1.

73

came in. ⁶*And Israel was brought very low because of Midian; and the people of Israel cried for help to the* LORD.

⁷*When the people of Israel cried to the* LORD *on account of the Midianites,* ⁸*the* LORD *sent a prophet to the people of Israel; and he said to them, 'Thus says the* LORD, *the God of Israel: I led you up from Egypt, and brought you out of the house of bondage;* ⁹*and I delivered you from the hand of the Egyptians, and from the hand of all who oppressed you, and drove them out before you, and gave you their land;* ¹⁰*and I said to you, "I am the* LORD *your God; you shall not pay reverence to the gods of the Amorites, in whose land you dwell." But you have not given heed to my voice.'*

¹¹*Now the angel of the* LORD *came and sat under the oak at Ophrah, which belonged to Joash the Abiezrite, as his son Gideon was beating out wheat in the wine press, to hide it from the Midianites.* ¹²*And the angel of the* LORD *appeared to him and said to him, 'The* LORD *is with you, you mighty man of valour.'* ¹³*And Gideon said to him, 'Pray, sir, if the* LORD *is with us, why then has all this befallen us? And where are all his wonderful deeds which our fathers recounted to us, saying, "Did not the* LORD *bring us up from Egypt?" But now the* LORD *has cast us off, and given us into the hand of Midian.'* ¹⁴*And the* LORD *turned to him and said, 'Go in this might of yours and deliver Israel from the hand of Midian; do not I send you?'* ¹⁵*And he said to him, 'Pray, Lord, how can I deliver Israel? Behold, my clan is the weakest in Manasseh, and I am the least in my family.'* ¹⁶*And the* LORD *said to him, 'But I will be with you, and you shall smite the Midianites as one man.'* ¹⁷*And he said to him, 'If now I have found favour with thee, then show me a sign that it is thou who speakest with me.* ¹⁸*Do not depart from here, I pray thee, until I come to thee, and bring out my present, and set it before thee.' And he said, 'I will stay till you return.'*

¹⁹*So Gideon went into his house and prepared a kid, and unleavened cakes from an ephah of flour; the meat he put in a basket and the broth he put in a pot, and brought them to him under the oak and presented them.* ²⁰*And the angel of God said to him, 'Take the meat and the unleavened cakes, and put them on this rock, and pour the broth over them.' And he did so.* ²¹*Then the angel of the* LORD *reached out the tip of the staff that was in his hand, and touched the meat and the unleavened cakes; and there sprang up fire from the rock and consumed the flesh and the unleavened cakes; and the angel of the* LORD *vanished from his sight.* ²²*Then Gideon perceived that he was the angel of the* LORD; *and Gideon said, 'Alas, O Lord* GOD! *For now I have seen the angel of the* LORD *face to face.'* ²³*But the* LORD *said to him, 'Peace*

be to you; do not fear, you shall not die.' ²⁴Then Gideon built an altar there to the LORD, and called it, The LORD is peace. To this day it still stands at Ophrah, which belongs to the Abiezrites.

²⁵That night the LORD said to him, 'Take your father's bull, the second bull seven years old, and pull down the altar of Baal which your father has, and cut down the Asherah that is beside it; ²⁶and build an altar to the LORD your God on the top of the stronghold here, with stones laid in due order; then take the second bull, and offer it as a burnt offering with the wood of the Asherah which you shall cut down.' ²⁷So Gideon took ten men of his servants, and did as the LORD had told him; but because he was too afraid of his family and the men of the town to do it by day, he did it by night.

²⁸When the men of the town rose early in the morning, behold, the altar of Baal was broken down, and the Asherah beside it was cut down, and the second bull was offered upon the altar which had been built. ²⁹And they said to one another, 'Who has done this thing?' And after they had made search and inquired, they said, 'Gideon the son of Joash has done this thing.' ³⁰Then the men of the town said to Joash, 'Bring out your son that he may die, for he has pulled down the altar of Baal and cut down the Asherah beside it.' ³¹But Joash said to all who were arrayed against him, 'Will you contend for Baal? Or will you defend his cause? Whoever contends for him shall be put to death by morning. If he is a god, let him contend for himself, because his altar has been pulled down.' ³²Therefore on that day he was called Jerubbaal, that is to say, 'Let Baal contend against him,' because he pulled down his altar.

³³Then all the Midianites and the Amalekites and the people of the East came together, and crossing the Jordan they encamped in the Valley of Jezreel. ³⁴But the Spirit of the LORD took possession of Gideon; and he sounded the trumpet, and the Abiezrites were called out to follow him. ³⁵And he sent messengers throughout all Manasseh; and they too were called out to follow him. And he sent messengers to Asher, Zebulun, and Naphtali; and they went up to meet them.

³⁶Then Gideon said to God, 'If thou wilt deliver Israel by my hand, as thou hast said, ³⁷behold, I am laying a fleece of wool on the threshing floor; if there is dew on the fleece alone, and it is dry on all the ground, then I shall know that thou wilt deliver Israel by my hand, as thou hast said.' ³⁸And it was so. When he rose early next morning and squeezed the fleece, he wrung enough dew from the fleece to fill a bowl with water. ³⁹Then Gideon said to God, 'Let not thy anger burn against me, let me speak but this once; pray, let me make trial only this once with the fleece; pray, let it be dry only on the fleece, and on all the ground let there be dew.'

[40]*And God did so that night; for it was dry on the fleece only, and on all the ground there was dew.*

In the first part of chapter 6 the Lord sets the scene, and in the second part he prepares the saviour. In fact, in a sense it is the Lord who is doing everything in the story of Gideon, and this is even clearer while Gideon himself is still a nonentity and has not yet taken the first step of obedient response to God's call.

a. The Lord sets the scene (6:1–24)

We recall that forty years of rest followed Israel's deliverance from Canaanite cruelty under the leadership of Deborah and Barak. What happened after that was, as usual, a lapse into sin and idolatry. If we ask what Israel was doing, the answer is, 'evil in the sight of the Lord'. We shall do better to ask what the Lord was doing. Of his activities we learn first in the words of the narrator of the book, then in the words of a prophet, and then in the words of an angel.

i. According to the narrator (6:1–6)

The Lord's name figures prominently in this opening paragraph of chapter 6. It is in his sight that Israel again does evil, he who gives them over to another oppressor, and to him that they once more cry for help (6:1, 6). Here are three of the Rs – rebellion, retribution, and repentance (of a sort) – and the next ninety-four verses will of course tell of the fourth R, the Lord's rescue of his people by the instrumentality of Gideon.

That outline we have seen before. What is new is the narrator's description of this latest oppressor, the people of Midian, together with their associates, the Amalekites and the 'people of the East'. It is a substantial insertion into the customary bare framework, and we should ask ourselves what the writer (and the Lord) want us to make of it. As far as the names are concerned, we are probably meant to hear echoes from the past. It is true that no less a person than Moses had married into the tribe of Midian,[9] and his Midianite relatives were welcome among the Israelites in the early days of the exodus journey.[10] But even before that visit, with the journey only just begun, we are told that 'then came Amalek and fought with Israel'.[11] The Amalekites were the first enemy actually to take up arms against Israel, years before Philistines or Canaanites or any of the nations of Mesopotamia, or even Moab, so long her

[9] *Cf.* Ex. 2:15–22.   [10] *Cf.* Ex. 18.   [11] Ex. 17:8.

antagonist; with a sharp paradox God condemns Amalek for ever – '*Remember* what Amalek did . . . *Blot out the remembrance* of Amalek.'[12] And by the time described in Numbers 25 and 31 Midian likewise had fallen foul of the Lord and his pilgrim people. The names Midian and Amalek, therefore, convey in themselves an active enmity which persists over many years, as Israel never succeeds in finally dealing with it.

If that is the allusion we are intended to catch (so *many* years of bad relations), it certainly chimes in with what the narrator actually tells us concerning the Midianite oppression of chapter 6. This is not occupation, like that of the Moabites in the days of Ehud, nor conquest, like that of the Canaanites in the days of Deborah; it is a 'wasting of the land' which left no sustenance in Israel. But what he stresses is how many times they invaded (note the word 'whenever', and the tenses of the verbs: they would come, they would attack, they would destroy, *whenever* the Israelites had crops to be plundered); how many miles they covered (as far as Gaza, in the deep south, having presumably crossed Jordan a very long way to the north of that, to judge by 6:33); and above all, how many men their host comprised (they were 'like locusts' not just for destructiveness, which is what locusts usually mean, but here specifically 'for number; . . . they . . . could not be counted'). Too many! Too many! And it is into the hand of this 'too-many' enemy that the Lord has given his people.

ii. According to the prophet (6:7–10)

Here again is something familiar: with the Midianite oppression God raises a prophet for his people, as with the Canaanite oppression he had raised Deborah to be their prophetess (4:4). But here also is something new, for the prophet's message is unexpected. He does not say what we might have hoped: 'The Lord has seen your rebellion, he has set the Midianites on to you as a retribution, and he has heard the cry of your repentance; so now he will raise up a rescuer for you.' That was the classic pattern in the days of Othniel, but things have moved on since then. That is what the immature believer expects, but life is more complicated than that.

However, if the prophet does not say what we might have hoped, neither does he say (to fly to the opposite extreme) what we might have feared: 'The Lord has seen your rebellion, and sent his retribution, and naturally your cries of anguish now assail his ears; but he doesn't think much of your so-called repentance, and intends

[12] Dt. 25:17–19; see also Ex. 17:14–16.

to tighten the screw till you really repent. Then he might think about rescuing you.'

No. What the Lord does say through his prophet is this: 'I led you up, brought you out, and delivered you from Egypt. I gave you this land. The one thing I asked of you was to reject the gods of this land. And you have not listened to me.' So . . . ? 'So I will give you another chance'? 'So I will give you no more chances'? No, 'so' nothing. Just a recital of what God has done, and of what Israel has failed to do.

What we have here is an explanation. We can recognize and applaud in our own day the desire for genuine heart-religion, which reacts against mere head-knowledge of the Christian faith. But something vital is lost when God's people begin to dislike the word 'understand'. The prophet of Judges 6 is sent to make Israel *understand* what is going on. (One thought-provoking way of defining the preacher's job: 'To explain what is really going on.') And how does this prophet uncover what is really going on? He recites the recent great mercies of God to his people. *He* has heard *their* voice, although they have not listened to his; and he has done for them – oh, so much! So many good things; *too many* mercies for God simply to overlook their sin. It is no coincidence that innumerable Midianites are sent as a punishment for the rejection of innumerable mercies.

iii.   According to the angel (6:11–24)
In 6:1 another repetition of the pattern; in 6:8 another prophet, as in 4:4; and now in 6:11 another angel, as in 2:1. This time there is no question but that the 'angel of the Lord' is supernatural, and is to be identified with the Lord himself (6:14, 16), although Gideon does not recognize it at once.

With arresting words the angel greets Gideon. Let us be arrested by them! 'The LORD is with you, you mighty man of valour' (6:12).

Israelite farmers are no longer free to winnow their wheat in the open air, where the breeze can catch it and separate chaff from grain. For seven years it has been so. For fear of marauding Midianites, Gideon has taken his wheat to a winepress, a hollow in the ground, to winnow it, and as he crouches there the sudden voice must make him jump out of his skin. Who is the stranger sitting under the oak? And more to the point, what is he saying?

To judge by appearances, Gideon is anything but a 'mighty man of valour' as he skulks in the winepress. However, some commentators take it that the angel is speaking actual truth. Gideon needs only to have his natural courage coaxed out into the open. He is like the Gilbert and Sullivan character who sings of himself as 'diffident, modest and shy' when he is really nothing of the sort.[13] I believe myself that this is the language of irony and faith – ironic at the time, and prophetic of what God will make of Gideon in the future.

There are two reasons for this view. First, Gideon represents Israel, and just as Israel has been 'brought very low' (6:6) so Gideon really is the least member of the weakest clan in his tribe (6:15). The central theme of these chapters is that God will work out his purposes in those who truly are helpless – 'lest Israel vaunt themselves against me, saying, "My own hand has delivered me" ', as he will put it in the next chapter (7:2). It is of the essence of the story that Gideon is *not* at the beginning a mighty man of valour, as is brought out, I think, by the way his courage grows so gradually (6:27, 36–40; 7:10); the angel is speaking prophetically about what God intends to make of him.

The second reason is that we are meant, I am sure, to see a parallel between Gideon and an earlier leader, not any of the judges, but the great Moses himself. The misery of Israel in 6:6 is there in Exodus 2: 'The people of Israel groaned under their bondage, and cried out for help.'[14] The conversation between the Lord and his chosen rescuer, here in 6:11–22, is there in Exodus 3: 'I will send you . . . that you may bring forth my people',[15] as in 6:14; 'Who am I that I should . . . bring the sons of Israel out . . . ?',[16] as in 6:15; 'But I will be with you,[17] word for word as in 6:16. In each account a confirming sign is promised, and in each the appalled interviewee realizes that he has been face to face with God.[18] If the parallel is intentional (and it is significant that there has already been a similar parallel between a Moses/God encounter and the Barak/Deborah one in 4:8–9),[19] then what was true of Moses will be no less true of Gideon, that his valour is not in himself but in what God is going to make of him.

What God will make of Gideon is then all the more remarkable. In this paragraph also we cannot miss the 'numbers' theme, increasingly clear as the angel presses relentlessly on: 'The LORD is with *you*' (6:12; 'with *thee*', singular, as the older translations make plain); 'Go in this might of *yours*' (6:14); '*You* shall smite the Midianites' – all those countless hordes! – '*as one man*' (6:16).

So the Lord sets the scene. If the special message of Deborah and Barak was that Israel might begin to know the fact and the necessity of conflict between Israel and the world around her, the message of Gideon clearly has something to do with the weakness

[13] Sir Ruthven Murgatroyd in *Ruddigore*.   [14] Ex. 2:23.   [15] Ex. 3:10.
[16] Ex. 3:11.   [17] Ex. 3:12.
[18] 6:17 and Ex. 3:12; Jdg. 6:22 and Ex. 3:6.   [19] See p. 63.

of God's people and the apparently overwhelming strength of the enemy, and with God's methods of perfecting his own strength in weakness.[20]

b. The Lord prepares the saviour (6:25–40)

Gideon, then, is the one who, with God, will be powerful 'and deliver Israel from the hand of Midian' (6:14), but who, without God, is indeed 'the least' (6:15). The sign that the angel of the Lord gives him to confirm that he has not imagined it all, that is, the burning up of Gideon's offering of meat and bread (6:21), is followed by a string of other confirmations as the Lord sets about preparing his servant for his task.

Again we put ourselves in Gideon's place, not necessarily because we aspire to be leaders, nor because Gideon is Everyman, but because he represents an Israel who is beginning to have to learn lessons for herself (Moses being long gone and David not yet come); and Israel's lesson at this time, the time of Gideon, is to learn just how great is the foe that faces her.

i. The enemy among us (6:25–32)

6:1 sets old alongside new: 'Israel did what was evil . . . the LORD gave them into the hand of Midian.' The foe without has been brought by God, and is, as we have seen, a foe of a new kind. The sin within is man's doing, and therefore depressingly unoriginal. It should be no surprise that Gideon's own father Joash has an altar and a pole beside it where, yet again, the worship of Canaanite gods takes place, for these are the pervasive influences of the world Joash lives in. And of our world too, even if the names and the structures are unfamiliar. The gods have not changed, for human nature has not changed, and these are the gods that humanity regularly re-creates for itself. What does it want? If it is modest, security and comfort and reasonable enjoyment; if ambitious, power and wealth and unbridled self-indulgence. In every age there are forces at work which promise to meet our desires – political programmes, economic theories, philosophical movements, entertainment industries – all having one feature in common: they are big enough to do things for us that we cannot do for ourselves, yet at the same time amenable to our manipulating them so as to get from them what we want. So the life of Ophrah revolves around these Baals. We put our money into this one, and vote for that one, and spend all our free time on the other one, expecting worldly

[20] *Cf.* 2 Cor. 12:9.

benefits to be produced by human efforts.

Here is the enemy among us. We, God's people, do know the Lord (why else would his angel have spoken to Gideon as he did?), but how much of the world around us has crept in among us! It seems to have taken over our thinking in such a way that we can hardly see how we can live without it.

So we are called first to stand up against this enemy. The divine plan is simply that these things which stand for the Canaanite world and its values should be removed, and sacrificed to God: simple, though not easy, and doing it by night because we are scared to do it by day matters nothing as long as the hard thing is *done* – as Davis says, 'Obedience was essential and heroism optional.'[21] The human reaction is as the Lord has calculated it will be. The people of Ophrah are shocked to find their place of worship desecrated, soon discover the culprit, and demand that the insult to Baal be avenged; Joash with robust common-sense retorts, 'If Baal is the god he is supposed to be, let him do his own avenging'; and, as in Egypt long before, the Canaanite gods are shown to be no gods – then, as now, more no doubt for the sake of the Israelites than for the sake of the heathen devotees of those gods.

So we – that is, Gideon – have taken the first step of obedience, and thereby our faith is confirmed. Our God is the real God.

ii. The enemy around us (6:33–35)

Once the enemy among us has been dealt with, the enemy around us must be looked to. The first was the subtle influence of Canaanite thinking; the second is the obvious evil of Midianite action.

This evil is not only allowed, but actually brought, by the Lord (6:1). It is directly related to the sin of God's people – if they trust one set of worldly forces to give them prosperity, they can hardly be surprised if another set takes it away. So God ordains that those whose hearts are set on the Canaanite gods of peace, plenty, and comfort shall regularly suffer the Midianite scourges of strife, deprivation, and misery. But all the same the punishment *is* an evil, and even as he is using it to teach his people hard lessons, the Lord is at the same time calling Gideon to rise and oppose it.

So we are called to stand up against this enemy too. As the word of the Lord has come to us (6:25) so the Spirit of the Lord comes to us (6:34); each has equal power; and as news arrives of the latest invasion, 'all the Midianites and the Amalekites and the people of

[21] Davis, p. 98.

the East . . . together' (6:33), we blow the trumpet and find perhaps to our own astonishment that the troops do indeed rally to the call. We have taken the second step of obedience, to stand for what is plainly right against what is plainly wrong, and again our faith is confirmed. As we have found that our God really *is* God, so our people really do turn out to be the people of God.

iii. The enemy within us (6:36–40)

Even now the weaknesses of our own character remain within us. We may have found the courage to repudiate the world, and the daring to call others of God's people to identify with us, but we have not yet found the confidence to be quite sure that we are on the right track. We ought not to blame Gideon for putting out his famous fleece. Setting up tests for God is not normally a good way of seeking guidance, but we need to balance the impiety of Israel's demanding signs from God in Psalm 95:8–11 against the equal impiety of King Ahaz's not doing so in Isaiah 7:10–17. The proper question, as ever, is to ask what God is doing with his people. As a rule he requires them to 'walk by faith, not by sight';[22] the important thing about guidance is not the method but the fact. They are expected to trust that as they make decisions on the basis of what he has already said, so he *is* guiding them; they are not expected to demand that he show them *how* he is guiding them, by telling them what decisions to make. But we may take Gideon's as a special case. Here the Lord is coaxing along a reluctant leader who really is 'diffident, modest and shy', and who needs to have his confidence built up step by step by a patient, loving, but determined God.[23]

So we learn to stand up against the enemy within us, the inadequacy of our faith, and to use every means we can to encourage ourselves in the greatness and the goodwill of our Lord.

Thus the scene is set, and the saviour prepared, for the confrontation between Israel and Midian in chapter 7. Victory is assured. But we must never forget that the Judge has designedly brought together two opposing forces which are totally disparate. The one hopelessly outnumbers the other. Aptly is the Israelites' rendezvous named '*Trembling* Spring' (Harod, 7:1).

> We go in faith, our own great weakness feeling,
> And needing more each day thy grace to know;

[22] 2 Cor. 5:7.
[23] 'He is hesitant, not unbelieving. It is not the absence of faith but the caution of faith we see here' (Davis, p. 99). Davis has a helpful extended comment on the passage.

Yet from our hearts a song of triumph pealing,
We rest on thee, and in thy name we go.[24]

3. The end of the story (8:1–35)

*And the men of Ephraim said to him, 'What is this that you have
done to us, not to call us when you went to fight with Midian?'
And they upbraided him violently.* [2]*And he said to them, 'What
have I done now in comparison with you? Is not the gleaning of
the grapes of Ephraim better than the vintage of Abiezer?* [3]*God has
given into your hands the princes of Midian, Oreb and Zeeb; what
have I been able to do in comparison with you?' Then their anger
against him was abated, when he had said this.*

[4]*And Gideon came to the Jordan and passed over, he and the
three hundred men who were with him, faint yet pursuing.* [5]*So he
said to the men of Succoth, 'Pray, give loaves of bread to the people
who follow me; for they are faint, and I am pursuing after Zebah
and Zalmunna, the kings of Midian.'* [6]*And the officials of Succoth
said, 'Are Zebah and Zalmunna already in your hand, that we
should give bread to your army?'* [7]*And Gideon said, 'Well then,
when the* LORD *has given Zebah and Zalmunna into my hand, I
will flail your flesh with the thorns of the wilderness and with
briers.'* [8]*And from there he went up to Penuel, and spoke to them
in the same way; and the men of Penuel answered him as the men
of Succoth had answered.* [9]*And he said to the men of Penuel, 'When
I come again in peace, I will break down this tower.'*

[10]*Now Zebah and Zalmunna were in Karkor with their army,
about fifteen thousand men, all who were left of all the army of
the people of the East; for there had fallen a hundred and twenty
thousand men who drew the sword.* [11]*And Gideon went up by the
caravan route east of Nobah and Jogbehah, and attacked the army;
for the army was off its guard.* [12]*And Zebah and Zalmunna fled;
and he pursued them and took the two kings of Midian, Zebah and
Zalmunna, and he threw all the army into a panic.*

[13]*Then Gideon the son of Joash returned from the battle by the
ascent of Heres.* [14]*And he caught a young man of Succoth, and
questioned him; and he wrote down for him the officials and elders
of Succoth, seventy-seven men.* [15]*And he came to the men of Succoth,
and said, 'Behold Zebah and Zalmunna, about whom you taunted
me, saying, "Are Zebah and Zalmunna already in your hand, that
we should give bread to your men who are faint?"'* [16]*And he took
the elders of the city and he took thorns of the wilderness and briers*

---

[24] Edith Gilling Cherry, *We rest on thee.*

and with them taught the men of Succoth. ¹⁷And he broke down the tower of Penuel, and slew the men of the city.

¹⁸Then he said to Zebah and Zalmunna, 'Where are the men whom you slew at Tabor?' They answered, 'As you are, so were they, every one of them; they resembled the sons of a king.' ¹⁹And he said, 'They were my brothers, the sons of my mother; as the LORD lives, if you had saved them alive, I would not slay you.' ²⁰And he said to Jether his first-born, 'Rise, and slay them.' But the youth did not draw his sword; for he was afraid, because he was still a youth. ²¹Then Zebah and Zalmunna said, 'Rise yourself, and fall upon us; for as the man is, so is his strength.' And Gideon arose and slew Zebah and Zalmunna; and he took the crescents that were on the necks of their camels.

²²Then the men of Israel said to Gideon, 'Rule over us, you and your son and your grandson also; for you have delivered us out of the hand of Midian.' ²³Gideon said to them, 'I will not rule over you, and my son will not rule over you; the LORD will rule over you.' ²⁴And Gideon said to them, 'Let me make a request of you; give me every man of you the earrings of his spoil.' (For they had golden earrings, because they were Ishmaelites.) ²⁵And they answered, 'We will willingly give them.' And they spread a garment, and every man cast in it the earrings of his spoil. ²⁶And the weight of the golden earrings that he requested was one thousand seven hundred shekels of gold; besides the crescents and the pendants and the purple garments worn by the kings of Midian, and besides the collars that were about the necks of their camels. ²⁷And Gideon made an ephod of it and put it in his city, in Ophrah; and all Israel played the harlot after it there, and it became a snare to Gideon and to his family. ²⁸So Midian was subdued before the people of Israel, and they lifted up their heads no more. And the land had rest forty years in the days of Gideon.

²⁹Jerubbaal the son of Joash went and dwelt in his own house. ³⁰Now Gideon had seventy sons, his own offspring, for he had many wives. ³¹And his concubine who was in Shechem also bore him a son, and he called his name Abimelech. ³²And Gideon the son of Joash died in a good old age, and was buried in the tomb of Joash his father, at Ophrah of the Abiezrites.

³³As soon as Gideon died, the people of Israel turned again and played the harlot after the Baals, and made Baal-berith their god. ³⁴And the people of Israel did not remember the LORD their God, who had rescued them from the hand of all their enemies on every side; ³⁵and they did not show kindness to the family of Jerubbaal (that is, Gideon) in return for all the good that he had done to Israel.

After the rout of chapter 7, the Ephraimite force which had joined in the chase of the fleeing Midianites captures the two generals Oreb and Zeeb. But their execution is not the end of the tale, for the Midianite kings Zebah and Zalmunna are still at large, and it is in that connection that the story of Gideon is to be completed. Up to now the genuineness of Gideon's judgeship has been clear from the way he has followed step by step the directions of his mentor, the great Judge, the Lord. But nothing ever goes right for long in the times of the judges, and chapter 8 is by way of being a warning – in fact a double warning, as the first part of it bids us 'Beware!' and the second bids us 'Remember!'

a. Beware! (8:1–21)

The previous two chapters have shown the development of Gideon from the nonentity at the winepress of Ophrah to the conquerer of his people's foes. Watch now, attentively, as he continues to develop. Increasing experience is not necessarily in itself a good thing. There is a 'maturity' which leaves behind the wise and humble attitudes of the early days of discipleship. Advancement can be a perilous thing.

Look at the diplomacy of 8:1–3. With the nation's enemy on the run, the tribe of Ephraim can indulge the luxury of picking a quarrel with their own victorious general. Their touchiness will surface again in the days of Jephthah, who will give them considerably shorter shrift (12:1–6). Whatever his private feelings (he may have been sorely tempted to beat them up, as Jephthah later did), Gideon reckons that for the moment he has more pressing matters on hand, and 'a soft answer' which 'turns away wrath'[25] defuses the explosive situation in the Israelite ranks.

So far so good. Look next at the determination of 8:4–9. It is a measure of the unlikelihood of this rout of the many by the few that, as pursued and pursuers rush past Succoth and Penuel, neither town is yet prepared to believe in an Israelite victory. But in spite of his own weariness and the unhelpfulness of the two towns, Gideon keeps up such an unrelenting pace that he will eventually take the Midianites completely by surprise as they pause for breath (8:11). The phrase 'faint yet pursuing' (8:4) is the memorable summing-up of his determination. We glimpse also, perhaps, in his replies to the people of the two towns, a new and disquieting development in his character; but leave that aside for the moment.

Look next at the skill with which he brings the campaign to an

[25] Pr. 15:1.

end in 8:10–12. The three hundred are no longer blowing trumpets and waving torches, nor are they now merely pursuing; they have become a fighting force, out to destroy the power of the Midianites (who now number a paltry 15,000 – 'all who were left of all the army of the people of the East'!). It is an account of strategy, manoeuvre, a surprise attack which throws 'all the army into a panic', and finally the pursuit and capture of the Midianite kings – in brief, total success. Where did Gideon learn these military skills? He has become a notable leader.

Well, we might say, that just about wraps it up. What the Lord had in mind for Gideon to do ('You shall smite the Midianites'), Gideon has done. What Gideon has in mind, however, is something more. A number of other notions have been growing there alongside his development as the saviour of his people. The men of Succoth and Penuel ought indeed to have had faith in him when he first passed that way; he had had every appearance of being on a winning streak; instead they had been cautious. Look at the ruthlessness with which he repaid their caution (8:13–17)! We may smile at the quaint phrase, that with thorns and briers he 'taught the men of Succoth', but it is an uneasy amusement when we recall his original threat, 'I will flail your flesh' (8:7), and find that as well as demolishing the tower at Penuel, as he said he would, he also 'slew the men of the city'. And this ruthless element becomes still more disturbing when we realize that these were his fellow-Israelites. File that away as a portent of things to come.

Look finally, in this part of the chapter, at the climax of the campaign in 8:18–21, when the Midianite kings are put to death. With a startling twist the narrator produces something of which we, the readers, have had no idea at all: out of the blue comes Gideon's question to the two kings, 'What about the men you killed at Tabor?' (8:18, GNB). Zebah and Zalmunna had, it turns out, 'been responsible for the death of his brothers. It is a personal vendetta which Gideon has been prosecuting with such ruthless determination in Transjordan.'[26] In chapters 6 and 7 his motivation was obedience to God, but here it is personal revenge. How he has changed! His son Jether is now the diffident faintheart that Gideon once was, while Gideon himself has become, even on the testimony of his enemies, a man of majesty (8:18) and strength (8:21). But there is something less than admirable at the heart of him, for all the development of his great abilities. Beware of the gifts of the Spirit without the fruit of the Spirit!

[26] Webb, p. 151.

b. Remember! (8:22–35)

For too long the life of Israel has been dominated by these heathen kings. It is perhaps natural that the killing of them should lead immediately to the desire for the rule of an Israelite king instead, and that king Gideon. His response could be taken in two ways. The obvious meaning of 8:23 is that he repudiates the suggestion. On the other hand, there may be an unspoken 'Yes, but': yes, I will continue to be your leader, but remember it will be the Lord ruling through me – just as it has been the Lord delivering Israel by my hand (6:14, 16, 36–37). In either case, verses 22 and 23 rebuke the simple popular view 'Saviour, therefore king', and tell us: Remember *the Lord* is King. *He* rules, and he decides how and through whom he will rule.

Whatever Gideon thinks of the offer of kingship (and certainly he has come to look increasingly like an autocrat), he intends to take up the matter of judgeship. He has an 'ephod' made, the priestly vestment which incorporated a gem-encrusted breastplate and the 'urim and thummim', objects which we cannot now picture but which were used to seek God's guidance. God as Judge had first appointed this method of directing his people, and it had been rightly used in the past and would be again.[27] But compared with the true ephod, which is presumably all this time at Shiloh (18:31), Gideon's is handier for his own family, as well as being a very splendid affair (8:26–27), and its prestige attracts 'all Israel'. This is the 'hankering', as Davis calls it, 'for more than what God has already given for our sustenance, nurture, direction . . . We are not content merely to walk obediently to the Scriptures, trusting God's providence and goodness . . . No, we must have more – a specific, direct word from God about what we should do in our particular problem.'[28] Verses 24–27, however, make it plain that an ephod of human origin – guidance as man likes to receive it – can be nothing but a snare and a delusion, and they tell us: Remember *the Lord* is Judge. *He* directs, in the ways he has laid down, not in the ways we set up, however legitimate they may sound.

Whether or not Gideon had agreed to 'rule' Israel, he lived the rest of his life in some style. If the Bible describes you as having a large family and dying 'in a good old age' it usually means you are rather eminent, and Abimelech – 'My father is king'? – is a sufficiently ambiguous name to give to one of your sons. Be that as it may, Gideon had seen off the people of the East for good, and through him Israel enjoyed forty peaceful years. But although

[27] Ex. 28:1–35; Nu. 27:21; 1 Sa. 23:9–12; 30:7–8.
[28] Davis, pp. 114–115; and see above, on Gideon's fleece, p. 82.

the Midianites never came back, the good time was not lasting, and when after Gideon's death the Israelites slid back into their old ways, it was a case of not remembering *the Lord*, who had rescued them from so many enemies, as well as not caring about all the good that Gideon had done. The closing verses of chapter 8 set these two negligences in parallel (ingratitude for Gideon's good deeds means forgetfulness of God's rescues) and tell us: Remember *the Lord* is Saviour. Gideon was in a secondary sense saviour, judge, perhaps even king; but as at the beginning, so in a different sense still at the end, he was only a man with all the weaknesses of humanity; and he needed to be, for only so can God stop the mouths of those who boast 'My own hand has delivered me' (7:2). The true King, Judge, and Saviour is the Lord alone.

Remember finally why later generations remember this man. He is weak in chapter 6 because of his inexperience and diffidence. He is weak in chapter 8 because of his self-will and lack of discernment. Both ends of the story teach the same lesson: when the foe is so strong and we are so frail, we have to cast ourselves on the Lord. That is why Gideon is one of the four immortals from the book of Judges in the gallery of faith in Hebrews 11. He, and Israel with him, finds authority and direction in the Lord as they practise the mathematics of Judges 7, the three hundred against the 135,000. 'When I am weak, then I am strong.'[29]

And notice that on the way to Hebrews 11, halfway down the span of history between these two books of the Bible, the 'day of Midian' provides the backcloth for Isaiah's great vision of the coming King, Judge, and Saviour. As we see ourselves at the mercy of the numberless hosts of darkness, 'to us a child is born', and entrusting ourselves to that one, so powerless and so grossly outnumbered, it would seem, we find that 'of the increase of *his* government and of peace there will be no end'.[30]

[29] 2 Cor. 12:10.   [30] Is. 9:4–7.

Judges 9:1 – 10:5

5. Abimelech: something completely different

Again Judges surprises the reader. The lead in to chapter 9 is a familiar enough scene-setting, as the people of Israel once more do what is evil in the sight of the Lord, although in keeping with the theme of general decline the sins of 8:33–35 are more specific than before, reminding us of the 'third-generation' wickedness of 2:16–19. But instead of the sequence we have grown used to, sin followed by punishment, then a cry for help, then a rescue, we now have something completely different. The first two verses of this chapter set the tone: the leading figure in it will not be a person raised up by God either as a scourge or as a saviour; what brings him to centre stage is the fact that he is a son of Gideon. The place and the people involved belong neither to Israel nor to Israel's enemies; they are Shechemite, and have a long-standing relationship with Israel dating back to the days of Jacob himself, before Jacob's family had even migrated to Egypt, let alone returned from it.[1] Authority in Judges 9 is a matter not of judging or of delivering, but of ruling, the ominous word first introduced when Israel offered the kingship to Gideon (8:22). And it may occur to us as we go on to read the whole story of Abimelech that nowhere in it, from 8:34 to 10:6, is the Lord mentioned by name.

All this unexpectedness re-opens the question of the value of the book for those who read it today. However they apply to themselves the narratives of Moses' time or of David's time, they have to re-tune in order to hear clearly what the judges are saying to them. But having worked out what kind of lesson they should learn from Ehud and Deborah and Gideon, they find that that method also now goes by the board. Surely Abimelech is not what I ought

[1] See Gn. 34.

to be? Or is he what I may be, or what I must try not to be? What is the connection between his experience and mine?

As always in hearing the voice of God in Scripture, we must take his revelation to be consistent, settle in our minds what are the unchanging facts behind the flux of events in Bible history, and discern what is common to the Bible world and our world.

For a start, there are distinctions between the way God is known in the Old Testament and the way he is known in the New Testament (though considerably fewer than, and different from, the distinctions that some would have us believe); he is nevertheless the same God. His people are at various times in history a family, a nation, a monarchy, and a supra-national church, but they are throughout the same people of God. The moral world they move in has been guided by the teaching of lawgiver, prophet, and apostle, but the law of God is one, and does not change. The physical world they inhabit bears on its face the marks of a dozen successive cultures, from the ancient Near East through classical Rome to the global village of today, but seedtime and harvest, cold and heat, summer and winter, day and night do not cease.[2] The life they lead may be that of herdsmen, slaves, pilgrims, farmers, soldiers, teachers, but it is always to be lived in the service of God. The responsibilities placed on them will vary, but there will always be some 'talent' to be used and improved.

So whatever Judges shows of these constants – God and his people, their moral and physical environment, their life of service and responsibility – we are bound to look for equivalents in our own experience. With this sideslip into the alien world of chapter 9, a narrative peculiar even by the standards of Judges, we must still try to do the same. 'Something completely different' obliges us to ask the difficult questions. What is really going on here? What is God doing, and what are his people doing? How are the right judgments to be made?

1. Truth and integrity undermined

Words used twice in chapter 9, in verses 16 and 19, provide a key phrase for understanding the story of Abimelech. *'Emeth* and *tāmim*, 'good faith and honour' in the RSV (the NIV is similar), they appear in what is to my mind the most helpful English form in the NAS as 'truth and integrity'. A decline in truth and integrity is one mark of the general downward trend of Israelite life throughout the book of Judges. We have already seen how events move not in

---

[2] See Gn. 8:22.

a cycle, but in a steadily declining spiral. In the last three chapters, the story of Gideon, it was becoming plain how in Israelite society truth and integrity were going out of fashion. There for the first time God questioned the sincerity of Israel's usual cry for help, with a well-deserved rebuke – You squeal 'on account of the Midianites', he said through his prophet, 'but you have not given heed to my voice' (6:7, 10). Bad relationships began to emerge within the Israelite camp, between the Ephraimites and Gideon and between Gideon and the men of Succoth and Penuel. Israel's apostasy after Gideon's death had already been foreshadowed by her 'playing the harlot' with his ephod even during his lifetime (8:33, 27); we had not seen that before. The time of peace which resulted from Gideon's victory will turn out to be the last one noted in the book, and something must have been going very wrong for that to be the case.

In chapter 9 this will be the dominant theme. 'Truth and integrity' is the key phrase of the story of Abimelech not because these things figure largely in it, but because they don't. They ought to be the characteristics of a people loyal to their God and to one another. Instead, the undermining of such values in recent chapters leads in this one to their general collapse.

2. Truth and integrity rejected (9:1–6)

Now Abimelech the son of Jerubbaal went to Shechem to his mother's kinsmen and said to them and to the whole clan of his mother's family, ²'Say in the ears of all the citizens of Shechem, "Which is better for you, that all seventy of the sons of Jerubbaal rule over you, or that one rule over you?" Remember also that I am your bone and your flesh.' ³And his mother's kinsmen spoke all these words on his behalf in the ears of all the men of Shechem; and their hearts inclined to follow Abimelech, for they said, 'He is our brother.' ⁴And they gave him seventy pieces of silver out of the house of Baal-berith with which Abimelech hired worthless and reckless fellows, who followed him. ⁵And he went to his father's house at Ophrah, and slew his brothers the sons of Jerubbaal, seventy men, upon one stone; but Jotham the youngest son of Jerubbaal was left, for he hid himself. ⁶And all the citizens of Shechem came together, and all Beth-millo, and they went and made Abimelech king, by the oak of the pillar at Shechem.

The tale begins with a paragraph which is a prime example of the writer's knack of raising questions rather than answering them. Judges is a profoundly unsettling book, this chapter for all its rumbustiousness deeply puzzling, and verses 1–6 thoroughly equivocal. In a moment we shall look at some of their ambiguities. In the event, what Jotham, Gideon's youngest son, will describe as 'truth and integrity' is going to be rejected. Already, as the scene is set, nothing is quite what it ought to be. Words are not true to their definitions, present facts are not true to their past histories. Nothing is integrated.

Here then is the son of Gideon. (Gideon, by the way, is always in this chapter called by the ambiguous name of Jerubbaal, which could have a pro-Baal flavour as well as the anti-Baal one evident in 6:32.) This is not one of the many sons borne to Gideon by his true Israelite wives, but the son of his concubine from Shechem. Like the father, the son has an ambiguous name, Abimelech, 'father-king'. It could be meant to honour Gideon ('My father is king') or even the Lord ('My real Father is the divine King'). At the same time heathen nations might use it too, with a different king in mind.[3] Maybe in this case it was meant to echo Gideon's pious statement in 8:23, 'I will not rule over you, and my son will not rule over you; the LORD will rule over you.' A seemly name; or then again perhaps not.

Abimelech goes to Shechem, where his mother's people live. He identifies with her and her family. Good boy; dutiful boy. And Shechem is a good place, not of course strictly Israelite, but with a long history of friendly association with Israel. There had been alliance and intermarriage in the old days, as we have seen, in spite of occasional strained relationships,[4] and when God's people returned from Egypt the conquering armies of Joshua had no quarrel with this town. Indeed it was honoured as the site of the great conventions described in Joshua 8:30–35 and 24:1–28.

The oak at Shechem in particular had an honoured place in the lore of the chosen people. There Father Abraham had pitched his first camp in Canaan, and the Lord had appeared to him with the promise that the land should be his.[5] There his grandson Jacob put away the foreign gods his household had brought from Mesopotamia, to renew his own dedication to the Lord.[6] The oak, we might say, was O.K.

And there was a shrine, too, at Shechem, the house of the Lord of *Berith*, the Covenant. To the true Israelite there is only one covenant, the agreement which has bound generation after generation of his people to the Lord their God. The shrine, the oak, the town, the name, can all be seen as integrated with the grand

---

[3] *Cf.* Gn. 20:2; 26:8.   [4] *Cf.* Gn. 34.   [5] *Cf.* Gn. 12:6–7.
[6] *Cf.* Gn. 35:1–4.

traditions of the true Israel.

But Abimelech breaks faith with all these meanings. In every aspect his story begins with the rejection of truth and integrity. For him, his own name is to be understood with the crassest literalism. It was his father Gideon who was the king, or as near as made no difference, so that with Gideon's death he himself is in line for the throne. For him, the tensions within the town of Shechem (reflecting those within his own character) can be made to serve his personal ambition, so he plays down the things that link Shechem with Israel and plays up the antagonisms between them. For him, the historic oak tree will bear witness to a trans-action far different from that between Abraham and God: here, as a result of his own scheming, the people of Shechem will make him king. And both for him and for them the local shrine, which they call (of all things) 'the house of the Lord of the *Covenant*', belies its name: the Lord worshipped there is not Yahweh but Baal.

And what actually happened? – for these verses are, after all, the beginning of a story. Well, Abimelech persuaded his Shechemite relatives that his Israelite half-brothers would seize control – per-haps of the nation (see 9:22), certainly of Shechem itself – unless they were eliminated, and he were made king instead. The leaders of Shechem agreed.[7] The massacre of Abimelech's rivals was financed by funds from the temple of Baal-Berith, and his coron-ation duly took place 'by the oak of the pillar at Shechem'.

You have only to set Judges 9:1–6 alongside Joshua 24 to see the great irony of these events. In that chapter in the earlier book the authority of Joshua brought together a gathering at which 'all the tribes of Israel' heard his challenge, and promised not to 'forsake the LORD, to serve other gods' (verses 1, 16). Where did this elaborate, solemn exchange take place? 'Joshua made a covenant with the people that day . . . *at Shechem*. And . . . he took a great stone, and set it up *there under the oak*' (verses 25–26). And in what terms had Joshua presented the challenge? 'Fear the LORD, and serve him in *tāmim* and *'emeth*', says verse 14, the only place outside Judges 9 where the two words are combined. Serve him in *truth and integrity*. The story of Abimelech is set at the heart of the book of Judges to show what happens when obligations are not kept, when truth and integrity are rejected. There is no longer

[7] They had found 'someone who belonged both to the invaders and to the city, and who had already shown a remarkable capacity for making decisions combined with a complete lack of scruples, a man who could restore to their city its ancient splendour, if necessary with the agreement of Israel, and otherwise independently of it' (Soggin, p. 182).

any Joshua to bring the weight of his authority to bear, but that places all the greater responsibility on an Israel who does in fact know very well how she should be serving the Lord.

3. Truth and integrity recalled (9:7–21)

When it was told to Jotham, he went and stood on the top of Mount Gerizim, and cried aloud and said to them, 'Listen to me, you men of Shechem, that God may listen to you. [8]The trees once went forth to anoint a king over them; and they said to the olive tree, "Reign over us." [9]But the olive tree said to them, "Shall I leave my fatness, by which gods and men are honoured, and go to sway over the trees?" [10]And the trees said to the fig tree, "Come you, and reign over us." [11]But the fig tree said to them, "Shall I leave my sweetness and my good fruit, and go to sway over the trees?" [12]And the trees said to the vine, "Come you, and reign over us." [13]But the vine said to them, "Shall I leave my wine which cheers gods and men, and go to sway over the trees?" [14]Then all the trees said to the bramble, "Come you, and reign over us." [15]And the bramble said to the trees, "If in good faith you are anointing me king over you, then come and take refuge in my shade; but if not, let fire come out of the bramble and devour the cedars of Lebanon."

[16]'Now therefore, if you acted in good faith and honour when you made Abimelech king, and if you have dealt well with Jerubbaal and his house, and have done to him as his deeds deserved – [17]for my father fought for you, and risked his life, and rescued you from the hand of Midian; [18]and you have risen up against my father's house this day, and have slain his sons, seventy men on one stone, and have made Abimelech, the son of his maidservant, king over the citizens of Shechem, because he is your kinsman – [19]if you then have acted in good faith and honour with Jerubbaal and with his house this day, then rejoice in Abimelech, and let him also rejoice in you; [20]but if not, let fire come out from Abimelech, and devour the citizens of Shechem, and Beth-millo; and let fire come out from the citizens of Shechem, and from Beth-millo, and devour Abimelech.' [21]And Jotham ran away and fled, and went to Beer and dwelt there, for fear of Abimelech his brother.

A voice cries from a crag[8] of the hill opposite Shechem, and catches the attention of the Shechemites with a story – not an

---

[8] Rather than the top of Mount Gerizim, 'from which Jotham would have been invisible to the people of Shechem' (and, more to the point, inaudible), Boling (p. 172) understands this to mean 'a promontory' on its lower slopes, suggesting one particular site as a possibility.

entertainment, but a message.

The voice is the voice of Jotham, the only one of the sons of Gideon to escape the slaughter at Ophrah when Abimelech and his thugs came to eliminate the opposition. He is the youngest son of a youngest son (if that is what 6:15 implies about Gideon), but there is apparently no-one more senior around Shechem who is prepared to stand up for the claims of truth and integrity. Not that that should surprise us, since the abiding image of Jotham's father's judgeship is of the three hundred standing up against the 135,000, with the forces of right deliberately reduced so that God gets the glory. Jotham will in fact run away into hiding after this, and disappear from the pages of Scripture. But then all he is called to do is to pronounce God's curse on those who abandon truth and integrity.

The place is in general terms Shechem, recalling the 'truth and integrity' covenant-making assembly of Joshua 24, but more specifically one of the two hills by the town, recalling two other historic events from the recent past. As Israel's long journey came to an end, Moses had instructed the people that when they had entered the promised land they should go to Shechem, and that there from the twin hilltops the summary of God's law should be proclaimed, the blessings from Mount Gerizim and the curses from Mount Ebal.[9] So in due course it happened, under the leadership of Joshua.[10] And now Jotham appears, on Gerizim, ironically, not Ebal, to tell his famous tale. It will, as things turn out, have the effect of a curse. But theoretically it could have been a blessing: 'If then you have dealt in truth and integrity with Jerubbaal and his house this day, rejoice in Abimelech, and let him also rejoice in you' (9:19, NAS).

The story Jotham tells is a fable like those which under the name of Aesop have come down to us from ancient Greece, with parallels in many other cultures besides. 'The trees decided to have a king. But neither the olive nor the fig nor the vine wanted the job. "We have better things to do", they said. So the trees asked the bramble; and the bramble said . . .'

What the bramble said is the point of the parable. If one of the objects of Judges was to make disapproving noises about monarchy in general, as is the view of some, then Jotham's fable would be saying how sensible the olive and the fig and the vine were to turn down the offer of kingship. But that is to miss the point. The fable is about Abimelech; it is not concerned with the olive and the fig

[9] *Cf.* Dt. 27:11 – 28:68.
[10] *Cf.* Jos. 8:30–35.

and the vine, which turned down the offer, but with the bramble's acceptance of it. ' "Are you *in truth*[11] asking me to be king?" said the bramble with well-feigned surprise. "Well, you are welcome to my shade, but you will have to grovel to get under it; and if things go wrong, don't forget that one thing I am good at is catching fire, and even the loftiest of you will need to beware of that." ' In other words, Jotham is saying how foolish is their choice, not of kingship in principle, but of this particular king.

The meaning of the fable thus reiterates the theme of this entire chapter. If the people of Shechem had acted with truth and integrity in respect of Gideon and his family, they might conceivably have looked forward to a decent government under Abimelech in which the same qualities would dignify public life. But of course they had not. Nobody had (8:35). So having abandoned truth and integrity by the very act of throwing in their lot with Abimelech, the Shechemites could only expect a future which would be as lacking in those virtues as the past had been. Each party would suffer at the hands of the other.

Which in the event was exactly what happened. The outcome was what Jotham had said it would be. He at any rate had spoken with truth and integrity.

4. Truth and integrity abandoned (9:22–49)

Abimelech ruled over Israel three years. ²³And God sent an evil spirit between Abimelech and the men of Shechem; and the men of Shechem dealt treacherously with Abimelech; ²⁴that the violence done to the seventy sons of Jerubbaal might come and their blood be laid upon Abimelech their brother, who slew them, and upon the men of Shechem, who strengthened his hands to slay his brothers. ²⁵And the men of Shechem put men in ambush against him on the mountain tops, and they robbed all who passed by them along that way; and it was told Abimelech.

²⁶And Gaal the son of Ebed moved into Shechem with his kinsmen; and the men of Shechem put confidence in him. ²⁷And they went out into the field, and gathered the grapes from their vineyards and trod them, and held festival, and went into the house of their god, and ate and drank and reviled Abimelech. ²⁸And Gaal the son of Ebed said, 'Who is Abimelech, and who are we of Shechem, that we should serve him? Did not the son of Jerubbaal and Zebul his officer serve the men of Hamor the father of Shechem? Why then

---

[11] *i.e.* with the emphasis 'Are you really asking *me*?' This follows Auld's suggestion (p. 184), as does the rest of this paraphrase of the fable.

should we serve him?' ²⁹Would that this people were under my
hand! then I would remove Abimelech. I would say to Abimelech,
"Increase your army, and come out." '

³⁰When Zebul the ruler of the city heard the words of Gaal the
son of Ebed, his anger was kindled. ³¹And he sent messengers to
Abimelech at Arumah, saying, 'Behold, Gaal the son of Ebed and
his kinsmen have come to Shechem, and they are stirring up the
city against you. ³²Now therefore, go by night, you and the men
that are with you, and lie in wait in the fields. ³³Then in the
morning, as soon as the sun is up, rise early and rush upon the city;
and when he and the men that are with him come out against you,
you may do to them as occasion offers.'

³⁴And Abimelech and all the men that were with him rose up by
night, and laid wait against Shechem in four companies. ³⁵And Gaal
the son of Ebed went out and stood in the entrance of the gate of
the city; and Abimelech and the men that were with him rose from
the ambush. ³⁶And when Gaal saw the men, he said to Zebul,
'Look, men are coming down from the mountain tops!' And Zebul
said to him, 'You see the shadow of the mountains as if they were
men.' ³⁷Gaal spoke again and said, 'Look, men are coming down
from the centre of the land, and one company is coming from the
direction of the Diviners' Oak.' ³⁸Then Zebul said to him, 'Where
is your mouth now, you who said, "Who is Abimelech, that we
should serve him?" Are not these the men whom you despised? Go
out now and fight with them.' ³⁹And Gaal went out at the head of
the men of Shechem, and fought with Abimelech. ⁴⁰And Abimelech
chased him, and he fled before him; and many fell wounded, up to
the entrance of the gate. ⁴¹And Abimelech dwelt at Arumah; and
Zebul drove out Gaal and his kinsmen, so that they could not live
on at Shechem.

⁴²On the following day the men went out into the fields. And
Abimelech was told. ⁴³He took his men and divided them into three
companies, and laid wait in the fields; and he looked and saw the
men coming out of the city, and he rose against them and slew
them. ⁴⁴Abimelech and the company that was with him rushed
forward and stood at the entrance of the gate of the city, while the
two companies rushed upon all who were in the fields and slew
them. ⁴⁵And Abimelech fought against the city all that day; he took
the city, and killed the people that were in it; and he razed the city
and sowed it with salt.

⁴⁶When all the people of the Tower of Shechem heard of it, they
entered the stronghold of the house of El-berith. ⁴⁷Abimelech was
told that all the people of the Tower of Shechem were gathered
together. ⁴⁸And Abimelech went up to Mount Zalmon, he and all

the men that were with him; and Abimelech took an axe in his hand, and cut down a bundle of brushwood, and took it up and laid it on his shoulder. And he said to the men that were with him, 'What you have seen me do, make haste to do, as I have done.' *49So every one of the people cut down his bundle and following Abimelech put it against the stronghold, and they set the stronghold on fire over them, so that all the people of the Tower of Shechem also died, about a thousand men and women.*

Now see how the grand covenant works out – the covenant, that is, by which (in Jotham's ironic words) Shechem rejoices in Abimelech and vice versa. For three years all goes well, and Abimelech seems even to have reached a position of some dominance in the nation as a whole (9:22). Then begins a series of events which can be read in three ways. The narrative is certainly an adventure story, full of incident and drama. It is also on the one hand comic, even farcical; and on the other, a deeply serious process of judgment. The mainspring for it lies in the word 'treacherously', in 9:23. Treachery is the breakdown of truth and integrity. Since both king and populace got where they were by breaking faith with the family of Gideon, they could hardly be surprised when in due course they broke faith with each other.

Once God himself has triggered the plot by sending an evil spirit to set the two parties at loggerheads, the first move is against Abimelech. (He started the trouble, after all.) To begin with, the men of Shechem, for whatever reason, now want to harm him. The robbers they station along the trade-routes will hurt both his pocket, depriving him of his dues, and his pride, showing that he cannot keep order in his own domains. Then Gaal and his crowd move into town, and at once gain a following. Not all that Gaal says is clear,[12] but what is clear is that in Abimelech's absence he is 'stirring up the city against' him (9:31). Here we see the 'fire' that Jotham had predicted beginning to 'come out from the citizens of Shechem . . . and devour Abimelech' (9:20).

The second move is from Abimelech's side, in retaliation. His henchman Zebul, partly out of loyalty and partly no doubt piqued at being called merely Abimelech's deputy when he holds no less a post than that of governor of the city, gets a message through to his chief, with suggestions about how to deal with the Gaal gang. Abimelech acts accordingly. The loud-mouthed Gaal suspects neither the antagonism of Zebul nor the sudden arrival of Abimelech's

---

[12] Davis (p. 125 n. 8) wonders whether the obscurity of 9:28b has anything to do with the fact that Gaal was half drunk!

armed bands. 'Men coming over the hills, Gaal? No, no! Where are your glasses?' By the time Gaal knows his eyes have not been deceiving him, it is too late. 'Where is your mouth now?' jeers Zebul, pushing him out of the town and shutting the gates on him. Gaal's Shechemite insurrection shrivels in the 'fire come out from Abimelech'.

There is more to come. Everyone in Shechem who had not actually signed on with Gaal assumes that the episode can now be quietly forgotten. But the fire is burning hotter in Abimelech. Ordinary work resumes next day as the Shechemite farmers go out into their fields, not realizing that both they and their kinsfolk inside the town are traitors in Abimelech's eyes, and are destined not to see the light of another day. They, like Gaal, perish in the heat of his anger.

And the fire rages on. It sounds as though the 'Tower of Shechem' is another place, distinct from Shechem itself, and here also are Shechemites who, with increasing justification as the news begins to filter through, fear that Abimelech will be after their blood too.[13] The fire becomes literal, and the stronghold, whether fortress or (as some think) cellar, becomes a deathtrap for a thousand of his enemies, suffocated or incinerated inside it.

Are we supposed to take it that a lack of truth and integrity really does lead to this kind of conflagration? Admittedly the way in which Gideon's family had been treated by Abimelech and the Shechemites was cruel and cynical. But I have little doubt that during the three years before the relationship between king and townspeople began to be snarled up, he and they would have agreed in laughing off the melodramatic threats with which Jotham had applied his fable. We may also guess that when fire did start shooting out in both directions, neither party paused to think why such an escalation of hatred should have emerged from what were (on their view) such unimportant beginnings. But that was what Jotham had predicted. The devouring fire was related directly to the fact that they had not kept faith with Gideon, who in his generation had done so much for them (9:16–20). And why should this be not a special case but a regular principle? Why, when truth and integrity are thus abandoned, should the effect be so far-reaching? The answer is plain in the story. It takes only the first tear in the fabric of good faith for the whole thing to begin unravelling.

[13] It may be that 9:46–49 describes an incident within 9:42–45, and that the Tower was geographically within Shechem. 9:46 would mean something like 'When the people heard the city gate being breached by Abimelech's attack.' So Bruce, p. 266; Boling, pp. 180f. Soggin (pp. 192–193) argues for the Tower's being a separate place.

And still Abimelech has not finished.

5. Truth and integrity maintained (9:50–57)

Then Abimelech went to Thebez, and encamped against Thebez, and took it. ⁵¹But there was a strong tower within the city, and all the people of the city fled to it, all the men and women, and shut themselves in; and they went to the roof of the tower. ⁵²And Abimelech came to the tower, and fought against it, and drew near to the door of the tower to burn it with fire. ⁵³And a certain woman threw an upper millstone upon Abimelech's head, and crushed his skull. ⁵⁴Then he called hastily to the young man his armour-bearer, and said to him, 'Draw your sword and kill me, lest men say of me, "A woman killed him." ' And his young man thrust him through, and he died. ⁵⁵And when the men of Israel saw that Abimelech was dead, they departed every man to his home. ⁵⁶Thus God requited the crime of Abimelech, which he committed against his father in killing his seventy brothers; ⁵⁷and God also made all the wickedness of the men of Shechem fall back upon their heads, and upon them came the curse of Jotham the son of Jerubbaal.

Presumably in Abimelech's eyes the nearby town of Thebez has joined the rebellion against his rule. Again the defenders barricade themselves inside a stronghold, again the attacker sets about smoking them out or burning them up. Again fire will come out from Abimelech and devour his former allies. Except that . . .

'And a certain woman threw an upper millstone upon Abimelech's head, and crushed his skull . . . Thus God requited the crime of Abimelech' (9:53, 56). Not only does the name of the Lord not appear anywhere in this chapter, but he is not even mentioned as God between 9:23 and 9:56. He it is, however, who is in control throughout. Let us see how he has been at work behind the scenes.

He has been working inexorably towards the punishment of both Abimelech and Shechem. Abimelech has been given a very long rein. Repeatedly trouble has arisen, but repeatedly he has been able to counter it. He deals with Gaal, then with Shechem, then with the Tower of Shechem, and in the end either presumption or paranoia drives him to teach Thebez a lesson too. 'See the naughty, restless child, Growing still more rude and wild',[14] till he comes to that ludicrous end. ('A *millstone*? Dropped by a *woman*? She had dragged it *up to the top of the tower*?') In the same process the Shechemites also come to destruction, having at the beginning

---

[14] Fidgety Philip, in Heinrich Hoffman's *Struwwelpeter*.

connived with Abimelech in the slaughter of Gideon's sons (9:18) and at the end been slaughtered in their turn by him (9:45, 49).

God has secondly been using the peculiar property which evil has of undoing itself. All he needs to do is to send the evil spirit to make, as I have said, the first tear in the fabric of the Abimelech/ Shechem covenant, and all begins to unravel. There is no other intervention. None is needed. God's almighty power is seen most chiefly in his showing mercy and pity;[15] he has little need to use it in judgment; he has but to take his restraining hand off the brake, and wicked men will run to their own destruction, and 'all who take the sword will perish by the sword'.[16] He does, says Auld in this connection, 'preside consistently over a world in which people reap what they sow'.[17] Jotham's curse expresses what happens anyway. Each side in turn lays ambushes, each double-crosses the other, and each is in the end destroyed.

God has thirdly been showing a broader consistency, for what happens here is a reflection of what happened in chapter 7. The mutual destruction of chapter 9 is what lies in wait in the end for every society which cares nothing for the truth, and this should have been as plain as a pikestaff to Abimelech and the Shechemites from the events of the previous generation. Of course they despised the victory won forty years before by Abimelech's father Gideon, but might nevertheless have remembered the facts – that Gideon's three hundred simply stood by while the Midianite host destroyed itself: 'the LORD set every man's sword against his fellow and against all the army' (7:22). Those who will not learn from history are doomed to repeat it. So although you might call this repetition poetic justice, it is perhaps more truly the way that God's world works in any case.

Fourthly, God has been declaring his power by the showing of mercy and pity in a quite positive way. He has been limiting the damage. Israel as a nation has inevitably been affected by the episode. Before the fire began to burn, Abimelech had 'ruled over Israel three years' (9:22), and after it had burnt itself out, 'Israel . . . departed every man to his home' (9:55). Just as the account is contained between the two mentions of God (9:23, 56), so the conflagration is held within bounds. It devours Abimelech, and it devours Shechem, but no-one else. If he afterwards attacked Thebez because he believed that that town had joined Shechem in rebelling against him, he may have been right in attributing to it that sort of guilt; but we may be pretty sure that Thebez had not joined in

[15] *The Book of Common Prayer*, the collect for Trinity 11.   [16] Mt. 26:52.
[17] Auld, p. 190.

Shechem's original guilt over the massacre at Ophrah, for God's retribution falls specifically on the heads of the men of Shechem, and Abimelech is killed before he can set fire to the tower of Thebez. As Abraham had learned long before when he pleaded with God not to destroy Lot along with the rest of Sodom, there are no mistakes. The guilty are punished, the innocent are spared. 'Shall not the Judge of all the earth do right?'[18] God distinguishes. He contains the evil. Within the boundary it runs its course; beyond, it cannot go.

Fifthly, God has been demonstrating his total control of all circumstances. He is the God of providence. As well as the close connections (such as Gaal's insurrection leading to Abimelech's revenge on Shechem), and those further removed (like the mutual killing in this chapter reflecting that in chapter 7), we have what could be seen as sheer coincidence – 'a certain woman' who happens to have her millstone with her (!) and who on the crowded rooftop of the tower of Thebez happens to be above the doorway, which Abimelech himself then happens to approach. She drops the stone, and she does not miss! So in the end several apparently unrelated things come together to bring about God's purposes. One is reminded of the similar wording in the account of the death of another king, Ahab, long afterwards: 'A certain man drew his bow at a venture, and struck the king of Israel between the scale armour and the breastplate',[19] again a blow not instantly fatal but none the less effective.

Finally, God has been using all the many denials of truth and integrity in the story in order to maintain his own truth and integrity. This irony underlies the whole narrative. The last two verses of the chapter summarize it by saying, in effect, 'Thus God acted justly against those who had acted unjustly.' He had begun the process by sending the evil spirit of 9:23, whose paradoxical task was to set in motion the punishment of evil, and who caused Abimelech and the Shechemites to break faith with each other so that God might keep faith with his own principles of justice. By their abandoning of truth and integrity towards each other, the truth and integrity of Jotham's fable is demonstrated, and the truth and integrity of God's own rule of law is displayed.

6. Truth and integrity overridden (10:1–5)

After Abimelech there arose to deliver Israel Tola the son of Puah, son of Dodo, a man of Issachar; and he lived at Shamir in the hill

---

[18] Gn. 18:25.   [19] 1 Ki. 22:34.

country of Ephraim. [2]*And he judged Israel twenty-three years. Then he died, and was buried at Shamir.*

[3]*After him arose Jair the Gileadite, who judged Israel twenty-two years.* [4]*And he had thirty sons who rode on thirty asses; and they had thirty cities, called Havvoth-jair to this day, which are in the land of Gilead.* [5]*And Jair died, and was buried in Kamon.*

We shall link the two judges of 10:1–5 on to the story of Abimelech, as Judges itself does, and see whether they are connected with him in any other way besides mere sequence. There is a variety of views as to what sort of people they were, they and the other 'minor' judges (Shamgar in chapter 3, Ibzan, Elon, and Abdon in chapter 12). Less important than the Gideons and the Samsons? In the language of the American West, 'lawmen' of the courthouse rather than 'lawmen' of the saddle? Administrators rather than soldiers? Or perhaps equally active and charismatic, but with their deeds simply undocumented? Let us see what we are actually told about Tola and Jair, remembering that their stories follow Abimelech's without a break, and should be read with that in mind.

No preacher could make much of a character-study or an 'example-to-follow' sermon out of Tola. Even Jair is slightly less nondescript ('Oh yes, Jair was the one with thirty sons who rode thirty asses, wasn't he?'). Practically every item in 10:1–2 has a parallel somewhere else; in other words, there is nothing distinctive about this next judge except the proper nouns, his name and tribe and home-town.

But it is the unoriginal items in this little vignette which in the circumstances have something to say to us. They may not tell us much about Tola, but they tell us something about God, and in particular about the Lord who is God of Israel at this low point in her fortunes.

For a start, this man who seems so insignificant was, all the same, one of those sent 'to deliver Israel'. He lines up with Othniel (3:9), Shamgar (3:31), and Gideon (6:14), of whom the same phrase is used, to say nothing of the judges who obviously were rescuers of Israel even if the actual word is not used of them. Whether the task he was called to was military, or administrative, or both, he is to be seen as a saviour-figure.

But more revealing are three other things we are told he did, again because of the echoes from elsewhere in the book. He 'arose' to rescue Israel, and that is a reminder of 5:7: 'The peasantry ceased in Israel, they ceased until you arose, Deborah, arose as a mother in Israel.' Tola 'lived' at Shamir, which seems a trivial enough point to make (all sorts of people are said to live, or dwell, in all sorts

103

of places in the course of the book), except that the word *yashab* has the basic meaning of 'sit' or 'preside', and seems to be used in that way particularly of – guess who? – Deborah: 'She used to *sit* under the palm of Deborah between Ramah and Bethel . . . and the people of Israel came up to her for judgment' (4:5). Which brings us to the third verb: Tola 'judged' Israel, and that word, used of the first judge, the model judge Othniel, and here of the sixth judge Tola, is perhaps surprisingly used of none of those between except (again) Deborah, in 4:4.

Now the story of Deborah and Barak is one of the more positive and encouraging sections of the book. Its background was the twenty years of cruel oppression by the ironclad forces of Canaan, when 'caravans ceased and travellers kept to the byways' (5:6). After that period of disarray Deborah's judgeship brought order and increasing confidence. So it may well be that when 'after Abimelech', that is, after the turmoils of Abimelech's misrule, Tola *arose*, and *presiding* at Shamir,[20] *judged* Israel for twenty-three years, – it may be that we are meant to see in his judgeship another like hers.

As for Jair, what is the importance of his thirty sons with their thirty asses and thirty cities? They might possibly be meant as a bad sign (indulgence, ostentation, dangerous worldly trends). But I am more inclined to see Jair's rule as twenty-two further years of the Lord's kindness to Israel added to the twenty-three years under Tola. Elsewhere in the Bible large families mean prosperity and divine blessing, and he who rides on an ass rather than a warhorse is one who comes in peace. Sound judgment on the Deborah pattern, and a time of relative prosperity and peace, were what the people of God needed at this juncture.

But not what they deserved. Robert Polzin comments on 'what happened to Israel in the period of the judges': 'in all fairness and honesty' – he is speaking of 9:16, 19, and the phrase we have become familiar with as 'truth and integrity' – 'in all fairness and honesty, Israel should not have survived'.[21] How it happened that Israel did survive, and what that tells us about Israel's God, is one of the most important issues in the book. Jotham, shouting his parable across the valley to the faithless men of Shechem and to his half-brother Abimelech, is the only person in the story who presses the claims of truth and integrity, and no-one else acts on those principles. Not even God! Justice must demand the rejection

[20] ' "Shamir", though here a place-name, as a word means "thorn/thornbush". Not the same word as in Jotham's parable' (*cf.* 9:14f., pp. 94–96 above), 'but good things can come from thorns too' (note from J. A. Motyer).

[21] R. Polzin, *Moses and the Deuteronomist*, quoted by Webb, p. 254 n. 101.

of this impossibly faithless people. By rights, as Polzin says, Israel should not survive. She has forfeited every claim on God's approval. And it is in that sense that God overrides his own truth and integrity. His own law requires the destruction of such sinners, but instead he gives them forty-five years of peaceful rule under Tola and Jair.

Of course the New Testament will explain to us that God's truth and integrity are not in fact overridden by his mercy. He is *both* just *and* the justifier of the one who believes in Jesus.[22] Already in Old Testament days it is known that mercy and truth can meet, that righteousness and peace can kiss each other.[23] None the less striking, for all that, is the message of Judges 10:1, that even 'after Abimelech', and the years of faithlessness in which he came to power, the Lord is prepared to give his people another chance, and to raise up a Tola and a Jair to provide space for repentance and renewal. That is what the Judge decrees. He is 'the gracious God who never allows "Abimelech" to be the last word for his people'.[24]

So it is of a piece with the overall message of the book that these brief notices of the sixth and seventh judges should form, not an unrelated item that happens to have been fitted in at this point, nor an introduction to the story of Jephthah, but a conclusion to the story of Abimelech. When they are left to themselves – in the period between Moses and David, so to speak – God's people are as likely as anyone else to abandon truth and integrity, to show themselves rebels against his judgment and incapable of a right judgment of their own. 'This infection of nature doth remain, yea in them that are regenerated.'[25] But the good news brought to us in Old Testament as in New, even (or perhaps especially) by a book like Judges, tells us that there is, in the words of the Bunyan title I have quoted in my Preface,[26] grace abounding to the chief of sinners.

[22] Rom. 3:26.   [23] Ps. 85:10.   [24] Davis, p. 130.

[25] Article 9, *Of Original or Birth-sin* (The Thirty-Nine Articles of the Church of England).

[26] See p. 8.

Judges 10:6 – 12:15

6. Jephthah: a man of his word

Jephthah the Gileadite strides on to the stage at the beginning of chapter 11. He is one of the great characters of Judges. He is also one of the most enigmatic, and his story will be perhaps the most gripping and the most moving, as well as the most confusing and puzzling, of all the stories in the book.

He is introduced at 11:1, but it is at 10:6 that his section of Judges begins. We may regard this latter part of the chapter, the greater part (10:6–18), as one type of background for Jephthah. It does not tell us about him personally, but it outlines the situation into which he came.

1. Jephthah's background: i (10:6–18)

And the people of Israel again did what was evil in the sight of the LORD, *and served the Baals and the Ashtaroth, the gods of Syria, the gods of Sidon, the gods of Moab, the gods of the Ammonites, and the gods of the Philistines; and they forsook the* LORD, *and did not serve him.* ⁷*And the anger of the* LORD *was kindled against Israel, and he sold them into the hand of the Philistines and into the hand of the Ammonites,* ⁸*and they crushed and oppressed the children of Israel that year. For eighteen years they oppressed all the people of Israel that were beyond the Jordan in the land of the Amorites, which is in Gilead.* ⁹*And the Ammonites crossed the Jordan to fight also against Judah and against Benjamin and against the house of Ephraim; so that Israel was sorely distressed.*

¹⁰*And the people of Israel cried to the* LORD, *saying, 'We have sinned against thee, because we have forsaken our God and have served the Baals.'* ¹¹*And the* LORD *said to the people of Israel, 'Did I not deliver you from the Egyptians and from the Amorites, from*

the Ammonites and from the Philistines? [12]*The Sidonians also, and the Amalekites, and the Maonites, oppressed you; and you cried to me, and I delivered you out of their hand.* [13]*Yet you have forsaken me and served other gods; therefore I will deliver you no more.* [14]*Go and cry to the gods whom you have chosen; let them deliver you in the time of your distress.'* [15]*And the people of Israel said to the* LORD, *'We have sinned; do to us whatever seems good to thee; only deliver us, we pray thee, this day.'* [16]*So they put away the foreign gods from among them and served the* LORD; *and he became indignant over the misery of Israel.*

[17]*Then the Ammonites were called to arms, and they encamped in Gilead; and the people of Israel came together, and they encamped at Mizpah.* [18]*And the people, the leaders of Gilead, said one to another, 'Who is the man that will begin to fight against the Ammonites? He shall be head over all the inhabitants of Gilead.'*

As well as being the start of the Jephthah story, these paragraphs mark the half-way point of the book. They remind us again that Judges describes not a circle but a spiral. We are back where we began – 'the people of Israel did what was evil' (2:11), 'the people of Israel again did what was evil' (10:6) – but we are now at a considerably lower level than we were then. It is true that other earlier oppressions have been as long as, or even longer than, the eighteen years during which Philistines and Ammonites now jointly oppress Israel. But there are plain signs of deterioration. 'All the people of Israel' are 'crushed' and 'sorely distressed' (10:8–9). What Israel does and what the Lord says both show how much worse things have become. Israel's offence is rehearsed at length as a sevenfold rebellion. She has turned from the Lord to serve instead the Baals and the Ashtaroth, and the gods of Sidon, Syria, Moab, Ammon, and Philistia (10:6). The Lord's complaint is that the Israelites are rebelling in spite of his sevenfold deliverance of them, from Egyptians and Amorites, Ammonites and Philistines, Sidonians and Amalekites and Maonites (10:11–12). One could say that with a merciful God who keeps rescuing them they have nothing to worry about. But of course the point is that a people that can still turn its back on a God who has helped it so often is placing itself almost beyond redemption, and certainly in the gravest of danger.

One of the main themes of the story of Jephthah will be that the rot which set in long ago has reached the core, and things central to the relationship between God and his people have now been affected. The national life lacks direction; Israel is a rudderless ship; the old standards have been forsworn, the old landmarks obliterated; the foundations are being eroded.

Listen to the exchange of 10:10–16. It begins with words which we have heard before – 'the people of Israel cried to the LORD' – but which in these chapters will repay our special attention. For one thing we observe the Lord's reaction to them. 'When the people of Israel cried to the LORD, the LORD raised up a deliverer'? That was what he did in 3:9. He did it again in 3:15, and again in 4:3–7. He did not do it quite so quickly in the time of Gideon, in 6:7–14. But now for the first time it sounds as though he may not do it at all. So here is something new. Why might the Lord react in this way?

Up to now we may have given Israel the benefit of the doubt, and assumed that when she cries to him it is a cry of repentance, shallow though the repentance may be. She is sorry for what she has done, and wishes she were different. But that assumption now has to be questioned. Yes, the cry is one of recognition: We realize, they say, that 'we have sinned against thee . . . forsaken our God . . . served the Baals' (10:10), and that is more explicit than anything they have admitted so far. Recognition is not however the same as repentance, as we see from the Lord's reply: 'Go and cry to the gods whom you have chosen' (10:14). It is as though he is saying: 'I know what this cry of yours is. It is merely a cry for help, which might just as well be addressed to the Baals as to me. If it were a cry of real repentance, it would tell me what you intend for the future, as well as what you admit from the past, and it would show a desire to turn *from* the Baals *to* me.'

Clearly this is how the Israelites understand his reply, since they respond by putting away these foreign gods (10:16a). The Lord's response is to become 'indignant over the misery of Israel'.

At this crucial point in the book we have to grasp what exactly is happening in 10:16b. It seems at first glance that we have here a parallel to verses elsewhere in Scripture such as Jonah 3:10. There God had said he would punish the people of Nineveh for their wickedness, but when they repented, he too 'repented of the evil which he had said he would do to them; and he did not do it'.[1] If this paragraph is like that one, then here Israel is crying for help; God is retorting 'Cry to the gods you have chosen'; at that Israel *really* repents, and the Lord in turn repents of the evil he is doing;

---

[1] In another sense, 'God is not man . . . that he should repent. Has he said, and will he not do it?' (Nu. 23:19). That means that he is true to his word and never changes his mind. But then the passages which tell how he *does* repent are, paradoxically, saying the same thing. They tell us that to the wicked he is constantly opposed, but that to the wicked man who is penitent he will with equal constancy be gracious.

which means that he will now raise up the next saviour, that is, Jephthah. But that is not what the text says. He is not repentant about the evil, as he will be in the case of Jonah and Nineveh, but 'indignant', or exasperated, over the 'misery' of Israel, or (perhaps more properly) over the whole complicated mess Israel has got herself into. It is not regret that he is expressing; or if it is, he is not sorry *for* them so much as sorry *about* them. As he said to Moses long before, 'It is a stiff-necked people; now therefore let me alone, that my wrath may burn hot against them and I may consume them.'[2] Here, as there,[3] the Lord does in the end 'repent', but this is not yet the place for it, nor could we at this point guarantee it.

What does happen next lays our hand on a thread which may lead us through the labyrinth of this darkest of the narratives of the judges. Remember the cry of Israel and the retort of God; hear now the call to arms among the troops of Ammon, followed by the consultation among the Israelite leaders in Gilead. Mouths are opened and voices speak. Listen with care to what is going to be *said* as the story unfolds.

2. Jephthah's background: ii (11:1-3)

Now Jephthah the Gileadite was a mighty warrior, but he was the son of a harlot. Gilead was the father of Jephthah. [2]*And Gilead's wife also bore him sons; and when his wife's sons grew up, they thrust Jephthah out, and said to him, 'You shall not inherit in our father's house; for you are the son of another woman.'* [3]*Then Jephthah fled from his brothers, and dwelt in the land of Tob; and worthless fellows collected round Jephthah, and went raiding with him.*

Now Jephthah himself appears, and the writer gives us background of a personal kind for him, to follow the general background of his times. At once the confusions of this confusing story begin.

The innocent reader's first perplexity: to be told that Gilead is Jephthah's father. But I thought Gilead was a place, not a person (10:17-18)? That question is readily answered. Personal names recur in the Bible, and are often linked with geographical names. We might well take it that an early Gilead[4] gave his name both to the area where his tribe settled, and to a descendant who later lived there.

[2] Ex. 32:9-10.   [3] Ex. 32:14.
[4] *Cf.* Nu. 26:29; see Boling, p. 197.

But the question sets the tone for a story which will be full of questions. These verses raise a clutch of them. Jephthah is illegitimate. He is an outcast. He becomes leader of a gang of brigands. He may be a 'mighty warrior', but a more unlikely saviour for the people of God we have yet to meet. His story will close with the words 'Jephthah judged Israel six years' (12:7), so he is indeed regarded as one of the judges, and his name will appear as one of the great men of faith in Hebrews 11:32. But is he really the kind of person who should be remembered like that? Whatever questions we may have had about Ehud and Shamgar, about Deborah, Barak, and Jael, and about Gideon, there is one about Jephthah which cannot be avoided, for nothing less than his right to his place in Scripture hangs upon it. Long before the climax of his story, which will sharpen that question to a degree, we may feel there is cause to ask it: is it appropriate for a man with this sort of record to be immortalized as a true judge of Israel and as a hero of faith?

All the same, we ought to note that the Jephthah of 11:1–3 was more sinned against than sinning. 'He could', says Davis, 'hardly help his being the leader of the Tob Raiders, an existence unlikely to nourish careful ethics or social graces',[5] and it was the tensions within his family which drove him to it. If so far he seems unsuitable for the Bible's hall of fame, it is less his own fault than the fault of others. And 'despised and rejected' is, we know, a label applied elsewhere to one chosen to be saviour of the people of God. The phrase in Isaiah 53:3 which points forward to Jesus also looks back to some of these forerunners of his. We have already linked it with Ehud the handicapped, undoubtedly despised for his withered hand, and can here link it with Jephthah the outlaw, rejected for his illegitimate birth. And remembering how Jesus warns his disciples that both master and servant can expect the same treatment ('If the world hates you, know that it has hated me before it hated you'),[6] we do not even need to look beyond this present book, let alone wait for the New Testament fulfilment of the phrase, to see Israel despising and rejecting God himself.

3. Jephthah's call (11:4–11)

After a time the Ammonites made war against Israel. *⁵And when the Ammonites made war against Israel, the elders of Gilead went to bring Jephthah from the land of Tob;* *⁶and they said to Jephthah, 'Come and be our leader, that we may fight with the Ammonites.'* *⁷But Jephthah said to the elders of Gilead, 'Did you not hate me,*

---

[5] Davis, p. 141.   [6] Jn. 15:18.

*and drive me out of my father's house? Why have you come to me
now when you are in trouble?'* ⁸*And the elders of Gilead said to
Jephthah, 'That is why we have turned to you now, that you may
go with us and fight with the Ammonites, and be our head over all
the inhabitants of Gilead.'* ⁹*Jephthah said to the elders of Gilead,
'If you bring me home again to fight with the Ammonites, and the
LORD gives them over to me, I will be your head.'* ¹⁰*And the elders
of Gilead said to Jephthah, 'The LORD will be witness between us;
we will surely do as you say.'* ¹¹*So Jephthah went with the elders of
Gilead, and the people made him head and leader over them; and
Jephthah spoke all his words before the LORD at Mizpah.*

'When the Ammonites made war against Israel, the elders of Gilead
went to bring Jephthah from the land of Tob . . . "Come and be
our leader." ' Thus 11:5–6 tells how Jephthah is called from exile,
and called to leadership.

And is that really God's call? Another question, another unexpected twist. The Lord raised up Othniel and Ehud (3:9, 15). 'The
LORD . . . commands you,' said the prophetess to Barak (4:6). 'I
send you,' said the Lord to Gideon (6:14). Is Jephthah's a divine call
in line with those – this delegation of not-very-admirable Gileadite
elders, swallowing their pride and hoping the despised outcast will
help them out of a mess? The Lord can hardly be involved in a
call like this, can he?

Yes, he can. The mention of his name three times in as many
verses (11:9–11) is no mere formality. These things are in truth
happening 'before the LORD'. We can see his involvement in at
least three ways.

He is bringing about the next repetition of the Judges pattern.
As Israel sinned again, 'the LORD . . . sold them into the hand of
the Philistines and into the hand of the Ammonites' (10:7). As
Israel cried for help again, 'the Spirit of the LORD came upon
Jephthah . . . and the LORD gave them', the Ammonites, 'into his
hand' (11:29, 32). The Lord who follows rebellion with retribution,
and then repentance with rescue, is in control of all that takes place
between, and the call of Jephthah, though more indirect than those
of other judges, is no less divine.

And we might guess that as he brings about the next rescue the
Lord will again include a new element in it, something unexpected,
as he has done each time before, in order that we may never assume
that we have him taped. We expected a second Othniel, and he
gave us instead an Ehud. We thought we had grasped how he
operated through Deborah, Barak, and Jael, and then found that
Gideon was quite different. Here too, then, there will probably be

something unforeseen, like Ehud's left hand, or Barak's unglamorous doing of what had to be done, or Gideon's three hundred, something which will make us admit again that God's ways are not our ways (and that even so they tend to be considerably more effective).

The Lord is, furthermore, watching over the interview between Jephthah and the Gileadite leaders. The paragraphs of chapter 10 where Israel cried, the Lord answered, the Ammonites were called to arms and the Gileadites consulted together, are seen to pave the way for this paragraph, where the thing that specifically happened 'before the LORD' was Jephthah's speaking with the deputation from Gilead. In each case mouths were opened and words were uttered.

The way the situation changes before our eyes in these five little speeches is fascinating. One: 'Be our leader in fighting the Ammonites.' It is condescending, magnanimous, a chance for the outlaw to be accepted back into society. He should jump at it. Two: 'First you didn't want me, now you need me!' Neither yes (pathetically eager) nor no (sulking), but a reply which seizes the advantage: he will not be manipulated. Three: 'Instead of "lead and fight", then, how about "fight and rule"?' They now admit that they are not making him an offer for his benefit, but turning to him for their own benefit, and they increase their bid from commander-during-the-campaign to tribal-chief-afterwards. Four: 'Provided *you* accept *my* terms, I agree.' The tables turned, 'Despised and Rejected' in control, thanks to his own negotiating skills. Five: 'We accept, and *the Lord is witness* to this transaction.'

Let us not miss what has happened under the Lord's supervising eye. The character given to Jephthah the moment he was introduced was 'mighty warrior', but as soon as he opens his mouth we see that he is notably good with words as well as with deeds.

The Lord is, thirdly, setting up a parallel between Jephthah and himself, between the judge and the Judge. Have we not heard this exchange before? The Gileadite leaders ask Jephthah for help, just as Israel asked the Lord for help in 10:10; he retorts that they have no claim on him, just as the Lord had retorted in 10:11–14; they admit it, and ask again, now with humility, just as Israel did in 10:15; and we may fairly say that the final word from Jephthah underlines the real meaning of 10:16, where the Lord becomes 'indignant over the misery of Israel'. At this point, neither the human judge nor the divine Judge is said to be *sorry* for the squealing Israelites. What we see here is not pity but a justified and resolute anger.

There will be a profound lesson to learn from this parallel when we get to the end of the story. Meanwhile we keep it at the back of our mind.

4. Jephthah's diplomacy (11:12–28)

Then Jephthah sent messengers to the king of the Ammonites and said, 'What have you against me, that you have come to me to fight against my land?' [13]*And the king of the Ammonites answered the messengers of Jephthah, 'Because Israel on coming from Egypt took away my land, from the Arnon to the Jabbok and to the Jordan; now therefore restore it peaceably'.* [14]*And Jephthah sent messengers again to the king of the Ammonites* [15]*and said to him, 'Thus says Jephthah: Israel did not take away the land of Moab or the land of the Ammonites,* [16]*but when they came up from Egypt, Israel went through the wilderness to the Red Sea and came to Kadesh.* [17]*Israel then sent messengers to the king of Edom, saying, "Let us pass, we pray, through your land"; but the king of Edom would not listen. And they sent also to the king of Moab, but he would not consent. So Israel remained at Kadesh.* [18]*Then they journeyed through the wilderness, and went around the land of Edom and the land of Moab, and arrived on the east side of the land of Moab, and camped on the other side of the Arnon; but they did not enter the territory of Moab, for the Arnon was the boundary of Moab.* [19]*Israel then sent messengers to Sihon king of the Amorites, king of Heshbon; and Israel said to him, "Let us pass, we pray, through your land to our country."* [20]*But Sihon did not trust Israel to pass through his territory; so Sihon gathered all his people together, and encamped at Jahaz, and fought with Israel.* [21]*And the LORD, the God of Israel, gave Sihon and all his people into the hand of Israel, and they defeated them; so Israel took possession of all the land of the Amorites, who inhabited that country.* [22]*And they took possession of all the territory of the Amorites from the Arnon to the Jabbok and from the wilderness to the Jordan.* [23]*So then the LORD, the God of Israel, dispossessed the Amorites from before his people Israel; and are you to take possession of them?* [24]*Will you not possess what Chemosh your god gives you to possess? And all that the LORD our God has dispossessed before us, we will possess.* [25]*Now are you any better than Balak the son of Zippor, king of Moab? Did he ever strive against Israel, or did he ever go to war with them?* [26]*While Israel dwelt in Heshbon and its villages, and in Aroer and its villages, and in all the cities that are on the banks of the Arnon, three hundred years, why did you not recover them within that time?* [27]*I therefore have not sinned against you, and you do me wrong by making war on me; the* LORD, *the Judge, decide this day between the people of Israel and the people of Ammon.' [28]But the king of the Ammonites did not heed the message of Jephthah which he sent to him.*

It should not escape us that the first action of the man of action, the mighty warrior, is not to mobilize troops but to send messages: not deeds yet, but words. A diplomatic exchange is set in motion. No doubt to the Ammonite king's astonishment, for the first time in eighteen years his military manoeuvres spark off a demand from the victims for an explanation. Equally astonishingly, he gives one – terse enough in all conscience, but there is apparently something about the Israelite leader who has asked for it that cannot simply be ignored. The territory east of the Jordan now occupied by Israel and called Gilead, a fifty-mile stretch between the rivers Arnon and Jabbok[7] (so runs the king's reply), was originally Ammonite land, which ought to be returned to its rightful owners.

Jephthah responds with a second message, of considerable length. As Davis helpfully suggests, it contains a fourfold argument: from history, from theology, from precedent, and from silence.[8] First the argument from history (11:15–22), a review of the facts. When Israel first arrived in those parts, says Jephthah, the land east of Jordan up to the Arnon belonged to Edom and Moab, and the Israelites did not even set foot in it. The land north of the Arnon, however, they did occupy. That had been *Amorite*, not *Ammonite*, territory; unlike the Edomites and the Moabites, the Amorites had risen in arms against Israel, and having been soundly defeated they lost their land to the newcomers, who then occupied it by right of conquest. 'Israel . . . took away *my* land' (11:13)? It was not your land; your people were not even there. That is the argument from history. The argument from theology (11:23–24) is based on an assumption common to all the peoples of the ancient Near East. It was our God who gave us that victory and this land, says Jephthah. You have a god, and he has given you a land to live in[9] (it was presumably south of the Arnon, related in some way to the territory of Moab, since the two nations were closely connec-

---

[7] The two rivers both flow westwards, the Arnon into the Dead Sea at the midpoint of its eastern shore and the Jabbok into the Jordan somewhat south of the midpoint of its course between the Sea of Galilee and the Dead Sea.

[8] Davis, pp. 142–145.

[9] Not that Jephthah, or any true Israelite, would believe that the gods of the heathen really existed as powers which could do such things. He is using an *argumentum ad hominem* – this is what the person addressed would have believed.

ted).[10] So you should be content to occupy that. The argument from precedent (11:25) compares this situation with that earlier one when the migrant Israelites were approaching the borders of Moab. Balak, the Moabite king of that time, was hostile enough, and would have liked to get rid of these unwelcome new arrivals, but he stopped short of going to war with them, and was content to maintain an armed truce.[11] If the real reason for the Ammonite's hostility is not a desire to recover lost land (see argument 1), but merely a dislike of Israel, why should he not do as his predecessor did? And finally, the argument from silence (11:26): we have already been here for three hundred years, so if there is genuine reason for your attacking us like this, how come no-one ever said anything about it before? It is you, not we, who are in the wrong; and – now speaks the true Israelite, who does not for a moment himself believe that Chemosh is on a par with the God of Israel – the authoritative decision between your claims and ours will be made by the Lord, who is the ultimate Judge over your nation, and every other nation, as well as over Israel (11:27).

We should not in the end, I think, be surprised that of all the judges it is Jephthah who puts into words this central truth of the book. It is fitting that here in the very middle of Judges we should hear this ringing proclamation of 'the LORD, the Judge'. The fact remains that Jephthah is a strange character, and the account of his judgeship is one of the most puzzling sections of the book. We have not yet solved its puzzles, indeed we have not yet reached the biggest one. For the time being there is something we cannot help noticing. In a way, what he says matters less than how he says it. Almost regardless of the content, what we have here is an impressive diplomatic note. He had no expectation that it would convince or disarm the Ammonite king ('Well, I never – I hadn't seen it in that light; how right you are! I do apologize'). It would, however, have made clear that he intended to dig his heels in, and wanted to force the issue (11:28); it could well have encouraged his own countrymen; and as the messages went to and fro, at the speed of riders, remember, not of radio waves, it would certainly buy time. We realize that again Jephthah has opened his mouth, and again it is his words which have shown him to be a man of great ability and authority, speaking almost as the Lord speaks through his prophets: 'Thus says Jephthah' (11:15).

[10] See Gn. 19:36–38; Dt. 2:17–19; Jdg. 3:13. The close relationship could account for the mention here of the Moabite god Chemosh as being on a par with, or even the equivalent of, the Ammonite god Molech/Milcom; and for the comparison between an Ammonite and a Moabite king in 11:25.

[11] See Nu. 22–24.

5. Jephthah's going out (11:29–33)

Then the Spirit of the LORD came upon Jephthah, and he passed through Gilead and Manasseh, and passed on to Mizpah of Gilead, and from Mizpah of Gilead he passed on to the Ammonites. ³⁰And Jephthah made a vow to the LORD, and said, 'If thou wilt give the Ammonites into my hand, ³¹then whoever comes forth from the doors of my house to meet me, when I return victorious from the Ammonites, shall be the LORD's, and I will offer him up for a burnt offering.' ³²So Jephthah crossed over to the Ammonites to fight against them; and the LORD gave them into his hand. ³³And he smote them from Aroer to the neighbourhood of Minnith, twenty cities, and as far as Abel-keramim, with a very great slaughter. So the Ammonites were subdued before the people of Israel.

The warrior-judge goes out, first on what seems to be a recruiting tour starting from and returning to Mizpah, and then on to what will be his successful campaign. After all, he is first and foremost a man of action, a 'mighty warrior' (11:1), and now the Spirit of the Lord has come upon him (11:29) and the Lord gives his enemies into his hand in a resounding and comprehensive victory (11:32–33).

But that is not the nub of the story. The Ammonites are disposed of, and disappear from the narrative in 11:33, while the tale of Jephthah himself has another fourteen verses to go. Hear now the crucial point of Jephthah's going out.

Before the campaign began, he had opened his mouth for a third time. What he said to the Gileadite leaders and what he said to the Ammonite king were part of the backdrop to this startling scene. We listen now to what, before he went forth to battle, he said to the Lord: 'If thou wilt give the Ammonites into my hand, then whoever comes forth from the doors of my house to meet me, when I return victorious from the Ammonites, shall be the LORD's, and I will offer him up for a burnt offering' (11:30–31).

Of all the questions in this perplexing story, this is the biggest. Did Jephthah really mean sacrifice? Yes. It would be comforting to think that when the first one to meet him on his return turned out to be his daughter, the terms of the vow were commuted to something less bloodthirsty, and that 11:37–38 implies perhaps that she was condemned to perpetual virginity. But he 'did . . . according to his vow' (11:39), and the vow was to offer a burnt offering.[12]

---

[12] We should not put on this the worst possible construction, that she was burnt alive. No doubt, as with Abraham and Isaac, what was envisaged was a quick death by the knife before the corpse was burnt (Gn. 22:2, 10).

Did Jephthah really mean 'whoever'? Yes. It is true that the term in Hebrew 'specifies neither species (man or animal) nor gender',[13] and he might have pictured a favourite dog leaping out to meet him. But obviously he took it that when his daughter came out the vow did apply to her. Then did he really mean the Lord? – she 'shall be the LORD's'? Yes. It would ease the problem if he were taking the Lord's name in vain, being a pagan at heart with the attitude of the heathen around him and no more than a veneer of Israelite religion. But that will not do either. The Lord's presence is recognized, not only in the words of men but in reality, more than a dozen times in this chapter, and most really and certainly in this paragraph.

The question cannot be evaded. The next paragraph will tell us what happened in respect of Jephthah's vow. But the vow itself is appalling enough, and no-one expostulates. This is simply not acceptable. In the very episode where the Lord uses this saviour-judge to rescue his people, we see something exceedingly wrong both in the man Jephthah and in Israelite society. Basic morality seems to have been eroded; and 'if the foundations are destroyed, what can the righteous do?'[14] Where have we got to when such things can happen in a supposedly God-fearing community? And even more mysterious, how can the Lord continue to work among people who have sunk to these depths? He is 'of purer eyes than to behold evil', and can 'not look on wrong'.[15] Will he not wash his hands of them?

6. Jephthah's coming home (11:34–40)

Then Jephthah came to his home at Mizpah; and behold, his daughter came out to meet him with timbrels and with dances; she was his only child; beside her he had neither son nor daughter. [35]And when he saw her, he rent his clothes, and said, 'Alas, my daughter! you have brought me very low, and you have become the cause of great trouble to me; for I have opened my mouth to the LORD, and I cannot take back my vow.' [36]And she said to him, 'My father, if you have opened your mouth to the LORD, do to me according to what has gone forth from your mouth, now that the LORD has avenged you on your enemies, on the Ammonites.' [37]And she said to her father, 'Let this thing be done for me; let me alone two months, that I may go and wander on the mountains, and bewail my virginity, I and my companions.' [38]And he said, 'Go.' And he sent her away for two months; and she departed, she and her

---

[13] Webb, p. 227 n. 51.   [14] Ps. 11:3.   [15] Hab. 1:13.

companions, and bewailed her virginity upon the mountains. ³⁹And at the end of two months, she returned to her father, who did with her according to his vow which he had made. She had never known a man. And it became a custom in Israel ⁴⁰that the daughters of Israel went year by year to lament the daughter of Jephthah the Gileadite four days in the year.

The answer to the natural question, Will God not wash his hands of them?, is apparently no. Vow or no vow, 'the Spirit of the LORD came upon Jephthah', and 'the LORD gave them', the Ammonites, 'into his hand' (11:29, 32). 'Then Jephthah came to his home at Mizpah; and behold, his daughter came out to meet him with timbrels and with dances; she was his only child; beside her he had neither son nor daughter. And when he saw her, he rent his clothes, and said, "Alas, my daughter! you have brought me very low, and you have become the cause of great trouble to me; for I have opened my mouth to the LORD, and I cannot take back my vow" ' (11:34–35). He had opened his mouth once too often.

People try to explain him, or to explain him away. With regard to his intention, perhaps he did not mean really to kill the girl? As we have seen, it is hard to get round the explicit statement that he had a burnt offering in mind. With regard to the action itself, perhaps he was a child of his time, in a primitive culture where human sacrifice was accepted, and in later ages he would have recoiled from it? But that does not hold, for earlier ages had already recoiled from it,[16] and with his background he should have known better. 'He is no early blob on some scale of moral evolution.'[17] With regard to his character, perhaps he was just plain wrong? But the confusion remains, for the Lord not only blessed him at that very time, but caused his name to appear afterwards as one of the four notables in Judges who are immortalized as the great believers of Hebrews 11.

No; as I read the story, it tells me that Jephthah killed his daughter, and he did so because he had opened his mouth in a thoughtless vow; and either in spite of this, or (incredibly) because of it, he is renowned in Scripture as a 'man of faith'. And I have to ask myself what conceivable lesson the God of Scripture intends his people down the ages to learn from the tale of this girl and her father, 'who did with her according to his vow which he had made' (11:39).

It could be the very simple lesson, needed by everyone who

---

[16] See Lv. 18:21; 20:2–5; Dt. 12:31; 18:10; and of course Ex. 20:13.
[17] Davis, p. 148.

opens his mouth and puts his foot in it (which means a good many of us), to be careful how we talk. 'Set a guard over my mouth, O LORD,' prayed the psalmist,[18] 'keep watch over the door of my lips!' It is more likely to be a rather different lesson, which will be intensified for us as Judges proceeds: namely, that how the Lord uses his servants in public is not necessarily related to what he knows them to be in private. This is not meant to be a cosy excuse ('He obviously uses my gifts, so I don't need to be too particular about keeping my heart clean'). Rather, it is a solemn warning: 'What matters to me is that my heart should be right with him, even if he does seem to use my gifts in spite of my sin.'

But neither of these lessons, however important, quite fits the story of Jephthah. I see something else there.

It has been a story full of the spoken word. Israel opens her mouth to complain, God opens his to rebuke, the Ammonites open theirs to call one another to arms and the Gileadites theirs to discuss what to do about it. When Jephthah comes on the scene, he opens his mouth to great effect, first in political bargaining and then in diplomacy, until the final, dreadful, careless 'opening of the mouth' that we have just been considering.

Now the age of the judges is one where there are open mouths everywhere, gabbling a confusion of messages. A car I drove a few years ago had a medium-wave radio, old-fashioned by today's standards, on which reception was fine during the day, until late afternoon. Then French and Dutch and German stations began to step up their signals, on wavelengths so close to the British ones that it became impossible to separate one broadcast from another. Just so were the crowded airwaves of Canaan in the time of the judges. Like Prospero's isle in *The Tempest*, the place was full of noises, conflicting and confusing voices mixing truth and half-truth and lies dressed up as truth. The voices of 'the Baals and the Ashtaroth, the gods of Syria, the gods of Sidon, the gods of Moab, the gods of the Ammonites, and the gods of the Philistines' (10:6), like the voices of our modern gods, with their plausible presentation and slick production, whose messages we take in because it doesn't occur to us not to, are in fact a medley of misleading propaganda. No wonder God had said that the nations of Canaan, the broadcasters of this confusion, had to be rooted out. No wonder he found it necessary here, half-way through Judges, to speak again in chapter 10 as he had spoken in chapter 2: when his people listen so readily to the clamorous voices, the gabbling mouths, he answers their cries for help not with rescue, but with rebuke.

[18] Ps. 141:3.

For among all these voices the voice of God is still speaking. Jephthah would be foolish to imagine that he can hear the true message only on occasions such as those when our writer tells us 'the LORD said', or 'the angel of the LORD . . . said', or 'the LORD sent a prophet . . . and he said'.[19] Our own generation also, in which 'words of prophecy' are given undue importance by many Christians, needs to remember this. The fact is that God had opened his mouth long before, in the days of Adam and Noah and Abraham and Moses, with words whose relevance and vitality had not lessened. Of those ancient words, ever sharp and clear for those whose ears are tuned to them, there was one which Jephthah failed to hear, and one which he did hear.

The first was the prohibition of human sacrifice. God had long before spoken plainly about that.[20] Whatever else Jephthah's vow might have obliged him to do, there was no way it could have obliged him to break that fundamental rule. Our Lord addresses the matter directly when he gives the Pharisees a drubbing-down for teaching that the man who vows his money 'to God' is thereby exempted from obeying the basic law of family responsibility, that is, from having in financial terms 'to do anything for his father or mother'.[21] So for Jephthah there is a similar basic law, the sanctity of human life, and he cannot hear it clearly enough to realize that it must override any foolish vow he may decide to make which would seem to exempt him from it.

But there is a word from God which he has heard, however wrongly he may apply it. 'Alas, my daughter! . . . *I have opened my mouth* to the LORD, and I cannot take back my vow.' 'My father, if *you have opened your mouth* to the LORD, do to me according to *what has gone forth from your mouth*' (11:35–36). If you have made a promise, you keep it. He should never have made that promise. He should have realized that keeping it might mean the breaking of other basic rules. But amid the welter of contradictory voices he had heard the voice of God saying '*You keep your word*', and he heeded the voice. It was a mark of paganism to shut one's ears to inconvenient messages, as he knew: 'the king of the Ammonites did not heed the message of Jephthah' (11:28). But Jephthah was a man of faith, and he did heed at any rate the message of God concerning faithfulness, whatever confusions may have accompanied it. What he did (the sacrifice of his daughter) is a thing all Scripture condemns; why he did it (in order to keep his word) is a thing all Scripture commends.

[19] E.g. 1:2; 2:1; 6:8, *etc.* [20] See above, p. 118 n. 16.
[21] See Mk. 7:9–13.

7. What happened afterwards (12:1–15)

The men of Ephraim were called to arms, and they crossed to Zaphon and said to Jephthah, 'Why did you cross over to fight against the Ammonites, and did not call us to go with you? We will burn your house over you with fire.' ²And Jephthah said to them, 'I and my people had a great feud with the Ammonites; and when I called you, you did not deliver me from their hand. ³And when I saw that you would not deliver me, I took my life in my hand, and crossed over against the Ammonites, and the LORD gave them into my hand; why then have you come up to me this day, to fight against me?' ⁴Then Jephthah gathered all the men of Gilead and fought with Ephraim; and the men of Gilead smote Ephraim, because they said, 'You are fugitives of Ephraim, you Gileadites, in the midst of Ephraim and Manasseh.' ⁵And the Gileadites took the fords of the Jordan against the Ephraimites. And when any of the fugitives of Ephraim said, 'Let me go over,' the men of Gilead said to him, 'Are you an Ephraimite?' When he said, 'No,' ⁶they said to him, 'Then say Shibboleth,' and he said, 'Sibboleth,' for he could not pronounce it right; then they seized him and slew him at the fords of the Jordan. And there fell at that time forty-two thousand of the Ephraimites.

⁷Jephthah judged Israel six years. Then Jephthah the Gileadite died, and was buried in his city in Gilead.

⁸After him Ibzan of Bethlehem judged Israel. ⁹He had thirty sons; and thirty daughters he gave in marriage outside his clan, and thirty daughters he brought in from outside for his sons. And he judged Israel seven years. ¹⁰Then Ibzan died, and was buried at Bethlehem.

¹¹After him Elon the Zebulunite judged Israel; and he judged Israel ten years. ¹²Then Elon the Zebulunite died, and was buried at Aijalon in the land of Zebulun.

¹³After him Abdon the son of Hillel the Pirathonite judged Israel. ¹⁴He had forty sons and thirty grandsons, who rode on seventy asses; and he judged Israel eight years. ¹⁵Then Abdon the son of Hillel the Pirathonite died, and was buried at Pirathon in the land of Ephraim, in the hill country of the Amalekites.

'The men of Ephraim were called to arms, and they crossed to Zaphon and said to Jephthah, "Why did you cross over to fight against the Ammonites, and did not call us to go with you? We will burn your house over you with fire" ' (12:1). But they were asking for trouble. 'Jephthah gathered all the men of Gilead and . . . smote Ephraim' (12:4), not only killing great numbers in the battle

but also picking off all the fugitives as they tried to escape homewards across the Jordan. Once before the tribe of Ephraim had
complained in this self-important way (8:1–3). Twice before it had
been involved in the slaughter of fugitives at a river crossing
(3:26–30; 7:24–25). How has the story moved on since those earlier
parallel incidents?

The previous complaint had been met with soft words from
Gideon. He had smoothed the ruffled feathers of Ephraim because
he still had an enemy in front of him and wanted friends behind
him. But in the case of Jephthah, the enemy has been dealt with,
and he is free to speak his mind to these arrogant fire-eaters.
He speaks, and acts, to good effect. With respect to the previous
slaughters, they had been by Ephraimites, of heathen intruders;
this one is by Gileadites, of Ephraimites – the killing of Israelites
by Israelites – and the casualty list is enormous. So these two
aspects of Jephthah's last recorded campaign leave us with an abiding impression of both the man and the nation at this stage in the
Judges account. First, his reaction to the Ephraimites' complaint
confirms Jephthah as a man memorably good with words as well
as with deeds. These were his gifts, even if the Lord who had used
them to defeat the Ammonites (12:3) stood aloof from this use
of them against fellow-Israelites. Secondly, the slaughter which
Jephthah instigated at the fords of Jordan confirms a double process
in the life of the nation. Israel's own sin and folly is leading towards
the break-up of the twelve tribes. The real reason for the quarrel
is tribal antagonism. The battle from which the Ephraimites ran
away had been caused precisely by their taunting of the Gileadites
as 'runaways' (12:4–5). The password 'sibboleth/shibboleth'[22]
traded on a difference in accent that had grown up between tribes,
and the use of it deepened the rift. Gideon's harshness towards his
fellow-Israelites at Succoth and Penuel (8:13–17) has intensified
into something that begins to look like civil war.

But at the same time, while Israel slides towards disintegration,
the Lord's mercy is at work holding the nation together. He is not
said to have given the Ephraimites into Jephthah's hand as he gave
the Ammonites, yet he is still ultimately in control of affairs, and
Jephthah's winning of this last battle puts a stop for the time being
to the separation between the tribes east and west of the Jordan.
We see both the human folly and the divine mercy in the last verse
which speaks of Jephthah (12:7): he is to the end a Gileadite,

---

[22] Meaning either 'ear of corn' or 'current of water'. If the latter, then perhaps
'any stranger trying to cross was directed to a section of the river and asked what
that was; and if he was from Ephraim he said "Sibboleth", and did not live much
longer' (Auld, p. 202).

identified with the Transjordan tribes, a 'shibboleth' man and not a 'sibboleth' one; yet he does go down to history as one who 'judged *Israel*'.

And in the continuing goodness of God, the brief notices of Jephthah's successors focus on the holding together, not the flying apart, of God's people. For three decades Israel will enjoy peace and unity. After Jephthah's six-year judgeship, Ibzan 'judged Israel seven years', then Elon 'judged Israel ten years', then Abdon 'judged Israel eight years'. These men are distinguished by the same marks of prosperity that we saw in the case of Jair,[23] and in addition Ibzan arranges marriages for his children which will help to bind Israelite clans together.

After all the questions that this story has raised, there remains the one that has to be asked of every story in Judges. How does God the Judge guide and govern his people? When they go to him for direction for their lives, how does he give it?

He answers first through Othniel: having rebuked his people, his overriding *purpose* is to deliver them. He adds, through Ehud, that his *method* may well be unexpected, the unorthodox deliverance of left-handedness. He shows, through Deborah and Barak, that his *requirement* is straightforward obedience to his revealed will. He demonstrates, through Gideon, that his *principle* is to use the weak and the humble to confound the powerful and the arrogant.

To put it another way, his working through his servants has meant that they reflect in themselves and their operations something of him and of his. Othniel is a saviour because his God is a Saviour. Ehud is left-handed, just as his God regularly saves 'left-handedly'. Barak obeys commands, just as his God always keeps his own rules.[24] Gideon's strength is made perfect in weakness, which is how his God works, supremely when in the end of the ages he comes himself in the frailty of human flesh. If this is a right reading of the book before us, what do we see of the work of God the Judge in the chapters about this latest of his deputy-judges, and does Jephthah himself reflect something of his Lord?

---

[23] 10:3–5; see p. 104.

[24] In the New Testament, where the persons of the Trinity are distinguished, it is the Son who is sent by the Father to save the world (1 Jn. 4:14). Even more clearly than the God of the Old Testament, that New Testament Saviour-God is reflected in Barak, who like him is a man under authority and does nothing apart from that authority (Lk. 7:6–8; Jn. 8:28–29), cannot act independently of the one who sends him (Jn. 5:19), and is victorious through obedience (Rom. 5:19; Phil. 2:8–11; Heb. 5:8–9). Perhaps these considerations shed further light on the question of why in Jdg. 4 Deborah is the judge, while in Heb. 11 it is Barak who is honoured. See pp. 63–64.

Throughout chapters 10–12 has run the theme of the spoken word, and its importance and power. This is what at the climax of the story has such terrible effects. 'I have opened my mouth,' says Jephthah, 'I cannot take back my vow'; 'You have opened your mouth,' agrees his daughter, 'do . . . according to what has gone forth from your mouth.' Jephthah like his predecessors is only human, even if he is God's chosen saviour, so the image of God in him is far from perfect. Especially at a time when Israel is readily listening to the sevenfold clamour of the voices of the false gods (the point has been underlined in 10:6), it is not to be wondered at that even the judge's ears are not very discerning. But the thing which our writer brings to the fore is the thing in which the human judge does reflect the divine Judge. In Old Testament and in New, God shows himself as the God who never goes back on his word. 'God is not man, that he should lie, or a son of man, that he should repent. Has he said, and will he not do it? Or has he spoken, and will he not fulfil it?' says the prophet.[25] 'He who calls you is faithful, and he will do it,' echoes the apostle.[26] And where God calls men and women to responsibility among his people, he expects the same quality in them, in New Testament as in Old: 'The fruit of the Spirit is . . . faithfulness'; 'Who shall dwell on thy holy hill? He . . . who swears to his own hurt and does not change.'[27] There was much that Jephthah needed to learn about the faith of the true God. But the dreadfulness of the deed for which he is most remembered points up by contrast the vital thing that he *had* grasped, and that he believed he must pursue, however misguidedly. He held true to such truth as he had attained, and that, as Paul tells us, is a firm stepping-stone towards God's showing us the truths we do not yet see clearly.[28]

---

[25] Nu. 23:19. Something we may note in passing: Balaam is a prime example of the important Judges truth (see pp. 61, 86, 119, 142f., 149) that a man may have real spiritual gifts without being a spiritual person (Nu. 23:16 with 31:16; Rev. 2:14).
[26] 1 Thes. 5:24.   [27] Gal. 5:22; Ps. 15:1, 4.   [28] See Phil. 3:15–16.

Judges 13:1 – 16:31

7. Samson: set apart for God

'This you have heard before,' says the writer to the reader. 'Without doubt you will groan "Tell me the old, old story", as I set the scene for the coming of the last of the judges: "And the people of Israel again did what was evil in the sight of the LORD" ' (13:1). Although Samson's is a self-contained story, those introductory words are enough to remind us that like the rest it belongs to the days when 'there was no king in Israel', and the people of God would be as unsuccessful as ever in coping with the challenge of such days.

Behind that immediate link between this episode and its predecessors there come flocking in a host of more subtle connections. 10:7 is recalled, 'Israel . . . sold . . . into the hand of the Philistines and into the hand of the Ammonites', the latter having come to the fore in Jephthah's time and the former doing so now in Samson's. Like Gideon's, this story has an angel and a burning sacrifice, and a troop of three hundred pyromaniacs to harass the enemy (animals this time, not humans!). Like Deborah's, this one has a dangerous woman 'thrusting a peg' with evil intent,[1] and bees and torches as notable items.[2] Like Shamgar's, this one has a judge noted for killing Philistines personally, and that with the oddest of weapons.[3] And like Othniel's, this one includes the judge's wife as an important factor.[4]

However, the connection between the last judge and the first is a contrast rather than a likeness. Othniel's marriage was 'exemp-

---

[1] The same phrase is used in 16:14 and 4:21.
[2] Curiously, these are the meanings of the Hebrew names Deborah and Lappidoth (4:4).
[3] An ass's jawbone (15:15); an ox-goad (3:31).
[4] See 1:11–15.

125

lary', and was 'his incentive to drive out the Gentiles';[5] Samson's is its opposite in both respects. And that reminds us of how much else in chapters 13 – 16 is new and different, often spectacularly so, from anything we have seen before. The way Samson killed a lion with his bare hands! – mobilized his three hundred jackals! – pulled up Gaza's city gates and pulled down its temple of Dagon! All the startling novelties are of a piece with a judgeship which is as far removed as it can be from the distant days of Othniel. Where now is the nationwide authority of the fourth judge, Deborah? Where even the military leadership of the fifth and the eighth, Gideon and Jephthah? Judges is not concerned to identify each of the twelve with one of the twelve tribes, but the first at any rate belongs to Judah and the twelfth to Dan, and the span of the whole sequence is clearly the span of chapter 1 writ large: at the beginning, ' "Who shall go up first . . . ?" "Judah shall go up; behold, I have given the land into his hand" ' (1:1–2); by the end, 'The Amorites pressed the Danites back . . . they did not allow them to come down' (1:34).

Across the historical span of the judges, then, Dan answers to Judah, the failure of the one to the success of the other, the eccentricities of Samson to the straightforwardness of Othniel; and we ask ourselves how we got from there to here. What is the process that has led from no. 1 to no. 12?

So far as Israel is concerned, it is a process of deterioration. The nation's experience is by no means merely cyclic, and the four Rs are too simple a way of describing what happens. Though rebellion followed by retribution is depressingly constant, repentance as a prelude to rescue is something we see less and less. Here in chapter 13 there is not even a cry of misery, let alone a cry of penitence. We realize that the successive enemies of Israel have hurt her in a variety of ways, ever more subtly and deeply: Moabite invasion (3:13), Canaanite cruelty (4:3), Midianite devastation (6:3–6). Now what worse thing can the Philistines do to the people of God?

The Samson saga tells us. To be given 'into the hand of the Philistines' (13:1) meant that Israelites fraternized readily with them, that even intermarrying with them was acceptable, that the once-patriotic men of Judah would rather be rid of Samson than rock the boat of harmonious relations with them (15:9–13), and that even the Lord had to be 'seeking an occasion' against them because every snag of hostility between them and Israel had been carefully smoothed over (14:4). In other words, Israel had totally sold out to the values of the Philistine world. There is scarcely a

---

[5] Webb, pp. 170, 257 n. 130 (quoting the second phrase from an article by D. W. Gooding).

single mention of the distinctive name of Israel's God on the lips of anyone in the whole of the four chapters,[6] and until the very last paragraph the climax looks as though it is going to be the triumph of the Philistine god Dagon (16:23–24). The Lord had left the heathen nations in the land expressly so that Israel 'might know war', and top of his list for the purpose of clearly setting his own nation over against the rest were 'the five lords of the Philistines' (3:2–3). Israel's ultimate rebellion lay in renouncing this conflict, accommodating herself to the ways of the Philistines, recognizing the rule of Dagon, and deliberately blurring the distinction between the people of God and the people of the world.

But while for Israel the process has been one of steady decline, for God it has been one of persistence in preserving and directing his people. It is fascinating to see how every event in this present story follows in cause-and-effect sequence from one or other of Samson's three recorded relationships with women (14:1–2; 16:1; 16:4). Each time he cheerfully falls for a quite unsuitable girl, and each time the Lord harnesses the young man's self-indulgence for his own purposes and makes sure that a string of consequences brings about, as ever, his long-term judgment.

1. The call of the judge (13:1–25)

And the people of Israel again did what was evil in the sight of the LORD; and the LORD gave them into the hand of the Philistines for forty years.

²And there was a certain man of Zorah, of the tribe of the Danites, whose name was Manoah; and his wife was barren and had no children. ³And the angel of the LORD appeared to the woman and said to her, 'Behold, you are barren and have no children; but you shall conceive and bear a son. ⁴Therefore beware, and drink no wine or strong drink, and eat nothing unclean, ⁵for lo, you shall conceive and bear a son. No razor shall come upon his head, for the boy shall be a Nazirite to God from birth; and he shall begin to deliver Israel from the hand of the Philistines.' ⁶Then the woman came and told her husband, 'A man of God came to me, and his countenance was like the countenance of the angel of God, very terrible; I did not ask him whence he was, and he did not tell me his name; ⁷but he said to me, "Behold, you shall conceive and bear a son; so then drink no wine or strong drink, and eat nothing unclean, for the boy shall be a Nazirite to God from birth to the

---

[6] The writer himself uses the name LORD (Yahweh), but everyone in the story says 'God' except the angel (once, 13:16) and Manoah's wife (once, 13:23). (Manoah's own word 'LORD' in 13:8 is not Yahweh but Adonai; the RSV nods.)

127

day of his death." '

⁸*Then Manoah entreated the* LORD, *and said, 'O,* LORD, *I pray thee, let the man of God whom thou didst send come again to us, and teach us what we are to do with the boy that will be born.'* ⁹*And God listened to the voice of Manoah, and the angel of God came again to the woman as she sat in the field; but Manoah her husband was not with her.* ¹⁰*And the woman ran in haste and told her husband, 'Behold, the man who came to me the other day has appeared to me.'* ¹¹*And Manoah arose and went after his wife, and came to the man and said to him, 'Are you the man who spoke to this woman?' And he said, 'I am.'* ¹²*And Manoah said, 'Now when your words come true, what is to be the boy's manner of life, and what is he to do?'* ¹³*And the angel of the* LORD *said to Manoah, 'Of all that I said to the woman let her beware.* ¹⁴*She may not eat of anything that comes from the vine, neither let her drink wine or strong drink, or eat any unclean thing; all that I commanded her let her observe.'*

¹⁵*Manoah said to the angel of the* LORD, *'Pray, let us detain you, and prepare a kid for you.'* ¹⁶*And the angel of the* LORD *said to Manoah, 'If you detain me, I will not eat of your food; but if you make ready a burnt offering, then offer it to the* LORD.' *(For Manoah did not know that he was the angel of the* LORD.) ¹⁷*And Manoah said to the angel of the* LORD, *'What is your name, so that, when your words come true, we may honour you?'* ¹⁸*And the angel of the* LORD *said to him, 'Why do you ask my name, seeing it is wonderful?'* ¹⁹*So Manoah took the kid with the cereal offering, and offered it upon the rock to the* LORD, *to him who works wonders.* ²⁰*And when the flame went up toward heaven from the altar, the angel of the* LORD *ascended in the flame of the altar while Manoah and his wife looked on; and they fell on their faces to the ground.*

²¹*The angel of the* LORD *appeared no more to Manoah and to his wife. Then Manoah knew that he was the angel of the* LORD. ²²*And Manoah said to his wife, 'We shall surely die, for we have seen God.'* ²³*But his wife said to him, 'If the* LORD *had meant to kill us, he would not have accepted a burnt offering and a cereal offering at our hands, or shown us all these things, or now announced to us such things as these.'* ²⁴*And the woman bore a son, and called his name Samson; and the boy grew, and the* LORD *blessed him.* ²⁵*And the Spirit of the* LORD *began to stir him in Mahaneh-dan, between Zorah and Eshta-ol.*

Once more, something old and something new: the old being, as before, that 'Israel again did what was evil in the sight of the LORD', and was duly punished. But 13:1 has a new kind of sequel. Instead of the introduction of a rescuer, the writer begins what seems for the moment to be an unrelated narrative. It has a real story-book flavour, like the opening verses of the next two books of the Bible ('A certain man of Bethlehem in Judah . . .', 'A certain man of Ramathaim-Zophim . . .'),[7] and if you had just a smattering of Bible knowledge, and were aware only that the tale of the famous Samson lay ahead, you might well wonder what this had to do with anything: 'There was a certain man of Zorah' (*where?*), 'whose name was Manoah' (*who?*).

What is more, not only is the fourth R (Israel's rescuer) not yet in sight, but the third R (Israel's repentance) is missing altogether. On reflection, though, we have to admit that it was hardly ever there anyway. Even the outline of what Israel was going to experience, set out in advance in chapter 2, should have warned us that our four Rs would be too simple and optimistic. You will review the entire period of the judges, said that chapter, and find that in the course of it Israel repeatedly sinned (2:11–13) and was repeatedly punished (2:14–15) and then repeatedly rescued (2:16–18), but that the attitudes of the two parties were on Israel's part mere remorse, not repentance, and on God's part first pity and then anger (2:18–20). As we noticed in the time of Jephthah, the Lord was 'indignant over the misery of Israel' (10:16), but the book is far more about his indignation with Israel herself than about his indignation with her oppressors.

All this is the background to the call of Samson. In a number of ways his call echoes that of Gideon, but those echoes apart it is different from all the other raisings-up, not least in that it comes not to Samson himself, but to his parents, and that even before he is born. We may make guesses as to why it should have been so, and one of the better ones would probably be that with a character whose doings are going to be so colourful and entertaining it is as well to establish in advance that God's doings are even more noteworthy, and indeed that it was he who set up the whole Samson event in the first place.

God's angel appeared in a Danite home in the village of Zorah, to announce to the couple whose home it was the birth of a child who would be the saviour of Israel. (Yes, this *is* Judges 13, not Luke 1! We shall bear the parallel in mind; it is something more than mere coincidence.) As the chapter unfolds, so does the character of these two whom the Lord has chosen. For all the startling novelties of the tale, the characteristics of this couple are, we begin to see, familiar ones. They were important in the stories of the

[7] Ru. 1:1; 1 Sa. 1:1.

earlier judges, and their reappearance here underscores their importance in God's dealings with his people throughout the book. As
we have noted how often the repetition of words and names and
phrases links this story with the previous ones, so now we see these
more substantial continuities: the way things are, as well as the
way they are described, when God sets about his judging and
saving work. As he prepared for the arrival of the last of the judges,
why did he choose this couple rather than another?

a. They were unlikely people (13:2–7)

'In this home', said the angel, 'Israel's saviour will be born; and he
is to be a Nazirite to God.' The lifestyle of a 'Nazirite', a person
'separate . . . to the LORD', is outlined in Numbers 6:1–21. If even
before his birth the child was destined to be saviour of his people,
then it was fitting that he should be brought up in a way that
marked him out as someone special. The Nazirite rules may seem
to us an odd collection, to do with drinks, carcasses, and haircuts;
and they were all negative. Grapes and all that might be made from
them; anything dead; and the barber's razor – all these were to be
kept at arm's length. As always, the sign is not so important as
what it signifies. The Nazirite would say a definite no to certain
perfectly natural things in order to show how definite was the yes
he was saying to something more important, his dedication of
himself to God.

Typically of God's way of working in Judges, the rule as the
angel decreed it for Samson was not quite as might have been
expected, and that in two ways. Samson's mother, not just Samson
himself, was affected by the prohibitions; his parents, not he, had
to make the vow.

If then the Lord's calling of the twelfth judge involved his
parents as much as, if not more than, him himself, what sort of
people do we find them to be as our attention is thus drawn to
them?

One notable fact is that no less than nineteen times between 13:2
and 14:9 Judges speaks of Manoah's wife, or Samson's mother, or
simply 'the woman'.[8] She is essential to the plot, yet in another
sense too unimportant even to be named. Her very obscurity is an
intrinsic part of the story. The other notable fact affects both her
and her husband. It is on her barrenness that the first sentence of
the first paragraph focuses, but the barrenness of one means of

---

[8] Even Manoah (some modern readers must find this hard to stomach) refers to
her as 'this woman' (13:11)!

course the childlessness of both.

So, as with other famous annunciations in Scripture, God's promise of the birth of a son comes to most unlikely people – a couple for whom such a thing was indeed not only unlikely but impossible, and therefore (if it were to happen at all) miraculous: the work of God himself.

Did we not see such things much earlier in the book? Once the pattern of judgeship had been established in Othniel, was not the chief characteristic of his successor his unlikelihood? We may think of Ehud as the left-handed man, which is how English translators naturally tend to describe him, but we remember that the way the writer put it in Hebrew was that he was 'restricted as to his right hand'. The emphasis was not on what he could do, but on what he could not do, and therefore on what God did through him. So the Ehud principle reappears in the Samson story.

What next do we learn about Manoah and his wife?

b. They were straightforward people (13:8–14)

The angel told the wife, and the wife told the husband, and the husband asked the Lord for a second visit from the one he assumed to be a 'man of God', not a supernatural messenger. We might wonder whether Manoah took his wife's report with a pinch of salt, and wanted it verified. But as we read on the artlessness of his prayer becomes plain. He is like Nathanael in the gospel story, 'an Israelite indeed, in whom is no guile'.[9] Like his wife, he believes the angel's message: he has no doubt that 'the boy . . . will be born',[10] that they are to become parents and will need to consider the child's 'manner of life'. He enquires matter-of-factly what the boy is to do and what they are to do with him; it sounds as though he has grasped the curious sharing-out of the three Nazirite vows – if it is the mother who is to give up the fruit of the vine and contact with anything unclean, does that mean that the son will have only the rule about the razor to observe? Surely there is more to it than that; 'what is he to do?' And equally clearly, Manoah intends to obey whatever instructions the 'man of God' will give him, since that was the object of his asking for a return visit.

Again the angel had come, indicating that Manoah's had been the kind of straightforward prayer that God delights to answer. Again it was to the woman that he had come, giving Manoah a

[9] Jn. 1:47.
[10] Notice also in 13:12 and again in 13:17: 'when' (not 'if') 'your words come true'.

further chance to show his uncomplicated faith as he 'arose and went after his wife'. He got little change out of the angel's reply to his questions, simply a repetition of what had been said the first time and nothing about the child's upbringing. But like the previous paragraph, this one is about the parents rather than about the child. If we are left somewhat in the dark about Samson, it is because we are meant to look rather at Manoah and his wife, a simple sincere couple who believe, and who enquire in order to obey.

Once more these are qualities we have seen before. The next lengthy story after Ehud's was the one about a leader humble enough to believe that through the woman-judge of Israel he would hear the words of God, to enquire what God's instructions were, and then to obey them. In fact Barak would not take a step forward unless he knew he would be in constant touch with that source of truth (4:8). In the same spirit, all those years later, would Manoah pray 'Come again to us, and teach us.' Tell us what to do and we will do it.

c. They were limited people (13:15–20)

There will be much in the course of these chapters about things that are not known. This recurring theme in the Samson narrative is not so much ignorance, as the irony of facts being known to some but not to others, or known to the reader but not known to the people in the story. Here in the opening chapter we find that 'Manoah did not know that he' (the divine messenger) 'was the angel of the LORD'. His wife did not know it either, since she referred to him as 'the man', 'a man of God', a man 'like . . . the angel of God' (13:10, 6). Samson's name is going to figure in the letter to the Hebrews, but his parents are there too as Old Testament examples to New Testament saints – two of those who 'have entertained angels unawares'.[11]

What Manoah did not know is followed by the mention of something he could not know. In all innocence he asked the supposed 'man of God' what his name was. 'It is wonderful,' replied the angel, meaning not that 'Wonderful' was his name but that Manoah was asking he knew not what, something he would not be able to take in even if it were told him. The psalmist years afterwards used the same word in a verse which helps us to understand this. The intimate knowledge that God has of me, he says,

---

[11] Heb. 13:2.

'is too *wonderful* for me; it is high, I cannot attain it.'[12]

It looks as if Manoah did not grasp even then quite what the angel's words implied. But the meat and bread he had brought as a meal for the visitor he was told to offer instead as a sacrifice, and he grasped the truth then. Even today, centuries later, the reader can feel a tingling of the scalp as he puts himself in the place of the awestruck couple, and sees in the rising flames of the sacrifice the nameless messenger himself rising into the air and disappearing above them.

Manoah and his wife are no fools, but they are all the same presented to us as people with limitations. There are matters they do not and cannot know, things in the plan of God which are not within their capacity. Their offering is made explicitly to a God who is beyond their grasp – 'to the LORD, to him who works wonders'.[13] Their limitations enhance the wonder of what God is doing and saying through his angel.

Yet again we ask ourselves how much of a novelty this is, and whether we have seen anything like it in the experience of earlier judges. Has there been one whose limitations were a necessary part of the plan of God to save his people? And of course there has. Our writer is underlining the lesson of Gideon, who was aware of limitations of his own (6:15) and had even greater limitations imposed on him by God (7:2–7), so that when the victory came the glory would be God's, and the people of Israel, like Manoah and his wife afterwards, would fall 'on their faces to the ground' and acknowledge that his 'name . . . is wonderful'.

d. They were confident people (13:21–23)

At least Mrs Manoah was. They had seen the angel of the Lord, which was tantamount to having seen God. It was again Gideon's story which told us that to see and hear the angel of the Lord meant in effect to see and hear the Lord himself (6:12–24). Thereupon Manoah, overcome with awe, was sure they would be struck dead. 'That can't be right, after all we have seen and heard,' countered his wife. 'If the Lord *said* we are to have a child, he has to let us live for us to have it.'

---

[12] Ps. 139:6. The angel's name is 'wonderful' (13:18) in AV mg., RV, RSV, NAS; NIV (putting 'wonderful' in a footnote) says it is 'beyond understanding', which is helpful, though it misses the link with Ps. 139. NAS's footnote suggests 'incomprehensible'.

[13] 13:19 RSV; so NEB. '. . . To the LORD, and he performed wonders while Manoah . . .' (NAS; cf. AV, RV, NIV) understands the syntax differently. See Webb, p. 166, and Boling, p. 222.

And where have we heard *that* before? We admire the woman's practical realism, but beyond that we ought to note the principle on which she bases her confidence. Was it not the mainspring of the story of Jephthah? 'I have opened my mouth . . . and I cannot take back my vow' (11:35). There, the circumstances were all awry, the vow was improper, and the results were terrible, but even so the principle was sound. And now, in this last and most disastrous time of rebellion, under the most unsatisfactory judgeship of all, the crucial fact is that the Lord has opened his mouth and he will not go back on his word, either in the promise of raising up Samson or in the guarantee of preserving Israel.

So the Lord kept his word, 'and the woman bore a son, and called his name Samson'. And with this home background, in which were combined all the elements characteristic of God's previous rescues, naturally 'the boy grew, and the Lord blessed him'. He was to be the next saviour. What seemed at first an unconnected stretch of rural railway in the neighbourhood of Zorah had after all arrived at the junction and connected with the main line that traverses all the territory of Judges; 'and the Spirit of the LORD began to stir him in Mahaneh-Dan'.

2. The emergence of the judge (14:1–20)

Samson went down to Timnah, and at Timnah he saw one of the daughters of the Philistines. ²*Then he came up, and told his father and mother, 'I saw one of the daughters of the Philistines at Timnah; now get her for me as my wife.'* ³*But his father and mother said to him, 'Is there not a woman among the daughters of your kinsmen, or among all our people, that you must go to take a wife from the uncircumcised Philistines?' But Samson said to his father, 'Get her for me; for she pleases me well.'*

⁴*His father and mother did not know that it was from the LORD; for he was seeking an occasion against the Philistines. At that time the Philistines had dominion over Israel.*

⁵*Then Samson went down with his father and mother to Timnah, and he came to the vineyards of Timnah. And behold, a young lion roared against him;* ⁶*and the Spirit of the LORD came mightily upon him, and he tore the lion asunder as one tears a kid; and he had nothing in his hand. But he did not tell his father or his mother what he had done.* ⁷*Then he went down and talked with the woman; and she pleased Samson well.* ⁸*And after a while he returned to take her; and he turned aside to see the carcass of the lion, and behold, there was a swarm of bees in the body of the lion, and honey.* ⁹*He scraped it out into his hands, and went on, eating*

as he went; and he came to his father and mother, and gave some to them, and they ate. But he did not tell them that he had taken the honey from the carcass of the lion.

¹⁰And his father went down to the woman, and Samson made a feast there; for so the young men used to do. ¹¹And when the people saw him, they brought thirty companions to be with him. ¹²And Samson said to them, 'Let me now put a riddle to you; if you can tell me what it is, within the seven days of the feast, and find it out, then I will give you thirty linen garments and thirty festal garments; ¹³but if you cannot tell me what it is, then you shall give me thirty linen garments and thirty festal garments.' And they said to him, 'Put your riddle, that we may hear it.' ¹⁴And he said to them,

'Out of the eater came something to eat.
Out of the strong came something sweet.'
And they could not in three days tell what the riddle was.

¹⁵On the fourth day they said to Samson's wife, 'Entice your husband to tell us what the riddle is, lest we burn you and your father's house with fire. Have you invited us here to impoverish us?' ¹⁶And Samson's wife wept before him, and said, 'You only hate me, you do not love me; you have put a riddle to my countrymen, and you have not told me what it is.' And he said to her, 'Behold, I have not told my father nor my mother, and shall I tell you?' ¹⁷She wept before him the seven days that their feast lasted; and on the seventh day he told her, because she pressed him hard. Then she told the riddle to her countrymen. ¹⁸And the men of the city said to him on the seventh day before the sun went down,

'What is sweeter than honey?
What is stronger than a lion?'
And he said to them,
'If you had not ploughed with my heifer,
you would not have found out my riddle.'
¹⁹And the Spirit of the LORD came mightily upon him, and he went down to Ashkelon and killed thirty men of the town, and took their spoil and gave the festal garments to those who had told the riddle. In hot anger he went back to his father's house. ²⁰And Samson's wife was given to his companion, who had been his best man.

If you read forwards, you arrive at Judges 14 with a picture of God's methods of judging and saving his people displayed in the careers of the first eleven judges and converging in the home background of the twelfth. You may well therefore expect the career of Samson as it unfolds to be the climax of the series. Furthermore, if you read (so to speak) backwards, you have already in your mind from much later in the Bible the New Testament accounts of the annunciation and birth of Jesus. You may well therefore see parallels with Samson, and your expectations will be even greater. So before we let such ideas run away with us, we must once more prepare ourselves for the unexpected. More than any of his predecessors, Samson will confound our assumptions. His emergence is as different from that of any of the previous judges as his 'call' was different from theirs, and the judge that emerges looks scarcely like a judge at all.

The writer tells the story as a sequence of journeys into Philistine country, using five times the phrase 'went down'. Another theme I have mentioned earlier, in this case not only running through chapter 14 but also linking it with much in earlier chapters, is that of unawareness or ignorance. 'His father and mother did not know' (14:4) is the first of several such statements here, of a piece with other ironies elsewhere in the story of Samson and with the same sort of thing earlier in the book.[14] To call the present chapter 'The emergence of the judge' is itself ironic, since apart from his parents no-one is aware that in Samson the next judge of Israel is emerging.

While the 'not-knowings' are central to the story, the 'down-goings' may be no more than a literary device, marking the chapter off into five smaller sections; although we may be meant to see a contrast with the 'up-goings' of Judah's conquering armies at the very beginning of the book (four of them in as many verses in 1:1–4). At any rate here they describe what actually happened.

a. Where the action is

Samson has grown up to be a man of action. Not that his actions have much to do with his call to be judge and saviour, or with a desire to serve Israel or obey God. If anything they move in the opposite direction, as his own desires and impulses dictate what he does.

He goes down to Timnah (14:1–4), and of the Philistine girls there one in particular catches his attention. Davis encourages us to imagine Samson's eyes and mouth wide open: 'Now *there's* a *woman*!'[15] Our writer leaves us in no doubt how improper the match is for a patriotic Israelite, stressing three times in three verses

---

[14] This frequent Judges theme has to do with facts which, for example, Eglon (3:16ff.), Sisera (4:17ff.), Gideon (6:11–22), Gaal (9:30–38), Jephthah (11:30–35), Manoah (13:16), the lords of the Philistines (16:24), and even we the readers (8:18–19), do not realize at the time. Klein's study *The Triumph of Irony in the Book of Judges* presents this as the keynote of the book.

[15] *Cf.* Davis, p. 169, on a literal rendering of 14:2 and the verse's proper emphasis.

the unsavoury name ('She was a Philistine. "She's a Philistine," said Samson. "She's a *Philistine*?" said his parents'). All that matters for Samson is that he wants her (14:3b).

He goes down to Timnah again, this time with his parents (14:5–6), and passing the vineyards between his village and the girl's he is attacked by a young lion. Or is he? What we are not told is tantalizing. Perhaps the lion never got as far as attacking, but just opened its mouth in a Metro-Goldwyn-Mayer growl, and got a response it had not bargained for.[16] And how did Samson's parents miss the incident? Why was the lad either prancing so far ahead, or dawdling so far behind, as to be out of sight and earshot *in a vineyard*? Is this a sidelong glance at Samson's Nazirite vow,[17] and a hint already of how little he will care about it?

A third time we are told 'he went down' (14:7), though this reads like the resumption of the second journey after the killing of the lion. At any rate there was later a third journey down to the girl's home (14:8–9), when 'he returned to take her', and this was the occasion when, finding a 'swarm of bees in the body of the lion, and honey', he certainly did abandon the Nazirite vow. Maybe he dealt with his conscience as summarily as he had dealt with the lion, telling himself (a) that the vow had been re-worded since the days of Numbers 6 – '*Eat* nothing unclean' (13:7) instead of 'Touch nothing unclean' – and though he touched the lion's carcass, what he ate was the bees' honey; and (b) that the vow had been shared out between himself and his mother, and the 'dead body' bit was hers, not his. Even so, while we may wonder whether his reticence in 14:6 was due to modesty about the lion or shame about the vineyard, it is a fair guess that shame and a bad conscience were the reason that in 14:9 he said nothing about having touched carrion.

The fourth journey is Manoah's, presumably for the official marriage formalities, and Samson is of course there too, the life and soul of the party. He turns the lion-and-honey incident into a party game, which begins to get out of hand. The thirty young Philistines, unable to guess the riddle, complain that the loss of the bet will 'impoverish' them, ignoring the fact that Samson will be thirty times as impoverished as any of them if he loses it. The result we know. As if in a dress rehearsal for chapter 16, the Philistines put pressure on the girl, and the girl puts pressure on Samson, and big strong Samson gives way.

But here as there, he, not his opponents, has the last word. The

---

[16] However, 'the roar in question (*šā'ag̱*) is the "pouncing roar" of a lion, intended to paralyse its chosen victim. Did ever a lion make a greater error of judgment?' (note from J. A. Motyer).

[17] *Cf.* Nu. 6:3–4.

fifth 'down-going' is his trip to obtain thirty outfits for the Philistines at Timnah from the Philistines at Ashkelon. The killing of the men of Ashkelon is a pre-echo of the final destruction at Gaza in 16:30, it is carried out in the power of the Spirit of the Lord, it is a fulfilment of the grim cry of Deborah and Barak in 5:31 ('So perish all thine enemies, O LORD'), and it is – too little and too late – what should have happened to all the peoples of Canaan years before. But none of this is in the mind of Samson. His are not the reflections, but simply the actions, and most of them are no more than reactions: reactions to the sight of a pretty girl or the roar of a beast of prey.

b. Where the ignorance is

The writer of Judges, a first-class story-teller, sometimes keeps even his readers temporarily in the dark, saving up last-page surprises for them. But in chapter 14 we are in the know, and we can appreciate the irony of what the people in the story do not realize.

In the first 'down-going' Samson's parents do not know that their son's infatuation is part of a divine plan (14:4). In the second, they are not told about his killing the lion (14:6), nor in the third about the source of the honey (14:9). In the fourth, the lion-and-honey riddle is a mystery to the Philistines (14:14). In the fifth, we might be tempted to say that the ignorance is that of the men of Ashkelon, who did not know what hit them! But there the significant 'thing not known' is hidden like a time-bomb in the very last verse of the chapter, with no attention at all drawn to it, so that not even we see it till the next chapter begins. Then it transpires that Samson himself, who in most of chapter 14 knew what other people did not, is the one who now is not aware that his wife has since been married to someone else.

This is what will carry the plot inexorably forward into the complications that lie ahead. But it turns the tables neatly on our hero. For we see that underneath all the action of this chapter, in which Samson has in a sense known what was going on when others did not, there is a profound ignorance on his part. He has no idea of his calling to be judge and saviour, nor of the real nature of his Nazirite vow. He cannot see how his relation with his Philistine 'wife' is the complete opposite of the marriage relationship of the first judge Othniel. He is quite unaware that his fraternizing with the Philistines generally, from which the entire story springs, runs counter to everything his predecessors stood for.

c. Where the judgment is

With such a man raised up to be judge, all action and no under-standing of anything that really matters, where can we expect to find the sound judgment that even now, with things so far gone, is directing the ways of Israel?

However thoughtless and irreligious Samson may be, we notice that the Spirit of the Lord is at work in him; though not (yet again) in ways we might have expected. He does not give him the gift of wisdom that Solomon knew was necessary to govern the people of God.[18] Still less does he begin to create within him the clean heart and the right spirit that David prayed for.[19] No; he enables him to kill a lion and thirty men who had done him no harm. So we need to ask what object the Lord can have in judging that these shall be Samson's first specific experiences of spiritual power, the first two occasions when we are told explicitly that 'the Spirit of the LORD came mightily upon him' (14:6, 19).

The key must be in 14:4. 'The LORD . . . was seeking an occasion against the Philistines.' Samson's fraternizing with the enemy expresses in one individual what the attitude of the nation at large had become. But the tribes of Canaan still *were* enemies of Israel, and Israel's distinctiveness was meant to be seen in confrontation and contrast with them. By the time of Samson, Israel has so accommodated herself to the world around her that (as we shall see in chapter 15) she wants no rocking of the boat. Like Samson, she is willing, even eager, to marry into Philistine society. The force of 14:4 is that the two communities are so interlocked that even the Lord can find nothing to get hold of to prise them apart. He uses Samson's weakness, therefore, to bring about the relation-ship with this irresistible girl from which so much ill-feeling will flow, and in the process he gives Samson his supernatural strength and the first opportunities to use it. With the lion the young man discovers his gift, and with the slaughter at Ashkelon he finds its purpose.

So *someone* is in charge, unsatisfactory though Samson may be as a judge. Someone is making judgments, in three senses: establish-ing how far Israel has sold out to the Philistines, deciding what now to do with either party, and then executing the decision as a sentence.

But we have not yet reached the third of these. That is to be prepared by 'the LORD, the Judge' in the next chapter.

---

[18] 2 Ch. 1:10.   [19] Ps. 51:10.

3. Judgment prepared (15:1–20)

After a while, at the time of wheat harvest, Samson went to visit his wife with a kid; and he said, 'I will go in to my wife in the chamber.' But her father would not allow him to go in. ²And her father said, 'I really thought that you utterly hated her; so I gave her to your companion. Is not her younger sister fairer than she? Pray take her instead.' ³And Samson said to them, 'This time I shall be blameless in regard to the Philistines, when I do them mischief.' ⁴So Samson went and caught three hundred foxes, and took torches; and he turned them tail to tail, and put a torch between each pair of tails. ⁵And when he had set fire to the torches, he let the foxes go into the standing grain of the Philistines, and burned up the shocks and the standing grain, as well as the olive orchards. ⁶Then the Philistines said, 'Who has done this?' And they said, 'Samson, the son-in-law of the Timnite, because he has taken his wife and given her to his companion.' And the Philistines came up, and burned her and her father with fire. ⁷And Samson said to them, 'If this is what you do, I swear I will be avenged upon you, and after that I will quit.' ⁸And he smote them hip and thigh with great slaughter; and he went down and stayed in the cleft of the rock of Etam.

⁹Then the Philistines came up and encamped in Judah, and made a raid on Lehi. ¹⁰And the men of Judah said, 'Why have you come up against us?' They said, 'We have come up to bind Samson, to do to him as he did to us.' ¹¹Then three thousand men of Judah went down to the cleft of the rock of Etam, and said to Samson, 'Do you not know that the Philistines are rulers over us? What then is this that you have done to us?' And he said to them, 'As they did to me, so have I done to them.' ¹²And they said to him, 'We have come down to bind you, that we may give you into the hands of the Philistines.' And Samson said to them, 'Swear to me that you will not fall upon me yourselves.' ¹³They said to him, 'No; we will only bind you and give you into their hands; we will not kill you.' So they bound him with two new ropes, and brought him up from the rock.

¹⁴When he came to Lehi, the Philistines came shouting to meet him; and the Spirit of the LORD came mightily upon him, and the ropes which were on his arms became as flax that has caught fire, and his bonds melted off his hands. ¹⁵And he found a fresh jawbone of an ass, and put out his hand and seized it, and with it he slew a thousand men. ¹⁶And Samson said,

> *'With the jawbone of an ass,*
> *heaps upon heaps,*

> *with the jawbone of an ass*
> *have I slain a thousand men.'*

¹⁷*When he had finished speaking, he threw away the jawbone out of his hand; and that place was called Ramath-lehi.*

¹⁸*And he was very thirsty, and he called on the* LORD *and said, 'Thou hast granted this great deliverance by the hand of thy servant; and shall I now die of thirst, and fall into the hands of the uncircumcised?'* ¹⁹*And God split open the hollow place that is at Lehi, and there came water from it; and when he drank, his spirit returned, and he revived. Therefore the name of it was called En-hakkore; it is at Lehi to this day.* ²⁰*And he judged Israel in the days of the Philistines twenty years.*

Samson as judge was 'called' before he was born, and has emerged into the limelight seeming as unconscious now as he was then of what he is intended to be. God has done it all, and God is now masterminding the plot's move towards its climax.

a. The Philistines provoked (15:1–8)

Even Gideon's three hundred with their blazing torches were to be outshone by Samson's. A pack of captured jackals! We may think this bizarre exploit cruel, or we may think it funny, but the point of it is still the Lord's resolve to provoke a confrontation between the two peoples. It is not in Samson to keep a quarrel going, not even a necessary one. Clearly his 'hot anger' of 14:19 has evaporated by 15:1, and equally clearly he reckons that the 'mischief' he plans in burning the Philistines' cornfields is a one-off retaliation, which should close the matter. The Lord knows very well that it will on the contrary lead to an escalation of the conflict, and sure enough the Philistines (to use an apt modern phrase) return the fire: not however upon Samson, but upon his intended in-laws at Timnah. Still, Samson takes this as a personal affront, and replies with an attack which he again fondly assumes will put an end to the dispute. But he is no match for the united determination of both the Lord and the Philistines that the end shall not be yet.

b. Israel shamed (15:9–13)

It was at the place afterwards known, from this incident, as Jawbone Hill (Ramath-Lehi, 15:9, 17) that the Israel of the judges touched her lowest point. The three-way exchange between Samson, the men of Judah, and the Philistine raiders is desperately revealing.

141

Samson was by now well aware of his gift of great physical strength. He was quite prepared to flex his muscles, literally and metaphorically, in combat with the Philistines, although, naïvely, he still seemed unable to see quite why they would not regard the quarrel as settled (15:11c).

The raiders were interested only in taking revenge on Samson. An attack on Israelite settlements was not on their agenda. That in itself speaks volumes; but it was the agitated Israelites who put into words the last blurring of distinctions between the people of God and the people of the world, the final sell-out. First, 'Why have you come up against us?' (15:10) – their question to the Philistines shows them mystified that there should be any semblance of conflict between their interests and the world's; secondly, 'Do you not know that the Philistines are rulers over us?' (15:11) – their question to Samson admits that there is in truth no such thing as harmonious co-existence between church and world, for where there is no conflict it is because the world has taken over.

This is the bottom of the spiral. We are back where we began in 1:1–20, with the foremost of the tribes; but then Judah swept away the power of the Philistine cities as one inconsiderable trifle ('also . . . Gaza' and the rest, 1:18; a drop from a bucket, the small dust of the balance),[20] in a great swathe of holy destruction throughout Canaan. Now even Judah is anxious only to live and let live, and would rather bind and betray its saviour than have him upset the balance of things.[21]

c. Samson empowered (15:14–17)

'When he came to Lehi', bound by his own countrymen, 'the Philistines came shouting to meet him.' They at any rate knew antagonism when they saw it. To them Samson represented the original Israel, the Lord's people as opposed to Dagon's people. And they were proved right as the Lord's Spirit came upon Samson for the third time, enabling him to snap the ropes that tied him, improvise a weapon, and slay a thousand Philistines.

The victory at Jawbone Hill underlines the paradox of Samson. He was so obviously now acting as the one through whom God would save Israel. Yet at the same time he was as clearly identified with Israel's sin as with God's salvation. He was a Nazirite, under a vow to distance himself from forbidden things, but reckoning that in practice the vow was unrealistic; you couldn't actually live

---

[20] Is. 40:15.
[21] In the broader sweep of history, it is to this point that Israel comes one last time in Jn. 11:47–50.

that way. The very weapon he used against God's enemies he must have taken from a carcass (not a skeleton; 'a *fresh* jawbone'). And that was just the attitude of his people. They were supposed to be devoted to the Lord. But they had reached the stage where so far from wanting to destroy the wicked ways of Canaan, they would not even distance themselves from these forbidden things.

So as his compatriots (and his enemies, for that matter) look at Samson, they see in him the power of God at work for salvation; but as God looks at him, he sees in him the sin of Israel at work for destruction. The twelfth judge may be in some ways the nearest we get in this book to a Christ-figure, but he is also a walking disaster. Let all who are given great opportunities, great responsibilities, and great gifts, take warning.

d. The Lord glorified (15:18–20)

However, the last paragraph of chapter 15 shows our hero in a favourable light. The encounter at Lehi left him gasping, and led to an experience the like of which we have not yet come across in this story. For the first time, he found himself in a situation he could not cope with, asked for God's help instead of taking it for granted, and had a prayer answered. These remarkable events registered even with simple Samson. The hill would be remembered by the name of the bizarre weapon with which he had won the victory there, but the hollow where God had done something that he could not do, and provided water for one who called out in need, would be remembered by that rare glimpse of his own helplessness and of the power which was really in control: Jawbone Hill, Caller Spring.

4. Judgment executed (16:1–31)

Samson went to Gaza, and there he saw a harlot, and he went in to her. ²*The Gazites were told, 'Samson has come here,' and they surrounded the place and lay in wait for him all night at the gate of the city. They kept quiet all night, saying, 'Let us wait till the light of the morning; then we will kill him.'* ³*But Samson lay till midnight, and at midnight he arose and took hold of the doors of the gate of the city and the two posts, and pulled them up, bar and all, and put them on his shoulders and carried them to the top of the hill that is before Hebron.*

⁴*After this he loved a woman in the valley of Sorek, whose name was Delilah.* ⁵*And the lords of the Philistines came to her and said to her, 'Entice him, and see wherein his great strength lies, and by*

what means we may overpower him, that we may bind him to subdue him; and we will each give you eleven hundred pieces of silver.' ⁶And Delilah said to Samson, 'Please tell me wherein your great strength lies, and how you might be bound, that one could subdue you.' ⁷And Samson said to her, 'If they bind me with seven fresh bowstrings which have not been dried, then I shall become weak, and be like any other man.' ⁸Then the lords of the Philistines brought her seven fresh bowstrings which had not been dried, and she bound him with them. ⁹Now she had men lying in wait in an inner chamber. And she said to him, 'The Philistines are upon you, Samson!' But he snapped the bowstrings, as a string of tow snaps when it touches the fire. So the secret of his strength was not known.

¹⁰And Delilah said to Samson, 'Behold, you have mocked me, and told me lies; please tell me how you might be bound.' ¹¹And he said to her, 'If they bind me with new ropes that have not been used, then I shall become weak, and be like any other man.' ¹²So Delilah took new ropes and bound him with them, and said to him, 'The Philistines are upon you, Samson!' And the men lying in wait were in an inner chamber. But he snapped the ropes off his arms like a thread.

¹³And Delilah said to Samson, 'Until now you have mocked me, and told me lies; tell me how you might be bound.' And he said to her, 'If you weave the seven locks of my head with the web and make it tight with the pin, then I shall become weak, and be like any other man.' ¹⁴So while he slept, Delilah took the seven locks of his head and wove them into the web. And she made them tight with the pin, and said to him, 'The Philistines are upon you, Samson!' But he awoke from his sleep, and pulled away the pin, the loom, and the web.

¹⁵And she said to him, 'How can you say, "I love you," when your heart is not with me? You have mocked me these three times, and you have not told me wherein your great strength lies.' ¹⁶And when she pressed him hard with her words day after day, and urged him, his soul was vexed to death. ¹⁷And he told her all his mind, and said to her, 'A razor has never come upon my head; for I have been a Nazirite to God from my mother's womb. If I be shaved, then my strength will leave me, and I shall become weak, and be like any other man.'

¹⁸When Delilah saw that he had told her all his mind, she sent and called the lords of the Philistines, saying, 'Come up this once, for he has told me all his mind.' Then the lords of the Philistines came up to her, and brought the money in their hands. ¹⁹She made him sleep upon her knees; and she called a man, and had him shave off the seven locks of his head. Then she began to torment him, and

his strength left him. ²⁰And she said, 'The Philistines are upon you, Samson!' And he awoke from his sleep, and said, 'I will go out as at other times, and shake myself free.' And he did not know that the LORD had left him. ²¹And the Philistines seized him and gouged out his eyes, and brought him down to Gaza, and bound him with bronze fetters; and he ground at the mill in the prison. ²²But the hair of his head began to grow again after it had been shaved.

²³Now the lords of the Philistines gathered to offer a great sacrifice to Dagon their god, and to rejoice; for they said, 'Our god has given Samson our enemy into our hand.' ²⁴And when the people saw him, they praised their god; for they said, 'Our god has given our enemy into our hand, the ravager of our country, who has slain many of us.' ²⁵And when their hearts were merry, they said, 'Call Samson, that he may make sport for us.' So they called Samson out of the prison, and he made sport before them. They made him stand between the pillars; ²⁶and Samson said to the lad who held him by the hand, 'Let me feel the pillars on which the house rests, that I may lean against them.' ²⁷Now the house was full of men and women; all the lords of the Philistines were there, and on the roof there were about three thousand men and women, who looked on while Samson made sport.

²⁸Then Samson called to the LORD and said, 'O Lord GOD, remember me, I pray thee, and strengthen me, I pray thee, only this once, O God, that I may be avenged upon the Philistines for one of my two eyes.' ²⁹And Samson grasped the two middle pillars upon which the house rested, and he leaned his weight upon them, his right hand on the one and his left hand on the other. ³⁰And Samson said, 'Let me die with the Philistines.' Then he bowed with all his might; and the house fell upon the lords and upon all the people that were in it. So the dead whom he slew at his death were more than those whom he had slain during his life. ³¹Then his brothers and all his family came down and took him and brought him up and buried him between Zorah and Eshta-ol in the tomb of Manoah his father. He had judged Israel twenty years.

With the opening of chapter 16, we move towards the climax of the drama. The scene is almost set, with the Lord carrying his plans remorselessly forward, Israel anxious not to have the status quo challenged, the Philistines increasingly provoked by Samson, and Samson blithely continuing to do his own thing.

The curtain goes up on a kind of prologue.

a. The judge's danger (16:1–3)

Samson was paying a visit to Gaza (whatever for? Even if Israelites generally now felt at home among their Philistine neighbours, how could Samson imagine that *he* would be welcome? Still, there he was), and he saw another girl he fancied; she was a prostitute, and 'he went in to her'.

No doubt at the time it meant nothing in particular to him. Not that anything ever did, much. But then when he is not *saving* Israel, he is *being* Israel, and that is most of the time. Sometimes he represents God as Israel sees him; much more often it seems that he represents Israel as God sees her, and here is a cheerfully representative episode. It is no use being shocked. In this we are all Samsons in some way or other, relishing the wrong thing in the wrong place, not least as we are persuaded that it doesn't particularly matter.

And, yes, in one way it was merely another insignificant piece of self-indulgence. But once more the narrative is heavy with irony. For we, the readers, know what Samson does not know. We are aware of how the story will end. He went to Gaza; he could not resist a pretty woman; and when he realized his enemies were lying in wait for him, he seized the town gates bodily, uprooted them, and carried them off. All good fun, at the time. But there would be another woman, with more far-reaching intentions; and another seizing, not of the gates but of the man who took them away; and another visit to Gaza, from which there would be no return.

That was the danger that lay ahead for Samson. He had as yet no inkling of it. When it came, it would bring the final irony: that in it, the judge would perish, but that by the very downfall of his deputy, *the* Judge would triumph.

b. The judge's folly (16:4–17)

We reach at last the most famous part of the story, perhaps the best-known episode in the book of Judges. Delilah, beautiful but treacherous; Samson, strong yet weak; a tragic infatuation, celebrated often since in painting and music and film. It captures the imagination, and once more (though not quite for the last time) irony gives it its power.

For neither the Philistines, now determined to destroy Samson, nor the woman, know why he has such strength, or how he may be deprived of it. And Samson does not know that his latest girl-friend is quite prepared to betray him for cash. And Delilah, even if she guesses that there is something supernatural about his strength, does not know that he still has a glimmer of respect for his Nazirite vow, and is willing to tell lies rather than give the secret away.

But one by one his deceptions are exposed, as she finds that he is not after all weakened by being bound with fresh bowstrings or new ropes, or even by the 'thrust of the peg' which weaves his hair into the threads of the loom and ominously recalls how treacherous Jael disposed of trusting Sisera.[22] Samson might not have remembered that incident, but he ought to have recalled how in his own experience another woman had 'pressed him hard' (16:16; 14:17) and succeeded in worming a secret out of him which was then used against him. This time also he gave way in the end.

c. The judge's downfall (16:18–22)

So she had his hair cut off. He must have known, the moment he awoke, that it had gone, yet still he assumed his strength would be unaffected (16:20b). Many have been the instances of unawareness throughout the story of Samson, but only twice before have we seen it at its plainest, in the words 'did not know' (13:16; 14:4). Now finally it is the judge himself who 'did not know that the LORD had left him' (16:20c).

The tragedy hurries to its close. Again there was a seizing, this time of Samson; again a seductive woman had betrayed him; again he went 'down to Gaza', but this time as a prisoner. Milton's *Samson Agonistes* describes this last scene but one of the drama in a single line, perhaps the most memorable in all that great poem: the fallen hero 'eyeless in Gaza at the mill with slaves'.

If, like the rest of Scripture, the account of the twelfth judge's downfall is God speaking to the reader, we have to ask what he was saying through it to its original readers. They were certainly meant to see themselves in it. The question would have been, where? Often in their history they must have been relieved to note that their ancestors in the days of Samson had been in very different circumstances from their own. They felt free therefore to wag their heads with sad disapproval over other people's follies. But if Samson represented Israel, and if the corporate sins of the nation were focused in this individual, it was much harder to avoid the implications. Israel's dubious relations with a seductive neighbouring community were rephrased as one man's dubious relations with the seductive girl down the road, and in becoming personal

[22] See p. 125 n. 1.

the lesson became universal, and unavoidable. Of this, more in a moment.

d. The judge's triumph (16:23–31)

The final irony concerns what the Philistines did not know. They had brought their enemy to book. They cannot have been so slow-witted as to miss the fact that his hair was growing again, but they must have assumed (quite rightly) that there was no magical connection between his strength and the length of his locks; by the one shearing his vow had been broken, and the Lord had left him. Nevertheless there was something, or rather someone, that they did not know. They knew nothing of the God who does the unexpected (Ehud), whose strength is made perfect in weakness (Gideon), and who never breaks his word (Jephthah). That God had said years before that Samson would be a Nazirite 'to the day of his death' (13:7). His abandonment of his servant at the time of his capture could not but be temporary. The promise was bound to hold, however Samson might despise it. There is grace abounding to the chief of sinners. 'If we are faithless, he remains faithful – for he cannot deny himself.'[23]

In those last days in the prison, did a re-run of the whole picaresque tragi-comedy pass before his blinded eyes? If the events of chapters 14 and 15 lead into the twenty-year judgeship of 15:20, and those of chapter 16 look back over the same period (16:31), then twice, once at the beginning and again at the end of that period, he had come into conflict with the Philistine neighbours with whom he and his people had tried to live in amity. Each time an attractive woman had captivated him, wormed a secret out of him, and passed it to his enemies. The first time the conflict had left the strong man exhausted, and he had called to the Lord for help, and had been given it. That too was going to happen again.

But before Samson, brought into the house of Dagon to entertain his captors, was given that last surge of strength which enabled him to bring down the entire building and them with it, there was a final twist of irony, and a triple one at that. The cry went up: 'Our god has given our enemy into our hand!' To the *Philistines*, not to Israel, was given the insight that a divine plan was overruling everything; but they attributed it to *the wrong god*; and then as without warning the house collapsed about their ears they must have realized with blinding clarity that that other God had turned the whole thing inside out, and that it would be Israel who would

[23] 2 Tim. 2:13.

cry '*Our* God has given *our* enemy into *our* hand'.

The story is dramatic in the extreme. If the pattern of a saviour's coming announced before his birth is meant to make us look forward in time to the gospel story, then perhaps when the saviour in his death destroys his people's enemies that too points ahead to a great New Testament event, and we shall hardly be surprised at the high drama of Judges 16.

But what does it all imply for the reader today?

We must learn from Samson himself, and a tragic lesson he provides. We cannot assume that each of Israel's judges is Everyman, with a life that sets examples and warnings before the attentive reader. But it is right to read Samson, at any rate, like this, because he is not only the saviour, with more than a passing resemblance to Christ, but also the sinner, unmistakably reflecting the face of Israel, and therefore our own face as the people of God: called by grace, bound by vow, repeatedly empowered, greatly gifted, yet faithless, self-indulgent, and only too ready to fraternize with the enemy. Milton again: 'O mirror of our fickle state!' says the Israelite chorus to Samson.

Much more, though, do we learn from *the* Judge, the Lord, and that is a momentous lesson. Where Samson/Israel is most self-willed, there, because of the contrast, the work of grace shines brightest. Before Samson's birth the Lord has prepared everything, throughout his life the Lord is masterminding everything, at his death the heathen god is defeated and the God of Israel triumphs.

Personally, Samson stands as a dreadful warning, the man of enormous potential who never grasped that the Spirit's call to holy discipline is even more important than the Spirit's gifts. But on the broader canvas, the plan of God goes inexorably on, and through Samson, tragic figure though he is, the Spirit of the Lord brings about the salvation of his people. He cannot in the end 'be like any other man', as he thought he would be once the secret of his strength was betrayed (16: 7, 11, 13, 17). That is why he is said, twice and truly, to have 'judged' Israel; why he rightly appears in Hebrews 11; and why his birth and death really are a reflection, however dim, of that other birth and death centuries later.

149

Judges 17:1 – 21:25

8. The top and bottom of it

There has been plenty in the long middle section of Judges to cause raised eyebrows. At the beginning we may have supposed that our four Rs, rebellion, retribution, repentance, and rescue, would 'furnish all we ought to ask' by way of a recurrent framework for the narratives of the twelve judges. What we found was that repentance figured less and less, and was pretty suspect when it did appear, while rebellion grew ever more serious, and the only regular feature was that sooner or later the Judge would raise up one of his deputies to set matters temporarily straight.

The five chapters that end the book are different. Up to this point we have been aware that however weird the activities of some of the characters on the stage, the Lord has been ultimately in charge of the production. But now he seems to have left the cast to its own devices, putting in a fleeting (and enigmatic) appearance in just one of the five chapters (20:18–28), and the result is an outlandish drama of the kind which would have led my grandmother, mystified by such a play on the radio, to comment dismissively, 'What a funny piece.' The events chronicled in these chapters are without exception the sort of thing on which one never hears sermons preached, even among Bible-loving people: 'Their hearts whisper softly and tenderly that there is no need to wrestle with such Scripture when they can be meditating on Philippians.'[1]

The writer of Judges has nevertheless given us this conclusion to his book. Without doubt it is meant to balance the introduction (1:1 – 3:6). The verse with which the latter began starts with the key words 'After the death of Joshua' (1:1); the verse with which the former will end contains the corresponding statement 'There

[1] Davis, p. 198.

was no king in Israel' (21:25).[2] The absence of the Lord from the closing chapters contrasts with his prominence in the opening chapters. Introduction and conclusion are intended to provide a frame for the long account of the judges themselves.

Listen again then to our admirable narrator, as he brings his series of tales to a close. For he is neither lecturing, nor preaching, nor even (you might think) taking sides: just telling stories. 'There was a man . . .' As a matter of fact, he writes here as if there were two of him, as if a couple of story-tellers were swapping yarns. 'Let me tell you', says the first, 'the story of the Levite who travelled from Bethlehem in Judah to the hill country of Ephraim . . .'[3] After which the second rejoins, 'Now have you heard the one about the Levite who travelled to Bethlehem in Judah from the hill country of Ephraim?'[4] The two tales look dispassionately at what it meant in practical terms to live as a weak, faithless, sinful people who no longer had a Joshua, and did not yet have a David, to keep them straight. The story of Micah and Jonathan and the men of Dan (chapters 17 – 18) conveys the view from above, the surface of things, the top side of life in the days of the judges. The story of the other Levite and his concubine, and the dire consequences of it (chapters 19 – 21), show how things were beneath the surface, the substance of them, the under side of life in those disconcerting times. The second will make plain how wrong were the underlying attitudes taken up by God's people. But before that stone is turned over and we see all the nastiness scurrying about underneath, the first story will show that superficially everything was as it should be, in that happy state of affairs which is a blend of ignorance and hypocrisy.

1. All the right procedures (17:1 – 18:31)

There was a man of the hill country of Ephraim, whose name was Micah. [2]And he said to his mother, 'The eleven hundred pieces of silver which were taken from you, about which you uttered a curse, and also spoke it in my ears, behold, the silver is with me; I took it.' And his mother said, 'Blessed be my son by the LORD.' [3]And he restored the eleven hundred pieces of silver to his mother; and his mother said, 'I consecrate the silver to the LORD from my hand for my son, to make a graven image and a molten image; now therefore I will restore it to you.' [4]So when he restored the money to his mother, his mother took two hundred pieces of silver, and gave it to the silversmith, who made it into a graven image and a

[2] See pp. 13ff.   [3] *Cf.* 17:7–8.   [4] *Cf.* 19:1–3.

molten image; and it was in the house of Micah. ⁵*And the man Micah had a shrine, and he made an ephod and teraphim, and installed one of his sons, who became his priest.* ⁶*In those days there was no king in Israel; every man did what was right in his own eyes.*

⁷*Now there was a young man of Bethlehem in Judah, of the family of Judah, who was a Levite; and he sojourned there.* ⁸*And the man departed from the town of Bethlehem in Judah, to live where he could find a place; and as he journeyed, he came to the hill country of Ephraim to the house of Micah.* ⁹*And Micah said to him, 'From where do you come?' And he said to him, 'I am a Levite of Bethlehem in Judah, and I am going to sojourn where I may find a place.'* ¹⁰*And Micah said to him, 'Stay with me, and be to me a father and a priest, and I will give you ten pieces of silver a year, and a suit of apparel, and your living.'* ¹¹*And the Levite was content to dwell with the man; and the young man became to him like one of his sons.* ¹²*And Micah installed the Levite, and the young man became his priest, and was in the house of Micah.* ¹³*Then Micah said, 'Now I know that the* LORD *will prosper me, because I have a Levite as priest.'*

¹⁸:¹*In those days there was no king in Israel. And in those days the tribe of the Danites was seeking for itself an inheritance to dwell in; for until then no inheritance among the tribes of Israel had fallen to them.* ²*So the Danites sent five able men from the whole number of their tribe, from Zorah and from Eshta-ol, to spy out the land and to explore it; and they said to them, 'Go and explore the land.' And they came to the hill country of Ephraim, to the house of Micah, and lodged there.* ³*When they were by the house of Micah, they recognized the voice of the young Levite; and they turned aside and said to him, 'Who brought you here? What are you doing in this place? What is your business here?'* ⁴*And he said to them, 'Thus and thus has Micah dealt with me: he has hired me, and I have become his priest.'* ⁵*And they said to him, 'Inquire of God, we pray thee, that we may know whether the journey on which we are setting out will succeed.'* ⁶*And the priest said to them, 'Go in peace. The journey on which you go is under the eye of the* LORD.'

⁷*Then the five men departed, and came to Laish, and saw the people who were there, how they dwelt in security, after the manner of the Sidonians, quiet and unsuspecting, lacking nothing that is in the earth, and possessing wealth, and how they were far from the Sidonians and had no dealings with any one.* ⁸*And when they came to their brethren at Zorah and Eshta-ol, their brethren said to them, 'What do you report?'* ⁹*They said, 'Arise, and let us go up against*

them; for we have seen the land, and behold, it is very fertile. And will you do nothing? Do not be slow to go, and enter in and possess the land. ¹⁰*When you go, you will come to an unsuspecting people. The land is broad; yea, God has given it into your hands, a place where there is no lack of anything that is in the earth.'*

¹¹*And six hundred men of the tribe of Dan, armed with weapons of war, set forth from Zorah and Eshta-ol,* ¹²*and went up and encamped at Kiriath-jearim in Judah. On this account that place is called Mahaneh-dan to this day; behold, it is west of Kiriath-jearim.* ¹³*And they passed on from there to the hill country of Ephraim, and came to the house of Micah.*

¹⁴*Then the five men who had gone to spy out the country of Laish said to their brethren, 'Do you know that in these houses there are an ephod, teraphim, a graven image, and a molten image? Now therefore consider what you will do.'* ¹⁵*And they turned aside thither, and came to the house of the young Levite, at the home of Micah, and asked him of his welfare.* ¹⁶*Now the six hundred men of the Danites, armed with their weapons of war, stood by the entrance of the gate;* ¹⁷*and the five men who had gone to spy out the land went up, and entered and took the graven image, the ephod, the teraphim, and the molten image, while the priest stood by the entrance of the gate with the six hundred men armed with weapons of war.* ¹⁸*And when these went into Micah's house and took the graven image, the ephod, the teraphim, and the molten image, the priest said to them, 'What are you doing?'* ¹⁹*And they said to him, 'Keep quiet, put your hand upon your mouth, and come with us, and be to us a father and a priest. Is it better for you to be priest to the house of one man, or to be priest to a tribe and family in Israel?'* ²⁰*And the priest's heart was glad; he took the ephod, and the teraphim, and the graven image, and went in the midst of the people.*

²¹*So they turned and departed, putting the little ones and the cattle and the goods in front of them.* ²²*When they were a good way from the home of Micah, the men who were in the houses near Micah's house were called out, and they overtook the Danites.* ²³*And they shouted to the Danites, who turned round and said to Micah, 'What ails you that you come with such a company?'* ²⁴*And he said, 'You take my gods which I made, and the priest, and go away, and what have I left? How then do you ask me, "What ails you?"'* ²⁵*And the Danites said to him, 'Do not let your voice be heard among us, lest angry fellows fall upon you, and you lose your life with the lives of your household.'* ²⁶*Then the Danites went their way; and when Micah saw that they were too strong for him, he turned and went back to his home.*

153

*²⁷And taking what Micah had made, and the priest who belonged
to him, the Danites came to Laish, to a people quiet and unsuspecting, and smote them with the edge of the sword, and burned
the city with fire. ²⁸And there was no deliverer because it was far
from Sidon, and they had no dealings with any one. It was in the
valley which belongs to Beth-rehob. And they rebuilt the city, and
dwelt in it. ²⁹And they named the city Dan, after the name of Dan
their ancestor, who was born to Israel; but the name of the city was
Laish at the first. ³⁰And the Danites set up the graven image for
themselves; and Jonathan the son of Gershom, son of Moses, and
his sons were priests to the tribe of the Danites until the day of the
captivity of the land. ³¹So they set up Micah's graven image which
he made, as long as the house of God was at Shiloh.*

These chapters are all about religion. As so often in Judges, things
are not what they seem. But for the people in the story, Ephraimites
and Danites and the Levite from Judah (a representative cross-
section of Israel), appearances are important. And the appearances
of the name of the Lord, the God of Israel, are frequent. This is a
very religious story. In the course of it he 'appears' – that is, he is
mentioned – repeatedly. After all, if you were the 'every man' of
those days, you would take the comment of 17:6 not as a condem-
nation but as a compliment – you were doing *what was right* in
your own eyes.[5]

The skill of our writer is a delight. Three times he opens a new
scene and brings in new characters, each occasion seeming at first
to be unrelated to what has gone before, so that each time we are
agog to know how the new episode will converge with the main
theme.[6] 'There was a man of the hill country of Ephraim . . . There
was a young man of Bethlehem in Judah . . . In those days the tribe
of the Danites was seeking for itself an inheritance . . .'

The curtain rises on a grotesque tableau in a home in Ephraim.

a. Enter Micah (17:1–6)

The opening exchange between the man and his mother sets out
brilliantly, in a single verse, the peculiar yet all-too-believable background for the rest of the story.

---

[5] 'Every man did what was right in his own eyes' (17:6; 21:25 RSV; so AV, RV,
NAS, NEB); 'Everyone did as he saw fit' (NIV), 'Everyone did just as he pleased'
(GNB). Sad to find NIV falling into GNB's bad habits and assuming that ordinary
readers cannot cope with metaphors, especially when one is as simple and as crucial
to the argument as this. See note on p. 10.

[6] *Cf.* pp. 129, 134.

What Micah says to his mother tells us that it began with a hoard of silver that she had amassed; that the silver was then stolen; that she called down a curse on the unknown thief; that Micah himself was the thief; and that he overheard the curse, and thereupon confessed and returned what he had stolen. All that in a single sentence.

What she says to him tells us both that she is relieved and forgiving, and that her instant reaction is to call down on her repentant son a blessing from the Lord, the God of Israel. How proper! So it would have been in the days of Abraham, or Moses, or Solomon, or Ezra. This is clearly a society in which God is real and his name comes naturally to the lips of his people. Mind you, without ever saying so the writer has already made plain that 'repentant' is perhaps the wrong word for Micah. His mother's enquiries may have failed to find him out, but a sweeping general curse addressed 'to whom it may concern' does make him very uncomfortable, and it is in order to wriggle out from under the curse that he owns up to the theft. At all events, he is forgiven in the name of the Lord. (For *robbing* his own *mother*? – but the particularly unpleasant nature of the crime is another aspect of the affair about which the writer blandly leaves us to draw our own conclusions.) The Lord has been invoked, so all is well.

So pleased is she to have the silver back that she consecrates it to the Lord. Again, how proper! So it would have been in the days of Abraham, *etc.*, even if such God-fearing times might possibly have reckoned that 'consecration' meant handing over rather more than two-elevenths of the sum involved. Mind you, there is something even odder about her notion of consecration: 'I consecrate the silver *to the* LORD . . . to make *a graven image and a molten image*'! Certainly we are meant both to look open-mouthed at this flagrant disregard of the second commandment, and to realize that the woman herself could not see the incongruity of it.[7] Clearly the new image took an honoured place in the shrine which Micah had apparently already set up in his home, along with everything else that a proper shrine required: an ephod like Aaron's or Gideon's,[8] teraphim or 'household gods' like Rachel's (though some would have said that these were no longer quite so proper),[9] and of course a priest. There being no-one of the tribe of Levi readily available, one of his own sons would have to do, but a priest there

[7] Boling, pointing out that Micah's name means 'Who is like Yahweh?', highlights the incongruity of the molten image in a supposedly God-fearing household by translating 17:4b as 'There it was, in the house of Yahweh-the-Incomparable!' (Boling, pp. 254f.).
[8] See p. 87.   [9] See Gn. 31:19–35; Jos. 24:14.

must be. It was important to Micah that he 'did what was right'. 'In those days there was no king in Israel' to tell him what was really right, and he had not learned where to look for authority at such times. With those significant words (17:6) the curtain is rung down on the first scene, and with the following verse the second scene opens.

b. Enter the Levite (17:7–13, 18:1a)

We shall be told at the end that his name was Jonathan (18:30). To begin with, it was not who he was, but what he was, that mattered. He left Bethlehem to look for a 'place', both a home and a job, and he arrived in the hill country of Ephraim without, it seems, necessarily intending to stop there. But he came by where Micah was living, and as he was a man looking for a post and Micah had a post looking for a man, that was where the Levite's quest ended.

At least, the post which Micah offered him was not exactly vacant. The summary way in which the job was made available to the newcomer ('Thanks for filling in, son – now back to the sheep-pen with you') shows again how important it was to these people that things should be done properly. Micah's shrine had to have a priest; he 'did what was right in his own eyes' and appointed one of his own boys to the job, but an Ephraimite priest did not sound quite right, and when the visitor seeking work turned out to be a Levite, Micah obviously saw him as a godsend: 'Now I know that the LORD will prosper me.' The first priest was all right at the time, but this one is the real thing.

For all that, the appointment was not exactly a matter of disinterested right conduct. It was the subject of an agreement which the two men had drawn up for their mutual advantage. Jonathan would get out of it a job of some prestige, a regular salary, a clothing allowance, and all found, as well as the stability and affection of a new home (17:10–11). Micah would get out of it a guarantee of the Lord's blessing (17:13), as if such a thing could be dependent on a piece of industrial bargaining.

But then he did not know any better. He ought to have done, but that is another question. As we are reminded by the closing words of this scene also, 'In those days there was no king in Israel' (18:1a). A king like Jehoshaphat or Josiah would have put a stop to these irregularities. The fact remains that Micah was eager to observe the proprieties as far as he understood them.

c. Enter the Danites (18:1b–31)

The migration of the Danites from a temporary southern settlement to a permanent northern one is the theme of this scene and this chapter. As it unfolds we see why Micah and his shrine and his mother's silver from Scene 1, and Jonathan and his 'levitical priest-hood' from Scene 2, were from the start an integral part of the plot.

For the third time, we shall notice how 'right' everything is. The rightness is more subtly woven into the narrative, and the name of the Lord is mentioned only once, but that mention is significant, and we must keep our ears open throughout the scene for echoes from the past. Someone, somewhere, laid down guidelines for what is going on here, and all the right procedures are being followed. Or something like them.

The first echo is not particularly obscure. What takes place in this scene arises from the fact that until now the tribe of Dan has not obtained its 'inheritance', its share of territory in the promised land. That was how chapter 1 ended. The tribes had had varying success in the occupation of Canaan, and Dan came at the bottom of the league table (1:34). So deciding eventually that this was just not good enough, the Danites took action.

Chapter 18 is in outline the account of two Danite journeys, the first an exploration by five spies and the second a military expedition by six hundred soldiers, the latter perhaps involving the general migration of the whole tribe (18:21). In each journey there is a break, when first the spies and then the soldiers arrive at the house of Micah in the hill country of Ephraim. To these breaks we shall return; they are the heart of the story. For the moment, however, we shall take the scissors to verses 2b–6 and verses 13–27a, remove those two sections, and paste together the cut ends. The result of this reprehensible exercise is a narrative that reads well enough, and surely reminds us of something we have read elsewhere.

'The Danites sent . . . able men . . . to spy out the land' (18:2), as the Lord had told Moses to do many years before, when Israel as a nation had yet to enter its promised territory.[10] In due course the five 'came to Laish, and saw the people who were there . . . lacking nothing that is in the earth, and possessing wealth' (18:7), like the people whom the earlier spies had found occupying a land which flowed with milk and honey.[11] When they returned, they urged the rest, 'Let us go up against them' (18:9), echoing Caleb's

---

[10] Cf. Nu. 13:1–2.   [11] Cf. Nu. 13:27.

encouragement on that earlier occasion;[12] and what, as men of understanding and obedience, he and Joshua had declared to be true ('The land . . . is an exceedingly good land . . . The LORD . . . will bring us into this land'),[13] the Danite spies now assumed to be true for their generation also ('God has given it into your hands, a place where there is no lack of anything that is in the earth', 18:10).

Thereupon the Danite troops set out on the second journey, from 'Dan's Camp' near Kiriath-jearim (18:12) all the way to Laish in the far north (18:27b). They 'went up' and 'defeated the Canaanites' and 'took possession' of the territory.

Those last three phrases are in fact quotations not from this chapter (though they well convey its substance) but from the very beginning of Judges (1:4, 5, 19). For as the five spies were following in the steps of the twelve spies of Numbers 13, so in due course the six hundred warriors were doing what all Israel ought to have done as a result of the spies' report, and what the tribe of Judah eventually did do 'after the death of Joshua' (1:1). And that is the ironic force of the single mention of the Lord's name in chapter 18. The first expedition broke its journey at the house of Micah, and finding the Levite there asked if the omens were favourable. 'The journey on which you go', replied Jonathan, 'is under the eye of the LORD.' What basis he had for saying that we do not know. It was of course true in the most general sense, and represents one of the chief themes of the book: the Judge is always presiding over all the fortunes of his people, even when they are most self-willed. But that was not what the Danites asked or what the Levite meant. For them, the whole project was a conscious fulfilling of a pattern which had been right twice before, once in Numbers 13 and once in Judges 1. They wanted to be reassured that as thus belatedly, and more from greed than from obedience, they set out to take some Canaanite land for themselves, it was still the right pattern, a venture that the Lord would approve. Whether *that* was true or not is beside the point. The important thing for the story is that the Danites wanted it to be true. They were as concerned with right procedures as Micah and Jonathan were.

The second expedition also stopped at Micah's house, at the suggestion of the five spies who had been there before. And for what? The Living Bible is not a translation one would ever use for study, but here its version is irresistible:

The five men went over to the house and with all of the

---

[12] *Cf.* Nu. 13:30.   [13] Nu. 14:7–8.

armed men standing just outside the gate, they talked to the young priest, and asked him how he was getting along. Then the five spies entered the shrine and took the idols, the ephod, and the teraphim.

'What are you doing?' the young priest demanded when he saw them carrying them out.

'Be quiet and come with us,' they said. 'Be a priest to all of us. Isn't it better for you to be a priest to a whole tribe in Israel instead of just to one man in his private home?'

The young priest was then quite happy to go with them, and he took along the ephod, the teraphim, and the idols. . . . When they were quite a distance from Micah's home, Micah and some of his neighbours came chasing after them, yelling at them to stop.

'What do you want, chasing after us like this?' the men of Dan demanded.

'What do you mean, "What do I want"!' Micah retorted. 'You've taken away all my gods and my priest, and I have nothing left!'

'Be careful how you talk, mister,' the men of Dan replied. 'Somebody's apt to get angry and kill every one of you.'

So the men of Dan kept going. When Micah saw that there were too many of them for him to handle, he turned back home (18:15–26, LB).

If you feel sorry for Micah, remember that he started by stealing from his own mother, and stealing silver worth more than five times the value of the image in the shrine ('My gods which I made', 18:24!). It is a case of the biter well and truly bit. And the Levite? He is for sale, and quite prepared to abandon his benefactor when he gets a better offer. And the men of Dan? They are mere bullies, and it is of a piece with their treatment of Micah that their eventual attack on Laish is made to seem cruel even by the standards of that cruel age. These doubts about the moral character of everyone concerned highlight by contrast the thing that really matters to the Danites. They end up not only with a proper tribal territory but with a proper priest, to say nothing of all the 'liturgical junk'[14] that goes with him. All the right procedures.

It worked, you see, says the writer in his deadpan way. Even if you apply the Gamaliel test ('If . . . this undertaking is of men, it will fail')[15] you have to admit it worked for a good long while (18:30–31). It was a success story. A rather dubious one? Whatever

[14] Davis, p. 200.   [15] Acts 5:38.

makes you say that?

But although all the right procedures have been followed (after a fashion), there is undeniably something very dubious about the state of a nation which thinks so superficially about the things that matter. Under the surface you find the substance, the real character of Israel in these testing times; as the remaining chapters of the book will show.

2. All the wrong attitudes (19:1–21:25)

In those days, when there was no king in Israel, a certain Levite was sojourning in the remote parts of the hill country of Ephraim who took to himself a concubine from Bethlehem in Judah. ²And his concubine became angry with him, and she went away from him to her father's house at Bethlehem in Judah, and was there some four months. ³Then her husband arose and went after her, to speak kindly to her and bring her back. He had with him his servant and a couple of asses. And he came to her father's house, and when the girl's father saw him, he came with joy to meet him. ⁴And his father-in-law, the girl's father, made him stay, and he remained with him three days; so they ate and drank, and lodged there. ⁵And on the fourth day they arose early in the morning, and he prepared to go; but the girl's father said to his son-in-law, 'Strengthen your heart with a morsel of bread, and after that you may go.' ⁶So the two men sat and ate and drank together; and the girl's father said to the man, 'Be pleased to spend the night, and let your heart be merry.' ⁷And when the man rose up to go, his father-in-law urged him, till he lodged there again. ⁸And on the fifth day he arose early in the morning to depart; and the girl's father said, 'Strengthen your heart, and tarry until the day declines.' So they ate, both of them. ⁹And when the man and his concubine and his servant rose up to depart, his father-in-law, the girl's father, said to him, 'Behold, now the day has waned toward evening; pray tarry all night. Behold, the day draws to its close; lodge here and let your heart be merry; and tomorrow you shall arise early in the morning for your journey, and go home.'

¹⁰But the man would not spend the night; he rose up and departed, and arrived opposite Jebus (that is, Jerusalem). He had with him a couple of saddled asses, and his concubine was with him. ¹¹When they were near Jebus, the day was far spent, and the servant said to his master, 'Come now, let us turn aside to this city of the Jebusites, and spend the night in it.' ¹²And his master said to him, 'We will not turn aside into the city of foreigners, who do not belong to the people of Israel; but we will pass on to Gibe-ah.' ¹³And he said to his servant, 'Come and let us draw near to one of these places, and spend the night at Gibe-ah or at Ramah.' ¹⁴So they passed on and went their way; and the sun went down on them near Gibe-ah, which belongs to Benjamin, ¹⁵and they turned aside there, to go in and spend the night at Gibe-ah. And he went in and sat down in the open square of the city; for no man took them into his house to spend the night.

¹⁶And behold, an old man was coming from his work in the field at evening; the man was from the hill country of Ephraim and he was sojourning in Gibe-ah; the men of the place were Benjaminites. ¹⁷And he lifted up his eyes, and saw the wayfarer in the open square of the city; and the old man said, 'Where are you going? and whence do you come?' ¹⁸And he said to him, 'We are passing from Bethlehem in Judah to the remote parts of the hill country of Ephraim, from which I come. I went to Bethlehem in Judah; and I am going to my home; and nobody takes me into his house. ¹⁹We have straw and provender for our asses, with bread and wine for me and your maidservant and the young man with your servants; there is no lack of anything.' ²⁰And the old man said, 'Peace be to you; I will care for all your wants; only, do not spend the night in the square.' ²¹So he brought him into his house, and gave the asses provender; and they washed their feet, and ate and drank.

²²As they were making their hearts merry, behold, the men of the city, base fellows, beset the house round about, beating on the door; and they said to the old man, the master of the house, 'Bring out the man who came into your house, that we may know him.' ²³And the man, the master of the house, went out to them and said to them, 'No, my brethren, do not act so wickedly; seeing that this man has come into my house, do not do this vile thing. ²⁴Behold, here are my virgin daughter and his concubine; let me bring them out now. Ravish them and do with them what seems good to you; but against this man do not do so vile a thing.' ²⁵But the men would not listen to him. So the man seized his concubine, and put her out to them; and they knew her, and abused her all night until the morning. And as the dawn began to break, they let her go. ²⁶And as morning appeared, the woman came and fell down at the door of the man's house where her master was, till it was light.

²⁷And her master rose up in the morning, and when he opened the doors of the house and went out to go on his way, behold, there was his concubine lying at the door of the house with her hands on the threshold. ²⁸He said to her, 'Get up, let us be going.' But there was no answer. Then he put her upon the ass; and the man rose up and went away to his home. ²⁹And when he entered his house, he took a knife, and laying hold of his concubine he divided her, limb

by limb, into twelve pieces, and sent her throughout all the territory of Israel. ³⁰And all who saw it said, 'Such a thing has never happened or been seen from the day that the people of Israel came up out of the land of Egypt until this day; consider it, take counsel, and speak.'

²⁰:¹Then all the people of Israel came out, from Dan to Beersheba, including the land of Gilead, and the congregation assembled as one man to the LORD at Mizpah. ²And the chiefs of all the people, of all the tribes of Israel, presented themselves in the assembly of the people of God, four hundred thousand men on foot that drew the sword. ³(Now the Benjaminites heard that the people of Israel had gone up to Mizpah.) And the people of Israel said, 'Tell us, how was this wickedness brought to pass?' ⁴And the Levite, the husband of the woman who was murdered, answered and said, 'I came to Gibe-ah that belongs to Benjamin, I and my concubine, to spend the night. ⁵And the men of Gibe-ah rose against me, and beset the house round about me by night; they meant to kill me, and they ravished my concubine, and she is dead. ⁶And I took my concubine and cut her in pieces, and sent her throughout all the country of the inheritance of Israel; for they have committed abomination and wantonness in Israel. ⁷Behold, you people of Israel, all of you, give your advice and counsel here.'

⁸And all the people arose as one man, saying, 'We will not any of us go to his tent, and none of us will return to his house. ⁹But now this is what we will do to Gibe-ah: we will go up against it by lot, ¹⁰and we will take ten men of a hundred throughout all the tribes of Israel, and a hundred of a thousand, and a thousand of ten thousand, to bring provisions for the people, that when they come they may requite Gibe-ah of Benjamin, for all the wanton crime which they have committed in Israel.' ¹¹So all the men of Israel gathered against the city, united as one man.

¹²And the tribes of Israel sent men through all the tribe of Benjamin, saying, 'What wickedness is this that has taken place among you? ¹³Now therefore give up the men, the base fellows in Gibe-ah, that we may put them to death, and put away evil from Israel.' But the Benjaminites would not listen to the voice of their brethren, the people of Israel. ¹⁴And the Benjaminites came together out of the cities to Gibe-ah, to go out to battle against the people of Israel. ¹⁵And the Benjaminites mustered out of their cities on that day twenty-six thousand men that drew the sword, besides the inhabitants of Gibe-ah, who mustered seven hundred picked men. ¹⁶Among all these were seven hundred picked men who were left-handed; every one could sling a stone at a hair, and not miss. ¹⁷And the men of Israel, apart from Benjamin, mustered four hundred

thousand men that drew sword; all these were men of war.

[18]The people of Israel arose and went up to Bethel, and inquired of God, 'Which of us shall go up first to battle against the Benjaminites?' And the LORD said, 'Judah shall go up first.'

[19]Then the people of Israel rose in the morning, and encamped against Gibe-ah. [20]And the men of Israel went out to battle against Benjamin; and the men of Israel drew up the battle line against them at Gibe-ah. [21]The Benjaminites came out of Gibe-ah, and felled to the ground on that day twenty-two thousand men of the Israelites. [22]But the people, the men of Israel, took courage, and again formed the battle line in the same place where they had formed it on the first day. [23]And the people of Israel went up and wept before the LORD until the evening; and they inquired of the LORD, 'Shall we again draw near to battle against our brethren the Benjaminites?' And the LORD said, 'Go up against them.'

[24]So the people of Israel came near against the Benjaminites the second day. [25]And Benjamin went against them out of Gibe-ah the second day, and felled to the ground eighteen thousand men of the people of Israel; all these were men who drew the sword. [26]Then all the people of Israel, the whole army, went up and came to Bethel and wept; they sat there before the LORD, and fasted that day until evening, and offered burnt offerings and peace offerings before the LORD. [27]And the people of Israel inquired of the LORD (for the ark of the covenant of God was there in those days, [28]and Phinehas the son of Eleazar, son of Aaron, ministered before it in those days), saying 'Shall we yet again go out to battle against our brethren the Benjaminites, or shall we cease? And the LORD said, 'Go up; for tomorrow I will give them into your hand.'

[29]So Israel set men in ambush round about Gibe-ah. [30]And the people of Israel went up against the Benjaminites on the third day, and set themselves in array against Gibe-ah, as at other times. [31]And the Benjaminites went out against the people, and were drawn away from the city; and as at other times they began to smite and kill some of the people, in the highways, one of which goes up to Bethel and the other to Gibe-ah, and in the open country, about thirty men of Israel. [32]And the Benjaminites said, 'They are routed before us, as at the first.' But the men of Israel said, 'Let us flee, and draw them away from the city to the highways.' [33]And all the men of Israel rose up out of their place, and set themselves in array at Baal-tamar; and the men of Israel who were in ambush rushed out of their place west of Geba. [34]And there came against Gibe-ah ten thousand picked men out of all Israel, and the battle was hard; but the Benjaminites did not know that disaster was close upon them. [35]And the LORD defeated Benjamin before Israel; and the men

of Israel destroyed twenty-five thousand one hundred men of
Benjamin that day; all these were men who drew the sword. [36]So
the Benjaminites saw that they were defeated.

The men of Israel gave ground to Benjamin, because they trusted
to the men in ambush whom they had set against Gibe-ah. [37]And
the men in ambush made haste and rushed upon Gibe-ah; the men
in ambush moved out and smote all the city with the edge of the
sword. [38]Now the appointed signal between the men of Israel and
the men in ambush was that when they made a great cloud of
smoke rise up out of the city [39]the men of Israel should turn in
battle. Now Benjamin had begun to smite and kill about thirty men
of Israel; they said, 'Surely they are smitten down before us, as in
the first battle.' [40]But when the signal began to rise out of the city
in a column of smoke, the Benjaminites looked behind them; and
behold, the whole of the city went up in smoke to heaven. [41]Then
the men of Israel turned, and the men of Benjamin were dismayed,
for they saw that disaster was close upon them. [42]Therefore they
turned their backs before the men of Israel in the direction of the
wilderness; but the battle overtook them, and those who came out
of the cities destroyed them in the midst of them. [43]Cutting down
the Benjaminites, they pursued them and trod them down from
Nohah as far as opposite Gibe-ah on the east. [44]Eighteen thousand
men of Benjamin fell, all of them men of valour. [45]And they turned
and fled toward the wilderness to the rock of Rimmon; five thousand
men of them were cut down in the highways and they were pursued
hard to Gidom, and two thousand men of them were slain. [46]So all
who fell that day of Benjamin were twenty-five thousand men that
drew the sword, all of them men of valour. [47]But six hundred men
turned and fled toward the wilderness to the rock of Rimmon, and
abode at the rock of Rimmon four months. [48]And the men of Israel
turned back against the Benjaminites, and smote them with the
edge of the sword, men and beasts and all that they found. And all
the towns which they found they set on fire.

[21:1]Now the men of Israel had sworn at Mizpah, 'No one of us
shall give his daughter in marriage to Benjamin.' [2]And the people
came to Bethel, and sat there till evening before God, and they
lifted up their voices and wept bitterly. [3]And they said, 'O LORD,
the God of Israel, why has this come to pass in Israel, that there
should be today one tribe lacking in Israel?' [4]And on the morrow
the people rose early, and built there an altar, and offered burnt
offerings and peace offerings. [5]And the people of Israel said, 'Which
of all the tribes of Israel did not come up in the assembly to the
LORD?' For they had taken a great oath concerning him who did
not come up to the LORD to Mizpah, saying, 'He shall be put to

death.' ⁶And the people of Israel had compassion for Benjamin their brother, and said, 'One tribe is cut off from Israel this day. ⁷What shall we do for wives for those who are left, since we have sworn by the LORD that we will not give them any of our daughters for wives?'

⁸*And they said, 'What one is there of the tribes of Israel that did not come up to the LORD to Mizpah?' And behold, no one had come to the camp from Jabesh-gilead, to the assembly. ⁹For when the people were mustered, behold, not one of the inhabitants of Jabesh-gilead was there. ¹⁰So the congregation sent thither twelve thousand of their bravest men, and commanded them, 'Go and smite the inhabitants of Jabesh-gilead with the edge of the sword; also the women and the little ones. ¹¹This is what you shall do; every male and every woman that has lain with a male you shall utterly destroy.' ¹²And they found among the inhabitants of Jabesh-gilead four hundred young virgins who had not known man by lying with him; and they brought them to the camp at Shiloh, which is in the land of Canaan.*

¹³*Then the whole congregation sent word to the Benjaminites who were at the rock of Rimmon, and proclaimed peace to them. ¹⁴And Benjamin returned at that time; and they gave them the women whom they had saved alive of the women of Jabesh-gilead; but they did not suffice for them. ¹⁵And the people had compassion on Benjamin because the LORD had made a breach in the tribes of Israel.*

¹⁶*Then the elders of the congregation said, 'What shall we do for wives for those who are left, since the women are destroyed out of Benjamin?' ¹⁷And they said, 'There must be an inheritance for the survivors of Benjamin, that a tribe be not blotted out from Israel. ¹⁸Yet we cannot give them wives of our daughters.' For the people of Israel had sworn, 'Cursed be he who gives a wife to Benjamin.' ¹⁹So they said, 'Behold, there is the yearly feast of the LORD at Shiloh, which is north of Bethel, on the east of the highway that goes up from Bethel to Shechem, and south of Lebonah.' ²⁰And they commanded the Benjaminites, saying, 'Go and lie in wait in the vineyards, ²¹and watch; if the daughters of Shiloh come out to dance in the dances, then come out of the vineyards and seize each man his wife from the daughters of Shiloh, and go to the land of Benjamin. ²²And when their fathers or their brothers come to complain to us, we will say to them, "Grant them graciously to us; because we did not take for each man of them his wife in battle, neither did you give them to them, else you would now be guilty." ' ²³And the Benjaminites did so, and took their wives, according to their number, from the dancers whom they carried off; then they went*

and returned to their inheritance, and rebuilt the towns, and dwelt in them. ²⁴*And the people of Israel departed from there at that time, every man to his tribe and family, and they went out from there every man to his inheritance.*

²⁵*In those days there was no king in Israel; every man did what was right in his own eyes.*

Where the previous two chapters were about religion, the remaining three are about morality. It would be a typically Israel-in-the-time-of-the-judges reaction to exclaim that surely religion is more important than morality? The fact is that you learn more about whether a man is really right with God from the quality of his life than from the style of his religion. So now we leave to one side the ephods and the teraphim, the priests and the shrines, and 'my gods which I have made', to see how the people of God actually *live* when they have to follow his authority for themselves instead of having an intermediary to tell them what to do.

We come then to the narrative of these three final chapters. Considered as a story, it is brilliantly told. But it is a dreadful story. What we might call the tale of the northbound Levite (17:8) was dreadful, but also comic: as is fitting, since it was concerned with the paraphernalia of religion, a subject never to be taken too seriously. On the other hand, the tale of the southbound Levite (19:1–3) is of an unrelieved dreadfulness, as is to be expected, since it is about that most serious of subjects, a morality adrift from its moorings. In it, the rules of holy living (which is true worship) are broken wholesale. Each chapter tells us how a particular set of rules was discarded, and how each abandonment led to another. All is connected. The pulling of the first loose end results in the unravelling of the whole.[16] We could think of the three chapters as three scenes, as we did with chapters 17 and 18; but they are really a continuous drama, more like a one-act play in three sections, and the curtain rises in 19:1 and falls in 21:25 with the two final statements of the motto theme: 'In those days there was no king in Israel.' And the drama is all about rules, because only a right attitude to the rules of weekday morality gives any meaning to one's attitude to the rules of Sunday religion.

a. *The rules of hospitality (19:1–30)*

'Now let me tell you about the other Levite . . .' This one had already at some time in the past been south to Bethlehem, where

---

[16] See God's dealings with Abimelech and Shechem, pp. 90, 101.

he had met a woman whom he subsequently married. At least she was not strictly a wife, only a concubine; but he reckoned her family as his in-laws. Out of that relationship were to come vast spreading waves of tragedy, in which the couple with whom it all began would be lost to view as the entire nation all but tore itself apart.

The story is 103 verses long, longer even than that of Gideon, but a mere three verses bring us to the crucial point, the trigger which sets off the action. The Levite had been south and brought the girl from there to his home in Ephraim, and then later she left him for some reason[17] and went back to her father; so he made another journey to Bethlehem to persuade her to return.

Now read on.

'When the girl's father saw him, he came with joy to meet him', and 'made him stay' (19:3–4). Thus begins the theme of hospitality, which pervades the chapter. The age-old custom is found in many cultures besides those of Bible lands, but in Scripture it has a special importance. The passages which speak of it explicitly, such as Hebrews 13:2 ('Do not neglect to show hospitality to strangers'), put into words an outlook common to, and expected from, all right-thinking people of those times. When you come to think of it, this is something more than an interesting social phenomenon. Second only to loving God is the commandment about loving your neighbour, and the fact that your neighbour might not necessarily be a friend of yours is underscored when it is a traveller who turns up in the role of 'neighbour'. After all, a visitor might be *anybody*! So the hospitality to visitors which is the mainspring of our present story is very near the heart of morality. We are eased in gently to the subject by the first people in the story being relatives who know and like each other, but soon it will be the attitude to unknown strangers which will put the sense of social duty to the test.

It was one big happy family to start with, the Levite and the girl apparently reconciled, his servant and the asses no doubt being well looked after, and her father delighted to play the host. Three days they stayed with him, and then the first cracks began to appear. Not that the visitors outstayed their welcome; just the opposite, in fact. It was the girl's father who was at fault. He so much enjoyed entertaining the company that he could not bear to let them go. With such a trivial thing – the unimportant sin of mere thoughtlessness – did the tragedy begin. On the fourth morning:

[17] They quarrelled (RSV, NEB, GNB): so Soggin, p. 284. She was unfaithful (AV, RV, NIV) is what the Hebrew text says. Or it was her walking out after a quarrel which technically constituted 'unfaithfulness' (Webb, p. 188; Boling, pp. 273f.).

'Surely you don't need to go quite so early? You've got all day!' And in the evening: 'You'd better stay overnight now, it's getting late.' And on the fifth morning: 'Surely, *etc., etc.*,' once again. So that by the fifth evening the Levite felt he simply could not stay any longer, and set off even though his party could not possibly get very far before nightfall. So his father-in-law's thoughtlessness was compounded by his own folly. There were plenty of periods in the days of the judges when 'caravans ceased and travellers kept to the byways' (5:6), when travel was not easy and night travel could be positively dangerous, and this was one of them.

Dusk found the three wayfarers near the town of Jebus. This town had been captured by the Israelites long before (1:8), but they had not disposed of the inhabitants as they should have done (1:21), and it was not, significantly, until the early days of the monarchy that David finally took possession of it, and it became Jerusalem, 'the city of the great king'.[18] Because in the time of Judges 19 it was still Jebusite, the Levite did not feel confident about the wisdom of spending a night there. That is to say, the next contributory factor to the plot of our story was a failure of nerve on the part of some Israelite general in the far-off days of the conquest; or, to put it bluntly, a lack of faith and obedience.

Ironically, the Levite might well have fared better among these pagans than he was destined to do among his fellow-Israelites in the place where eventually the party did stop for the night. 'The sun went down on them near Gibeah.' Well, Gibeah 'belongs to Benjamin' (19:14), so they would be all right there. But something – two things – about Gibeah must have aroused their suspicions. First, although as it was sunset most people would be disappearing indoors, even those who did see the travellers arrive did not speak to them, or enquire of them, or welcome them. 'No man took them into his house to spend the night' (19:15). What had happened here to the universally-accepted code of hospitality? And then when someone did speak to them he was a visitor himself, an old Ephraimite living temporarily in this Benjaminite town; and he said, in words that even today rivet the reader's attention and make him wonder just what was going on, (I paraphrase) 'You had better come and stay in my house; whatever you do, *do not spend the night in the square*' (19:20).

What *was* going on, as the Levite and his party duly discovered, beggars the imagination. The only comparable passage in the whole of the Bible is the description of what led to the Lord's obliterating of Sodom and Gomorrah in Genesis 19; but then they were heathen

---

[18] *Cf.* 2 Sa. 5:6–10; Ps. 48:2.

cities – this one was Israelite. It was not just that the rowdies of Gibeah got together after nightfall for an orgy, that they came out on to the streets to enjoy it openly, that it was going to involve not only rape but male rape, and that it did in fact lead to the death of the girl. All that was incredible enough. It was that all this was apparently expected, as part of the regular night-life of the town. And not among Jebusites and Canaanites, but among the people of God!

Here then is the next ingredient in the mix, after thoughtlessness, folly, unbelief, and disobedience: the downright wickedness of this Israelite town, its inhabitants, like the men of Sodom, 'great sinners against the LORD'.[19]

If any icing is needed on the cake, it is provided by the old man. Again the linking thread is hospitality, which was excessive at Bethlehem, not looked for from Jebus, and not forthcoming from the people of Gibeah. The old Ephraimite considers it very important. The Levite is his guest; he could not possibly hand him over to the mob – that would be a 'vile thing'. Rather than break the rules of hospitality, he is prepared to break a few others: 'Here are my virgin daughter and his concubine . . . Ravish them and do with them what seems good to you; but against this man do not do so vile a thing' (19:23–24).

Icing, did I say? That was just the marzipan. The icing is supplied by the Levite himself. When the uproar continued unabated, he 'seized his concubine, and put her out to them; and they knew her, and abused her all night until the morning'. (It is an impertinence to try to paraphrase this prince of story-tellers: let him go on in his own words.) When the Levite 'rose up in the morning . . . to go on his way, behold, there was his concubine lying . . . with her hands on the threshold. He said to her, "Get up, let us be going." But there was no answer . . .' (19:25, 27–28). She is dead, of course. The writer does not need to say so. The final gruesome touch to this part of the tale is the sending out, one to each tribe, of twelve bloody packages – a severed head to Judah, say, a hand and forearm to Zebulun – each with a covering letter (!) to tell what had happened and to appeal to whatever might be left of the conscience of Israel.

b. The rules of justice (20:1–48)

With a nation in such moral disarray as the Israel of Judges 19, it is not surprising that the rules of justice have gone the same way

---

[19] Gn. 13:13.

as the rules of hospitality. How the latter are observed has shown us something of the state of social morality; how the former work will now show us something of Israel's grasp of how to deal with breakdowns in it; and neither is exactly admirable.

Nothing is more obvious than that the men of Gibeah had behaved outrageously, and that outrage was the Levite's proper reaction. But chapter 20 underlines chapter 19 in revealing that here too nothing was quite what it should have been, and some things were altogether what they should not have been.

The public demonstration of sympathy for the Levite was an impressive one. For once, a rare thing in Judges, Israel was united – well, nearly – and the presence of so many armed men showed that the tribes meant business (20:1–2). But one could scarcely call it a reasoned response. After all, the appeal had been a thoroughly emotive one. Though the Levite may have lacked the facilities that modern media could have given him, he had three things which produced the desired result: a corpse, a knife, and an unerring instinct for what the public relishes.

It was not quite a united Israel that gathered at Mizpah. Prudently, the Benjaminites stayed away, no doubt judging quite rightly that given the state of public feeling they, like the girl, would probably have been torn limb from limb. But the rest wanted to hear the story (20:3). They knew the gist of it already, for that was what had brought them, but it was the kind that people like to hear again. Besides, this was by way of being an official gathering, which would reckon it had the authority to make decisions and take action. So, perhaps, it had; not many would be able to remember a precedent. At all events it wanted an official charge laid, on which it could act.

Just as we needed to remind ourselves not to feel too sorry for the wronged Micah in chapter 18, we have to admit that here likewise the wronged Levite is steadily forfeiting our sympathy. He has heavily edited the version of the affair at Gibeah which he presents to the assembly at Mizpah. No-one would suspect from it that any folly or callousness of his own might have contributed to the death of the girl.

Inflamed by the startling publicity and misled by the selective evidence, the assembly instantly resolved on a quite disproportionate punishment for Gibeah. Perhaps the Israel in which we have already seen signs of disintegration in the days of Deborah,[20] of Gideon,[21] and of Jephthah[22] cannot quite believe it is acting 'as one

[20] See p. 65.
[21] See p. 86.   [22] See pp. 122f.

man' (20:8), 'united as one man' (20:11), and wants to strike while the iron is hot.

Some cooler heads within the leadership propose that the absent Benjaminites should be given the opportunity to take action themselves against their own erring relatives before the Israel sledgehammer is brought down to crack the Gibeah nut. This initiative too causes more problems than it solves, as it brings out in the Benjaminites a fierce, misplaced loyalty towards the scoundrels in Gibeah. The upshot is that instead of a police action against a gang of hooligans, Israel finds herself facing a full-blown civil war, and one whose outcome is not a foregone conclusion, for the Benjaminites though vastly outnumbered are no mean warriors (20:15–17). All the signs are that the fabric of the nation is about to be torn apart. And the whole thing began with the Levite's father-in-law's well-meaning thoughtlessness in detaining his guests just one more day!

All this was happening in days 'when there was no king in Israel'; but it seems to have been a time when there were no judges and no heathen oppressors either, so it is hard to know where it fits in historically.[23] The mention of Aaron's grandson as being still alive (20:28), with other less definite pointers, persuades most commentators that the civil war took place very early in the period, soon 'after the death of Joshua'. But from a literary and theological point of view the end of the book is the right place for it.[24] There can be no doubt that Judges 20 is meant to answer to Judges 1. The book begins and ends with a gathering of all Israel, and with what flowed from it. The correspondences are striking, and the differences are instructive.

Again a national assembly had been convened, coming 'as one man to the LORD at Mizpah' (20:1). Just so had gathered the assembly of 1:1. Again battle loomed, and again the Lord's guidance was sought. The identical question was put: 'Which of us shall go up first to battle?' (20:18; cf. 1:1). This time also the Lord replied, and his answer was what it had been on the previous occasion: 'Judah shall go up.'

But now notice the differences. They all relate to those places in chapter 20 where the Lord's name appears. 'Israel . . . assembled as

---

[23] I take it that the phrase 'there was no king in Israel' (19:1; 21:25) is intended to locate this story, like the rest, in the period between the exodus and the monarchy, rather than to locate it in a time within that period when there happened to be no *judge* in Israel ('king', on that view, being equivalent to 'judge'). See pp. 13ff.

[24] Perhaps the civil war does belong at the end chronologically also. Though 20:28 may seem to us to refer to Aaron's grandson, there are many biblical examples of 'stretched' genealogies in which 'son' means 'descendant', and this could be a Phinehas of a later generation. The name is a recurrent one in the priestly families of the Old Testament. See Boling, pp. 286f.

one man *to the* LORD' (20:1) not now as an obedient people eager to blot out the wickedness of Canaan, as in chapter 1, but as a people mortified that it should itself have become so contaminated by that wickedness. Israel heard *the Lord* say 'Judah shall go up first' (20:18), to lead the attack not now on their enemies the Canaanites, as in chapter 1, but on their 'brethren the Benjaminites' – twice the tragic phrase is stressed (20:23, 28). Fighting began, and at once things went wrong for the Israelites. Night after night they came to *the Lord* (20:23, 26–28), with increasing perturbation, to receive orders which were not, as they had once been, guarantees of success, but recipes for disaster, as the armies of the eleven tribes suffered heavy losses; and when he did finally promise victory, that was no comfort, for it meant the practical wiping out of the twelfth tribe.

For the valour evident in chapter 1 was here turned to a vicious orgy of destruction which left the Benjaminite countryside strewn with the carcasses of men and beasts, every town a smoking ruin, and of the entire tribe only six hundred survivors. And this was *the Lord's* doing (20:35), as much as the destruction of Canaanite nations through all the time of the judges was his doing; but here it brought the virtual destruction of a tribe of *Israel*.

c. The rules of restitution (21:1–25)

Wrong having been punished, by a process of justice which leaves the reader wondering, it was now a matter of putting things right. The law contained rules for restitution where there had been loss or hurt or damage; the trouble was that in this case it was beyond the wit of man to work out who owed what to whom. The only thing that was beyond question was that to all intents and purposes there was now 'one tribe lacking in Israel' (21:3). It was unthinkable that Israel should not be a twelve-fold structure. The way the 'twelve' is made up shows a good deal of variation in Scripture, but twelve it always is, and we should try to imagine the dismay of the eleven tribes as it dawned upon them that they might have destroyed this basic feature of their national life. They might have been able to cope with the fact that the Lord himself had ordered the campaign against Benjamin, since what he had taken away he might somehow give back. What was harder was that they remembered one of their own follies, when in the heat of the moment at Mizpah they had sworn that there would be no more marriage-contracts between Benjamin and the rest of them (21:1). So although six hundred Benjaminites had survived, since all were male they could have no more (Israelite) offspring.

Then someone suggested that the problem might be solved by Israel's implementing the other foolish vow that had been made at Mizpah, a 'great oath' that anyone who had failed to join in should be put to death (21:5). Jabesh-gilead had not sent representatives; therefore all that was needed was for the population of that town to be slaughtered, men, women, and children, all except the unmarried girls. This clever and humane idea meant that of the Benjaminite survivors four hundred at any rate could now have Israelite wives. A blind eye was turned to the fact that neither oath was being strictly adhered to. But two hundred men of Benjamin were still wifeless.

'The elders of the congregation said, "What shall we do . . . ?" And they said, "There must be an inheritance for the survivors . . ." . . . So they said, "Behold, there is the yearly feast . . ." ' (21:16–19) – the final inspiration being that the required number of girls should be kidnapped at the Shiloh village festival, so they would not actually have been *given* to Benjamin by their families, and to that extent the first oath would still hold (21:22).

That was what happened; and everything having thus been brought to a satisfactory conclusion, everybody went home. (Do not forget, by the way, that 'in those days there was no king in Israel; every man did what was right in his own eyes'.)

And here endeth the book of Judges.

But can that really be how hospitality is practised, and justice administered, and restitution made among the people of God? Only when they have failed to understand where authority is to be found, even in the absence of a king. The story of the first Levite in chapters 17 and 18 showed the religious life of God's people not as it should be, but as it only too easily can be: a ludicrous veneer of rightness, all the right procedures, with attractive liturgy and the proper paraphernalia, and the Lord nodded to incessantly. The story of the second Levite with all its ramifications in chapters 19–21 showed the moral life of God's people not as it should be, but as it only too easily can be: under the surface, a shambles of wrongness, all the wrong attitudes, with the Lord appealed to only in extremity and then answering your prayer in a way you don't like; for the rest, the decisions are reached – we noticed a moment ago who makes them when the Lord is not asked his opinion: 'they said' the questions, then 'they said' the answers (21:16–19) – the decisions are reached by Israel talking to herself. Those are the two baleful views of life among the people of God with which Judges is brought to an end. Under a brisk coat of paint, the house rots and crumbles.

But the process of decline had been quite unnecessary. The recurrent reminder that 'in those days there was no king' is no more than a statement of fact. It does not mean that godliness inevitably declined because there was no king, and that when David appeared on the scene all would be well. The kings when they came would have the power (not necessarily the will) to check ungodliness; though the days of the monarchy would spawn plenty of sins of their own. In the days of the judges that power was largely in the hands of the people – to quote E. M. Forster's title, *Two Cheers for Democracy!* – and the other recurrent refrain, 'Every man did what was right in his own eyes', means that the people themselves, individually and corporately, had the responsibility of checking ungodliness and promoting holiness. The question was, where did Everyman's 'own eyes' look to find the authority which would tell him how?

In practice he regularly looked into his own sinful heart. But in theory there was no reason why he should not have looked somewhere much more trustworthy. As the time of the judges is about to begin, the reply of all Israel to Joshua's reiterated challenge at Shechem is: 'We ... will serve the LORD ... we will serve the LORD ... the LORD our God we will serve, and his voice we will obey.'[25] As it ends, the Lord tells the last judge[26] that a rejection of his, Samuel's, rule is in fact a rejection of his, the Lord's, rule.[27] And in the middle of it Gideon reminds Israel that her real ruler is the Lord (8:23).

There need be no doubt as to where that authority is to be found, even in the absence of Moses and Joshua, David and Solomon. The revealed will of God in the words he has given is there all the time, and may be read plainly by the clear-sighted and obedient. 'If your eye is sound, your whole body will be full of light',[28] and doing what is right in your own eyes will take on a new meaning. It would have been – and was, as we learn from the book of Ruth – perfectly possible to live as a true people of God in the times of the judges. Instead of the skin-deep religion of chapters 17 and 18, the true worship and use of the Lord's name, aware of the perils of both sacramentalism and subjectivism (the need to have the right *things* and the right *feelings*).[29] Instead of the moral chaos of chapters 19–21, every circumstance of daily life acknowledging the

[25] Jos. 24:18, 21, 24.
[26] The fourteenth, not the twelfth. Samson would be followed by Eli the priest-judge (1 Sa. 1:9; 4:18) and Samuel the prophet-judge (1 Sa. 3:20; 7:15) before the days of the monarchy began with the first king Saul (1 Sa. 8–12).
[27] 1 Sa. 8:7.   [28] Mt. 6:22.
[29] Davis has an excellent page opening up these two dangerous subjects (p. 208).

Lord's authority and reign.

And why is it possible? Because even when, as in all five chapters, the Lord sits disapprovingly on the sidelines, speaking only when he is spoken to and for the rest leaving Israel to muddle through in her own way, since that is what she has decided she wants to do, – even then, he is *there*. He has not abandoned his people. Indeed, unasked and unobtrusive, he is ensuring that they will never finally destroy themselves by their own wilful folly. What we have here is in the end a story of grace. Two great gospel truths from the pen of the apostle Paul might sum up the final message of Judges, this book about a people to whom the Lord had bound himself by unbreakable promises, though they did their level best to free themselves from those bonds of love. 'Where sin increased, grace abounded all the more'; 'If we are faithless, he remains faithful – for he cannot deny himself.'[30]

[30] Rom. 5:20; 2 Tim. 2:13.

Other titles in The Bible Speaks Today series

New Testament

The Message of the Sermon on the Mount (Matthew 5 – 7)
Christian counter-culture
John Stott

The Message of Matthew
The kingdom of heaven
Michael Green

The Message of Mark
The mystery of faith
Donald English

The Message of Luke
The Saviour of the world
Michael Wilcock

The Message of John
Here is your King!
Bruce Milne

The Message of Acts
To the ends of the earth
John Stott

The Message of Romans
God's good news for the world
John Stott

The Message of 1 Corinthians
Life in the local church
David Prior

The Message of 2 Corinthians
Power in weakness
Paul Barnett

The Message of Galatians
Only one way
John Stott

The Message of Ephesians
God's new society
John Stott

The Message of Philippians
Jesus our Joy
Alec Motyer

The Message of Colossians and Philemon
Fullness and freedom
Dick Lucas

The Message of Thessalonians
Preparing for the coming King
John Stott

The Message of 1 Timothy and Titus
The life of the local church
John Stott

The Message of 2 Timothy
Guard the gospel
John Stott

The Message of Hebrews
Christ above all
Raymond Brown

The Message of James
The tests of faith
Alec Motyer

The Message of 1 Peter
The way of the cross
Edmund Clowney

The Message of 2 Peter and Jude
The promise of his coming
Dick Lucas and Christopher Green

The Message of John's Letters
Living in the love of God
David Jackman

The Message of Revelation
I saw heaven opened
Michael Wilcock